I0129419

The Multiplex in India

During the decade of its existence in India, the multiplex cinema has been very much a sign of the times – both a symptom and a symbol of new social values. Indicative of a consistent push to create a 'globalised' consuming middle class and a new urban environment, multiplex theatres have thus become key sites in the long-running struggle over cultural legitimacy and the right to public space in Indian cities.

This book provides the reader with a comprehensive account of the new leisure infrastructure arising at the intersection between contemporary trends in cultural practice and the spatial politics that are reshaping the cities of India. Exploring the significance, and convergence, of economic liberalisation, urban redevelopment and the media explosion in India, the book demonstrates an innovative approach towards the cultural and political economy of leisure in a complex and rapidly-changing society.

Key arguments are supported by up-to-date and substantive field research in several major metros and second-tier cities across India. Accordingly, this book employs analytical frameworks from Media and Cultural Studies and from Urban Geography and Development Studies in a wide-ranging examination of the multiplex phenomenon, and as such it will be relevant to anyone interested in cultural practice and social change in India.

Adrian Athique is a lecturer in Media at the Department of Sociology, University of Essex. His research interests include film exhibition in South Asia, unofficial networks of media distribution, new media technologies and the transnational reception of media in Asia – all of these part of a wider interest in cultural sociology, geography and history.

Douglas Hill is a lecturer in Development Studies in the Department of Geography at the University of Otago, New Zealand. His research engages with comparative political economy, especially in South Asia.

Routledge Contemporary South Asia Series

The Multiplex in India

A cultural economy of
urban leisure

Adrian Athique and Douglas Hill

Routledge
Taylor & Francis Group

LONDON AND NEW YORK

First published 2010
by Routledge
2 Park Square, Milton Park, Abingdon, Oxfordshire OX14 4RN

Simultaneously published in the USA and Canada
by Routledge
711 Third Avenue, New York, NY 10017

First issued in paperback 2014

Routledge is an imprint of the Taylor and Francis Group, an informa business

© 2010 Adrian Athique and Douglas Hill

Typeset in BaskervilleMT by Swales & Willis Ltd, Exeter, Devon

All rights reserved. No part of this book may be reprinted or
reproduced or utilised in any form or by any electronic,
mechanical, or other means, now known or hereafter
invented, including photocopying and recording, or in any
information storage or retrieval system, without permission in
writing from the publishers.

British Library Cataloguing in Publication Data
A catalogue record for this book is available
from the British Library

Library of Congress Cataloging in Publication Data
Athique, Adrian.
    The multiplex in India : a cultural economy of urban leisure /
    Adrian Athique and Douglas Hill.
    p. cm. – (Routledge contemporary South Asia series)
    Includes bibliographical references and index.
    1. Multiplex theaters–India. 2. Motion picture industry–India.
    3. Middle class–India. 4. Leisure–India. 5. India–Economic conditions.
    6. India–Social life and customs. I. Hill, Douglas. II. Title.
    PN1993.5.I8A87 2010
    384'.80954–dc22
    2009026730

ISBN 978-0-415-46837-4 (hbk)
ISBN 978-0-415-53359-1 (pbk)
ISBN 978-0-203-86214-8 (ebk)

Contents

Illustrations, maps and tables

Illustrations

Maps

Tables

About the authors

Dr Adrian Athique

A graduate in Media Arts from the University Of Plymouth, UK, Adrian Athique was a learning and teaching technologies officer at the Open University before relocating to Australia from 2002–2007. His doctoral research reconsidered the formulation of the media audience as a social body, and as a subject of social analysis, under the impact of media globalisation. After completing this work in 2005, Adrian spent two years as a post-doctoral research fellow at the Centre for Critical and Cultural Studies, University of Queensland, before joining the Department of Sociology, University of Essex in 2007. Adrian has published a wide range of work on the Indian media industries encompassing the disciplines of cultural geography and history, sociology, political economy and media studies. His current interests include the social practice of film exhibition, media distribution, new media technologies, leisure architecture and the transnational reception of Asian media.

Dr Douglas Hill

Dr Hill completed his Bachelor of Arts (Hons) at the Australian National University and a PhD at Curtin University. Dr Hill was a Research Fellow at the University of Wollongong for two years. His research engages with comparative political economy, especially in South Asia. Recently published work includes studies of contemporary issues in rural and urban development in Bengal, water resources in South Asia and the reorganisation of port facilities in South and Southeast Asia. Dr Hill is currently a lecturer in Development Studies, Department of Geography, University of Otago, New Zealand.

Acknowledgements

We would like to acknowledge the contributions of Graeme Turner and the Centre for Critical and Cultural Studies, University of Queensland and the Department of Geography, University of Otago, who funded the fieldwork for this study. We would also like to acknowledge the assistance of the Department of Sociology, University of Essex and the Department of Geography, University of Otago with the production costs of this monograph. We would also like to thank Tracy Connolly at Otago for producing the urban maps.

For their assistance in the conduct of our research, we would like to thank S. V. Srinivas and the Centre for the Study of Culture and Society, Bangalore for their kind invitation in 2007 and, also in Bangalore, we would like to thank Lawrence Liang at the Alternative Law Forum and Ramesh Patel at the Sagar cinema. In Kolkata, we would like to thank Abhijit Roy and the Department of Film Studies at Jadavpur University. Special thanks go to Palash Ghosh for his assistance with survey work and photography in Kolkata and Durgapur. Warm thanks also go to Gita Viswanath for recruiting focus and survey groups in Bangalore and Baroda. In Baroda, we would also like to thank the students and staff of the Department of English, Maharaja Sayajirao University as well as P. C. Kar and the Forum on Contemporary Theory, as well as Darshna Bhatt at the Chandan multiplex. We are particularly grateful to the multiplex companies who shared their vision of the industry with us: Alok Tandon, Rajesh Jindl, Snehal Chitneni, Mohit Bhargava, Deepak Srivastava and everyone at INOX Leisure, Tashur Dhingra at Adlabs Films, Shriram Krishnan at Shringar Cinemas, Ashish Shukla and Gagan Bindra at PVR Cinemas, Anand Moorthy at FUN Cinemas and Parveen Kumar at Wave Cinemas. Arjit Dutta in Kolkata and Vimal Doshi in Baroda were kind enough to share their insights on the distribution sector. We would also like to thank Kabir Khan and Vipul Shah for taking time to talk to us about filmmaking in Mumbai. In New Zealand, we would like to thank Jamie Pickford and Peter Prosser at Walker and Associates. In the UK, thanks go to Emma Mawdsley and Ira Bhaskar at the British Association of South Asian Studies for their early interest in this work and to the Institute of Development Studies, Oxford University. Similarly, in Australia, we would like to thank Tom O'Regan at the University of Queensland and Tim Scrase at CAPSTRANS, University of Wollongong. Last but not least, we would like to thank the hundreds of movie fans across India who took time to talk to us over the course of the study.

1 Situating the multiplex as a research object

The multiplex cinema is a site of major significance for anyone interested in understanding not only the operating logic of the media industries, but also the contemporary dynamics of urban development, public culture and social change. In the Indian case specifically, an account of the multiplex must be informed by India's great cultural diversity, its colonial and socialist pasts, its dense and contested spatialities, its vibrant audio-visual culture, the strengths and contradictions of its mixed economy and its complex arrangements of civil and political society. At the present time, the story of the multiplex in India is also widely perceived as being part of a wider narrative through which India is variously described as 'rising', 'shining', 'poised' and 'unbound'. Such epithets are mobilized in support of an unfolding regime of economic liberalisation, which began in earnest in 1991. During this era, successive Indian governments have relaxed stringent licensing laws that gave overwhelming control of the economy to the government. As a result, India has attracted significant inflows of foreign investment and is increasingly returning to its historically significant role in international trade. As part of this process, a new popular image of India is emerging in the pages of English-language news and business glossies as a dynamic, modernising, capitalist society amenable to incorporation into the global knowledge economy. This process of 're-branding', while far from uncontested, has been enormously influential both internationally and within India itself.

The shift towards a 'New Economy' represents a validation of new patterns of consumption associated with an aspirational middle class that has become increasingly offered as a model of social progress. It is this new middle class, seen as being forged amongst an environment of international brands and in an increasingly globalised workplace, which has been closely linked in the popular imagination with the constituency of the multiplex film theatre. It is hardly surprising then, that in a society where consumerism has been actively disparaged for several decades in the name of social cohesion, and where it still remains out of reach for the majority of the population, the impact of the multiplex on public culture has very particular connotations. This book demonstrates how the advent of the multiplex has significantly altered the nature of cinema as public space in India and thus, crucially, what it means to be in the cinema hall. In doing so, the case is also made that the multiplex craze could not have occurred in India until precisely the time that it did, and that this was due to a number of reasons that could variously be called economic, political, cultural and geographic – although in practice they are hard to separate and these stories must therefore be told together.

It is also important to note that the rise of the multiplex in India is far from a uniform process. Multiplexes appear to be springing up everywhere in some parts of the country, whilst being as noticeably absent in others. Again, there are reasons, and precedents, for this geographic dispersal that is explored in this study. It is equally important to recognise that whilst the multiplex is certainly an icon of the present, it is also responsive to a longer historical process of social change. In that sense, even though India's first multiplex has only been in operation since 1997, the story of the multiplex in India has been a century in the making. The multiplex is clearly part of a very particular industrial history that needs to be told, that of film exhibition. However, it is only in the most recent phase of this history that the media industries have emerged from the realm of India's informal economy as major benefactors of (and spokesmen for) the era of deregulation. For their part, the belated granting of official industry status to the film business in 2001 by the Indian government indicates their recognition of the importance of the entertainment and leisure sectors. Consequently, major changes are taking place in the ways that Indian films are produced, marketed and received, and it is of little surprise, therefore, that the form and content of the films themselves have also been changing rapidly over the last 15 years. These are all developments germane to any account of the multiplex, ensuring the arrival in India of this 'global' exhibition format and its important place in the wider story of Indian business and public culture.

Like the New Economy more generally, the rise of the multiplex is also overwhelmingly an urban story. Nowhere are the changes occurring in India today more apparent than in its cities, which are being extensively transformed by the rapid growth in car ownership and the parallel spread of an interconnected network of residential complexes, flyovers and country clubs. The multiplex cinema is an intrinsic part of this new leisure infrastructure, and is further indicative of a wider shift towards a Western-inspired commercial society with massive investments being made in consumer advertising and the building of thousands of shopping malls nationwide. The reorganisation of Indian cities in this way is now becoming possible because of a raft of regulatory changes that have favoured public–private partnerships and commercially-oriented development projects. The impetus behind this re-shaping of Indian cities is guided by the desire to create global cities capable of bringing together flows of international capital. Land for New Economy developments is becoming available through re-zoning at urban fringes, renovation of former industrial areas and the demolition of slums and illegal settlements. In this sense, the creation of valuable new public space within Indian cities, which the multiplex undeniably represents, is to the benefit of the inhabitants of new residential suburbs and at the expense of farmers, industrial workers and the urban poor. As such, multiplex theatres are powerfully implicated in the spatial politics of Indian cities.

The richness of the multiplex cinema as a research object is demonstrated by its obvious importance to these various overlapping histories and the fields of enquiry that surround them. In telling the story of the multiplex in India over the course of its first decade, there are many different players that we need to consider, and many different voices that need to be heard. As such, this study engages at various points with corporate managers, college students, film directors, investment advisors, architects, distributors, public relations officers, academics and others. Before opening up this broader discussion, however, this chapter begins by unpacking the title of this book, which not only demarcates the multiplex both as a physical arte-fact and as a social phenomenon taking place in contemporary India, but also implies a concerted attempt at an interdisciplinary intervention that is illustrative of the ways in which we have attempted to understand that phenomena. As such, this introductory chapter takes the multiplex as both the starting and finishing point of a journey that extrapolates from the question 'What is a multiplex?'. Along the way, we seek to clarify the terms under which it becomes possible to understand the mul-tiplex variously as a commercial, architectural, geographic, aesthetic and social intervention.

What is a multiplex?

In its most literal sense, a multiplex is most obviously a building where films are shown on more than one screen. The multiplex can therefore be most simply described as a contemporary setting for the time-worn practice of storytelling. The projection of feature films provides multiplex patrons with gratification by means of narrative entertainment, and it simultaneously engenders ideological exchanges that articulate the mythic logic of the society that they inhabit. Even from the most functionalist perspective, however, there is much more to the multiplex than this alone. It is equally obvious that in capitalist societies, a multiplex is constructed for the purpose of serving a paying public. As such, it has to be considered not only as a place of entertainment, but also as a site of commercial activity where money changes hands on the basis of large-scale participation in a series of complex eco-nomic interactions that cumulatively combine into a social structure referred to as an 'industry'. A multiplex, therefore, is primarily a site of social practice, a place where people congregate for the purpose of watching films. Members of such crowds are encouraged by the physical layout of the multiplex and by social con-vention to behave in a certain manner within its limits. In this way, a multiplex is a site for the performance of certain social rituals that are at least as significant as the narrative products that are consumed in the process.

In addition, since the multiplex is a piece of flagship architecture that makes a major intervention in urban space, the production of meanings at a multiplex facil-ity is by no means limited to its interior functions. A multiplex is most typically a highly decorated landmark, and hence is itself a text of a certain kind. Within a city, each multiplex occupies a particular place to which large numbers of people travel by various routes and means during the course of their everyday lives. The multi-plex impinges on the consciousness of even larger numbers of those who are, for now at least, just passing by. Whether it is constructed on a greenfield site at the frontier of development or in the space previously occupied by a building of another kind, a multiplex is almost invariably part of a major reconfiguration of urban space around which large numbers of people are required to reorganise their lives. Both the narrative and the behavioural influence of the multiplex can therefore be seen to spread far beyond its own confines. In each case the multiplex emerges from the pages of a particular urban history, laden with the ghosts of past aspirations and pregnant with the metropolitan fantasies of tomorrow. Ultimately, it is for all these various reasons that the multiplex has a particular salience for those interested in understanding the experience of contemporary urban life.

Of course, the multiplex has a well-known precedent in the form of a famous parent. The multiplex is instantly recognisable as a sub-genre of a type of building known as a cinema, a form which has existed for almost exactly a century and which displays many of the qualities discussed above. The multiplex, however, is generally recognised as being a new incarnation of the cinema with particular distinctive features. Across the world, the reconfiguration of the social spaces in which the theatrical exhibition of films takes place, from dedicated single-screen, large-capacity cinema halls to multiplex venues subdivided into several smaller auditoriums, has visibly re-written the paradigm of cinematic exhibition. In that sense, the multiplex is held as something new in that it offers us a range of choices oriented around our contemporary understanding of what it is to be modern and to be pleasured. The multiplex therefore provides some useful indications of the forms of public, discourse and environment we currently consider to be of value, and of the latest techniques for exploiting those desires commercially. It is highly significant then, that from the 1980s onwards the rise of the multiplex has been an integral part of the worldwide spread of mall culture. As such, the deployment of the multiplex in a number of culturally distinctive societies in different regions of the world during an era of increasing global economic integration and rapid urbanisation makes an even more pressing case for a detailed exposition of this phenomenon.

The multiplex story began, perhaps unsurprisingly, in North America, the world's single most profitable market for feature films. It took place, seemingly, in three stages. First of all, as Charles Acland recounts, the practice of 'twinning' was pioneered in Ottawa, Canada by the subdivision of a movie theatre (to use the American expression) into two screens by Nat Taylor in 1948. The first purpose-built two-screen theatre is subsequently held to be have been opened at the Ward Parkway shopping mall in Kansas City in 1963 by Stan Durwood (Acland 2003: 103). Twinning held certain advantages for distributors. The second screen was cheaper to run than a second theatre and therefore represented a lower overhead, while also enabling loss-making or low-performing films to be moved rapidly to the smaller screen, thus increasing the overall efficiency of the main auditorium (ibid.). In the American context, the twinning of theatres has also been seen as a response to the growth of television and the decline of audience numbers at the cinema, with theatres having to try harder to get people out to the cinema. From this perspective, the multi-screen cinema can be related to the wider screens and elaborate sound systems of the 1950s and 1960s. The twin cinema was also sporadically taken up in India not long after its American manifestation. Bangalore in particular still has several twin cinema sites from the early 1970s. They are constructed in a distinctive style of one big and one small screen operating as different cinemas but sharing the same lot. Since India at that time had a rapidly growing cinema audience and no national television service, this would appear to suggest that, in this case at least, the imperatives for twinning came from within the film industry itself rather than in response to the television threat.

Returning to the North American account, the second stage of multiplex development was the true multiplex, a cinema designed to operate with four or more small auditoriums. This format offered patrons a menu of entertainment, while placing a particular focus on the provision of ancillary activities, such as video games and expanded food and beverage facilities, referred to as 'concessions' but usually run in-house. Although potentially a stand-alone operation, the true multiplex was more typically in, or adjacent to, shopping malls. Over several decades, the ongoing suburbanisation of American cities led to the steady relocation of retail facilities to the ever-expanding suburbs. These new suburban commercial complexes grew in pace with the scale of suburbanisation. By the 1980s they had reached massive proportions. The large-scale of such developments, their position at the hub of new residential districts and the ready availability of floor space for lease that they provided made them a natural location for cinemas. At the same time, mall developers keen to attract a high turnover of visitors to their site in order to make leases attractive to retailers had a natural interest in the crowd-forming capacity of the cinema. Thus, the logic of multi-screen cinema was massively extended during the 1980s, which became the era of the in-mall-multiplex.

The multiplex can be seen as a response by the leisure economy to the general shift of the population. The first generation of cinemas were often downtown or in older residential districts close to the centre. By contrast the shopping malls in the 1980s served the sprawling Fordist suburbs of the 1960s and the youth that had grown up there. As part of the spread of suburban malls and their growing size, the multiplex became the standard out-of-home visual entertainment experience for the MTV generation. A variant on the competing media explanation discussed previously was again offered for their success in that the multiplex boom of the 1980s was seen as a response to the advent of home video and cable, which compelled the exhibition sector to extend, if not exactly match, the range of titles on offer due to the increased choice that people were becoming accustomed to at home. However, as Thomas Guback (1987) argues, the adoption of the multiplex was as much the result of a drive to improve the efficiency of profit-taking in a stagnant market. More screens meant greater efficiency in terms of admissions per square foot and also minimised the risks from films that failed. New and refurbished facilities also justified rising admission prices. As such, multiplexes increased both the number of screens and their overall profitability without significantly increasing the overall number of cinemas or the size of the cinema audience as a whole.

What was also highly significant about the multiplex boom of the 1980s in North America was that it occurred alongside the re-integration of the audio-visual market by ever-larger multi-media corporations. In that sense, the boom in multiplex construction was not simply a device for defending a shrinking audience or for improving internal market efficiency. Rather, it was indicative of a 'crisis in exhibition and distribution' as the interests of distributors and exhibitors collided, and were then resolved, within an era of mergers, acquisitions and deregulated economics (Acland 2003: 85–106). In this context, the multiplex was deeply implicated in the 'resurrection' of 'vertical integration' in the US film industry (Guback 1987: 71–73). Following indications in the mid-1980s that the United States government would no longer enforce the separation of production, distribution and exhibition in the film industry, the major players in the media sector embarked upon a flurry of mergers and acquisitions. Producers and distributors acquired their own exhibition arms for the first time since the Paramount decisions in 1948 had forced the major players to relinquish their theatrical holdings (Acland 2003: 96). This new era of vertical integration meant that the multiplex was not primarily a device employed by exhibitors in response to the TV/video threat since exhibitors were rapidly being subsumed by the expanding media empires who also acquired the video distribution infrastructure. Instead, the multiplex became just one of the many profit windows in an organised value chain operated by a handful of media conglomerates. The multiplex was therefore symptomatic of market reorganisation, but more than that, it was an operating environment conceived and constructed for an era of corporate oligarchy and sophisticated market control.

In the process of competitive acquisition of market share by rapidly expanding media corporations, what was at best a stagnant market in terms of audience size was paradoxically furnished by major investments in new infrastructure. Indeed, by the time that the new media giants had bought out or forced out the old exhibitors, there was considerable over-screening in the US market. This rapid expansion of multiplexes in the 1980s also created something of an image problem. Whereas the old movie theatres that they had gradually replaced became objects of nostalgia, the mall multiplexes rapidly became disparaged for smaller seats, less legroom and poor sound. The industry responded to this (at least partially self-generated) crisis in the 1990s with a new wave of construction. The adoption of a lease model, however, increasingly meant that the new operators could easily divest themselves of unprofitable sites and move on to new pastures. What followed was the third stage of the multiplex story, the age of the megaplex. Theatres were reconstituted as cinematic theme parks based at the city limits, where a dozen screens or more were augmented by extensive shopping and dining franchises (see Acland 2002). Left in their wake were not only the closures of old heritage theatres downtown, but also suburbs littered with deadmalls and greyfields shopping developments, where the leading retail brands and cinema chains had moved on to bigger things. The story of the multiplex in America was thus intimately entwined with the increasing rapidity of regeneration and decay set by the paradigm of the retail property market.

The rise of the multiplex was by no means confined to this particular history, however, insomuch as the changes to the media industries that went with it had reverberations worldwide. Whilst the United Kingdom had some examples of twinned theatres by the 1970s, the exhibition infrastructure was still dominated by single-screen cinema halls in relatively central locations well into the 1980s. Indeed, according to Phil Hubbard (2002), traditional cinemas still constitute three-quarters of British cinemas at the present time. The acquisition of many British exhibition concerns by US companies as part of their expansion during the 1980s nonetheless saw the first multiplex being opened in Milton Keynes, a post-war resettlement city some 50 miles north of London, in 1985. Adjacent to what was then the country's largest shopping mall, The Point was operated by UCI as a ten-screen cinema complex which also incorporated a nightclub, a gaming arcade and several bars and restaurants. In many ways, this facility was more akin to the contemporary megaplex than what were then its peers in the suburban malls of the United States. Ultimately, however, it was to suffer the same fate, with UCI even-tually selling out in 2003 after the opening of a rival facility, Xscape, boasting 16 screens, numerous restaurants and a full-sized interior ski slope, in a new leisure dis-trict situated less than half a mile away. By this time, some 200 multiplex cinemas had been constructed in the UK, for the most part in new retail developments on the edge of existing towns.

As Phil Hubbard describes it, the advent of the multiplex in Britain 'fundamen-tally changed patterns of cinema-going in Britain' since

> two thirds of cinema screens (and 90% of admissions) are now in out-of-town locations. In this sense, it appears that any explanation of the resurgence of cin-ema attendance needs to pay careful attention not just to the design of multi-plex cinemas, but also to their locations.
>
> (2002: 1240)

As in America, the story of the multiplex in Britain has represented a shift of con-sumption away from urban centres and towards the periphery. Although towns and cities in the UK do not generally display the degree of suburbanisation that charac-terises many of their American counterparts, the sheer density of the existing metropolitan landscape and the heavily congested traffic in an increasingly car-dependent country (where the majority of town layouts pre-date the automobile) typically requires that any large new structures be built at the margins of conurba-tion. As such, an increasing proportion of the supermarkets that now dominate British life have been sited out of town and, similarly, this is where the multiplexes are to be found. As a result of this trend, town centres have dwindled in commercial importance, despite official policies designed to discourage the shift from High Street to Ring Road. The continuing decay of town centre retail districts has encouraged this centrifugal process of redevelopment. In doing so, it has exacer-bated the emergence of 'two-speed or "dual" cities, divided between the safer spaces of a mobile, affluent consumer elite and the more dangerous, marginalised spaces of the less affluent' (Hubbard 2002: 1240). Thus, whilst the multiplexes represent only one-quarter of the UK's cinemas, they nonetheless constitute the majority of screens and the vast bulk of box office, despite remaining beyond the reach of, as Hubbard puts it, the 'older, poorer, carless population' (2002: 1249).

After examining the relocation of cinema sites and the reorganisation of the tra-jectories of movement associated with leisure in the city of Leicester, Hubbard (2002: 1252) notes two other important, and closely related, aspects of the multiplex as a social space. First, unlike a traditional cinema, the multiplex is primarily intended to extend a single-commodity activity (i.e. going to the pictures) into a multi-media experience of consumption. As such, multiplexes are not simply places to see films; they are one-stop shops for out-of-home entertainment that variously combine eating, gaming and shopping with the practice of watching films. The mix of activities on offer, in combination with a sanitised and controlled interior space with ample free parking, represents a concerted effort to target families as consumers, as opposed to the youth groups, which was the mainstay of the cinema for decades. Thus, the multiplex constituted a transformation of British cinemas into 'Family Entertainment Centres' or 'FECs' (ibid.: 1239). This leads to the second aspect of the multiplex phenomenon: relegating the watching of films to a lesser component of the overall operating rationale. The wider impli-cation of this is a major shift from a content-driven to an experiential mode of understanding the exhibition trade. In the era of playback media, you do not go to the multiplex simply to view a feature film that you could not otherwise consume. Rather, you go there to encounter a particular sensorial experience: the multiplex itself.

In this respect, Hubbard emphasises the intensely 'embodied' nature of the film-going experience at the multiplex (2003). In ethnographic research, Hubbard finds that the sensory pleasures of the lobby, auditoria and seating were extremely impor-tant to patrons. Even more important was the ontological security that they drew from the orderly queues, the presence of other patrons who belonged to similar social categories as themselves and an overall experience of 'cleanliness' that went beyond any physical description of grime (ibid.: 261). According to Hubbard, the audiences at the multiplex are made to feel 'comfortable' through the mutually agreed maintenance of social distance between patrons since the architectural arrangement of the multiplex format encourages anonymous flows of people and 'participation, talking and other forms of social interaction with strangers are strictly curtailed in multiplex cinema auditoria' (ibid.: 262–264). All of this extended the sense of social-cocooning that they brought with them to the multiplex as car-owners (ibid.: 264–266). Both the one-stop shop and the social-cocooning effect are attributes of the multiplex experience that are consciously designed to cater to the desires and motivations of an atomised nuclear social unit. Thus, there are psychological and behavioural assumptions associated with the multiplex for-mat which have wider social implications.

During the early 1990s, when the multiplex was making its mark in Europe, it was also transforming the exhibition sector in Australia and in parts of Asia. The rapid adoption of retail mall development models in the megacities of northeast and southeast Asia got underway during the property booms of the 'Asian Tigers' era. As such, the construction of multiplex cinemas in Seoul, Bangkok and Singapore were part of the reordering of commercial and residential spaces in those cities under a certain economic paradigm. The particularities of the metropolitan politics of each city dictated a range of outcomes which variously served developers, con-sumers and local authorities in different measures – ranging from the ad hoc to sig-nificant integration with major planned reorganisations of urban space. For example, Ravenscroft et al. point to the development of multiplexes in Singapore as a particular outcome of comprehensive planning directives that suburbanised a major component of the cities' population, thus giving rise to the need for new integrated leisure and retail developments:

> Through successive master plans, the government has ensured that new residential areas have been served by cinemas with low admission prices . . . This has undoubtedly offered the possibility of social, cultural and ethnic accessibility and inclusion for all citizens – an offer that has been widely taken up. Yet it also implies that such spaces offer compensation for the highly regulated and inherently discriminatory world beyond the cinema.
>
> (Ravenscroft et al. 2001: 226)

Ravenscroft et al. describe the conjoined mall-multiplex as a spatial device which conditioned Singaporeans to a new way of living that was closely orientated towards centrally-planned consumerism. Singapore, with its ability to closely manage its population and visibly demonstrate the possibility of an orderly, sanitised urban environment in Asia, has long been an object of envy for India's metropolitan planners – and an arcadia for both the Indian traders and the unskilled labourers who travel across the Bay of Bengal to the island city.

The multiplex as an international standard, both as an icon of urban planning and as a generic format for consuming pleasures, clearly represents a new incarnation of cinema. As such, its uptake across the world during the 1980s and 1990s has constituted a repetition of the rapid global spread of new media formats that has been consistently demonstrated since the early days of cinema. Based upon its impacts elsewhere, the 'universal' multiplex has to be seen as marking an intervention into public life that needs to be considered along three distinct but converging vectors of social change: 1) the economic restructuring of the film industry to favour integrated operations and corporate capital 2) the rise of a new leisure economy that increasingly requires the watching of films to be augmented with other activities and behaviours 3) the wider spatial re-organisation of the urban environment undertaken with the intention of favouring certain modes of living and therefore leading to the re-making of existing public spaces and the social conventions that surround them. Brenner and Theodore describe these processes as constituting 'moments of creative destruction' that 'ultimately lead to the intensification of socio-spatial polarization as cities become shaped by market oriented development and elite consumption practices' (2002: 368).

The cultural economy of urban India

By comparison to the other markets discussed previously, and despite its enormous movie-going public, India has been a relative latecomer to what has arguably been the biggest shake-up to film exhibition since the introduction of colour. In general terms this is because (for various historical reasons that we will go on to explore in more detail) the Indian cinema market is not quite like the others mentioned thus far. In this context, the multiplex boom that is currently underway in Indian cities is all the more notable since it represents such a radical departure from the social practices traditionally associated with the cinema in India. In the environmental context, the physical architecture of the multiplex itself also represents a radical, dynamic intervention into a very different urban landscape from the North American Fordist suburbs for which it was originally designed. For both these reasons, Aparna Sharma (2003) has previously commented that: 'the Indian multiplex experience has been smattered with instances that stand in opposition to its immediate environs. Incoherent, inconsistent, possibly transitional yet aggressively attentive, these lend to it markings of an indigenous, self-derived and developed nature'.

What does remain constant in re-situating the story of the multiplex in India's towns and cities is that its story inevitably, and of necessity, draws together the strands of commercial culture, popular fantasy, political struggle, behavioural geography and public history that constitute the fabric of social change. For this reason, we should keep in mind Charles Acland's claims that:

> The manifest nature of public film exhibition carries the assumptions of a particular time. It is an ideologically invested marker of cultural and public life. An array of forces, intentions, determinations, and logics produces the semblance of the inherent taken-for-grantedness of industrial and cultural practice. Unpacking the forces underlying the process of that production here entails the concepts of a spatially and temporally defined pastime, city development zones, exhibitor/distributor relations and changing audiovisual entertainment. But a starting point, a foundational determination, is a set of assumptions about the free-market economy in which the merger of major communication and cultural industries 'made sense'.
>
> (2003: 95)

All of the components of the phenomenon identified here by Acland (i.e. spatial, temporal, developmental, operational, audiovisual, economic and pleasurable components) will prove to be pertinent categories of analysis for the Indian experience. We cannot, however, accept Acland's claim in its entirety for the sole reason that a conception of the market in any form as a foundational determination is a particularly loaded one in any sociology of culture, a point to which we will return shortly. Rather, if a general cause is needed at the outset, for the purposes of this study it is more defensible to assume that the foundational determinate of the Indian multiplex is history, from which the manifestation of past desires and contests constitute the social geography of the present. Without falling prey to economic determinism, it nonetheless remains the case that in order to understand the lived experience of the multiplex, we need to locate our enquiry within the industrial economy of leisure in India. This study provides ample evidence of the fact that, despite its serious neglect over five decades of film studies, the exhibition sector does indeed drive the Indian film industry, both financially and aesthetically. However, we must identity not only its capital formations, but also their operation within real social spaces. Thus, an industrial investigation inevitably becomes an exposition of social relations, which in turn implies a political dimension.

As such, while the critical connections between economic and cultural enquiry might seem either obvious or irrelevant at first glance, depending on your point of view, it remains the case that we still need to consider the unresolved schism between cultural and economic approaches to social change with some care and, at the very least, make our own position in the context of the present study as clear as possible. As Janice Peck (2006) observes, the antagonistic relationship between adherents of cultural approaches and adherents of political economy arises as much upon the convergence of their ontological frameworks as it does upon their disparity. On the one hand, many scholars in the disciplinary field of cultural studies reject the notion that economic structures have a credible determining effect on human subjectivity and social practice. On the other, political economists have a tendency to reject the culturalist notion that economic relations are just one determinant of a loose, relativistic operation of power – often on the grounds that the contestation of subjectivities, or identity politics, is seen as negating socio-economic struggle. These mutually antagonistic positions thus remain closely linked by their shared adherence to the utility of the base-superstructure paradigm and the attendant bifurcation in modernist thought between cultural and economic practices as distinct realms of human activity. Thus, as Peck observes, the disciplines of cultural studies and political economy appear to have carved up the social realm amongst themselves upon a mutually agreed basis that allows them to tackle the back-end and front-end of commercial society without making any sustained attempt to resolve their necessary relationship (2006: 93).

By contrast, in this study we rejected from the outset the proposition that the realms of culture and commerce are distinct, or as Pierre Bourdieu (1993: 32) has described them, homologous fields. Rather, economic structures are understood here as social relations that are inherently cultural, while simultaneously recognising that cultural practices in modern societies display a tendency towards complex economic organisation. As such, it becomes less than useful to ask whether such relations are primarily culturally or economically determined, since in practice it is impossible to maintain a meaningful distinction between the two. At the multiplex, the commercial organisation of cultural products is as important as the distinctive culture of doing business. This neither suggests the utility of a reductionist position, nor does it support the theoretical proposition of discrete spheres of influence.

We would further critique the culture/economy dualism on the grounds that followers of both economic and cultural approaches have been equally guilty on occasion of downplaying the material dimension of society – whilst paradoxically materialising the subject of their own enquiries. On the one hand, many political economies overly focus on the power wielded by capital concentrations figured as monetarist abstractions functioning externally to the social order. This is the world of dollar figures, depersonalised corporate entities, policy euphemisms and the work of capitalist ideology where money itself ultimately becomes the material under analysis. Subsequently, the material environments of offices, shops, homes and factories, and the experiences of those who are enshrined by them, are often neglected. It is upon this basis that the cultural studies school has frequently made the charge that political economists ignore the importance of everyday life

(Grossberg 1995: 74). However, cultural studies in turn displays a similar tendency to reify culture as a series of abstract discursive codes (signifying structures) or quantify it as a form of ontological substance or *materiel* (identity) in its own right. This in turn gives rise to the location of culture at the level of personal or textual symbolism without paying enough attention to the social spaces where culture practices are manifested. In this sense, the schism between cultural and economic analysis within sociology is itself instigative rather than indicative of the reductionist logic that pulls them apart.

Within the interdiscipline of media studies, but also in the wider domain of sociology, the result of the culture/economy dualism has been an ongoing bifurcation between different strands of radical critique. Commenting on this phenomenon, Toby Miller (2006) has recently observed that 'media studies has been overly functionalist on its political economy side, and overly conflictual on its active-audience side'. Miller further suggests that, in order to fix this, 'We need political economy to register struggle, and active-audience work to register structure' (ibid.). The book that you are now reading is thus part of a wider intent to overcome the limitations of disciplinary dualism and essentialism in research practice inherited from Western Marxism. This wider intent is referenced in the field of cultural economy which has emerged in recent years, although by its very nature this body of work lacks doctrinal specificity and encompasses approaches which juxtapose the cultural and the economic in different ways (Scott 2000, Du Gay and Prycke 2002, Amin and Thrift 2003). Our intention is to incorporate three major strands in cultural economy: the political economy of the cultural industries; the interrogation of commercial activity as a cultural practice; and the cultural specificity of the social worlds in which these practices take place. The research approach that we adopt could thus be seen as an attempt towards either a culturally-aware political economy of urban leisure or towards a politically-aware cultural economy of urban leisure and remain equally valid.

A crucial argument that we make here is that the missing dimension of enquiry required to reconcile the dualism between the cultural and economic must always be the environmental dimension – without which either the cultural or economic are more or less abstractions. This argument is made following Henri Lefebvre's (1991) influential observation that space is always socially produced, and that public space is therefore not only structuring of, but also structured by, cultural and economic behaviours. As this study demonstrates, it is upon the terrain of lived social relations and within the spaces that we occupy at the everyday level that the necessary intellectual relation between the material and symbolic realms (and the relations of power) can be most clearly seen. This relationship is by no means elusive, unintelligible or even inimical, but it is instead demonstrably both manifest and complementary – even if its ideological and/or systematic components may well remain unsatisfactory from a number of political standpoints. The spatialisation of our enquiry thus brings us into contact with the new geographies of recent years, including the cultural turn in urban and economic geography, and their mutual recognition that economic spaces are inhabited, contested and represented in ways that are evident at various scales (Amin and Thrift 2007, Castree 2004, Hudson

2004). Conversely, our approach also converges with those calling for a spatialised understanding of the cultural industries (Curtin 2003, Pratt 2004). In examining the multiplex, we are also attentive to critiques of studies of consumption that fall prey to the unsatisfactory dualism of locating such practices as either blind submission to global capitalism or as acts of unrestrained agency and individualised identity formation (Crewe 2003, Goss 2003).

In the context of understanding the changing social environment in India specifically, it is also worth recognising a further dimension to the question of interdisciplinarity. The pressing issue here is that whatever the so-called 'cultural turn' might have been, or is becoming, in European or North American scholarship, the disciplinary nature of, and the contribution to be made by, such a turn in Asia has yet to be determined. Claims of a cultural turn for India may well appear disingenuous at first glance. Culture has not, after all, been a neglected sphere in the description of India. As such, it is logical that Indian scholarship is likely to draw much more explicitly upon the rich tradition of anthropological work in this regard than its Western counterpart (despite the fact that anthropological definitions of culture lurk everywhere, often uncredited, behind cultural studies in the West) (see Hobart 2000). Nonetheless, there does appear to be a significant shift in thinking about Indian society that makes space for the serious consideration of the contemporary cultural formations that operate within the flux of social change; formations which interact with, but are not wholly constructed by, the legacies of India's famous ethnic diversity as mapped out by two centuries of anthropological records. Thus, the past two decades have witnessed a sustained attempt to rescue culture from the distant de-politicised heritage role to which it was banished during the Nehruvian era of developmental modernism, with much to be gained from the re-evaluation of the tradition/modernity binary that has structured cultural discussions in the past (see Prasad 1998: 7–8). It is no longer tenable to equate the modern simply with Westernisation and as antithetical to a concept of culture bound to indigeneity in a pre-modern form. However, since Indian society and its constituent cultures in their modern forms are undeniably particular in their nature, the anthropological mode of enquiry remains well suited to elucidating the social context in which the Indian media operate.

Specificity is important here. Approaches to contemporary cultural practice within India offer different challenges and rewards than similar undertakings in the Philippines or Japan, and the theorisation of culture in all those places will be noticeably distinct from the traditions laid down in Britain, Australia or the United States. Nonetheless, there are clearly going to be some mutual influences and concerns that remain, not least because the Marxist tradition from which the study of Western popular culture emerged – and against which it continues to differentiate itself – also has a rich and important history in modern India. As India reinvents itself in a post-Marxist, post-socialist era, it is already apparent that thinkers such as Foucault and Gramsci, who have proved crucial to a similar epistemological shift made in the West, are also seen to have salience for the contemporary Indian experience. This common intellectual heritage, powerfully transformed via the work of the Subaltern Studies scholars, is reflected in the polemical traditions laid down by post-colonial studies in the 1980s and 1990s, with its strident critiques of Western hegemony and of the democratic deficit inherited by the post-colonial state (see Ahmad 1994, Bhabha 1994, Chatterjee 1993, Guha and Spivak 1989, Nandy 1989, 1998, 2003).

The convergence of cultural materialism with the steel frame of empiricism laid down during five decades of socialist development also provides fertile ground for highly particular dynamics (combative, complementary and otherwise) arising from the reconfiguration of positivist and interpretative traditions within the field of Indian sociology. The explosion of popular commercial media in the liberalisation era, with which this study engages wholeheartedly and unashamedly, provides much of the impetus for the appropriation of India's media from the previously bifurcated domains of developmental communications studies and literary film studies. The popular media have begun instead to occupy the central terrain of debates on social change in India, much as they have elsewhere in the world. It is impossible to ignore, therefore, the obvious significance of the fact that a sociological engagement with popular culture follows the resurgence of cultural nationalism in India (since at least the 1980s, and most obviously after Ayodhya). So while a cultural turn in India will certainly not be about unravelling the popular successes and/or failures of the Western world after 1968, it must, inevitably, engage with the politics of popular culture and with the culture of political populism.

Given that the international genealogy of the multiplex consistently indicates an intervention into the spatial organisation of the urban environment, an appropriate conceptual approach to urban space is just as crucial to our enquiry. The cinema in India has, of course, been bound up throughout its history with the shock-tactics of metropolitan life (see Kaarsholm 2004). In order to understand how the changing political economy of leisure embodied by the multiplex in particular converges with the contemporary upheaval that has become so visible in India's towns and cities in the last decade, it becomes useful to situate our enquiry in the context of the tradition of critical urbanism that is now emerging in South Asia. This work draws upon the traditions of enquiry that have been upheld for some years in the political sciences by scholars such as Partha Chatterjee and Ashis Nandy. To risk the loosest of generalisations, the emerging field of critical urbanism seeks to operationalise these and other concerns within a multi-dimensional environmental model that encompasses the smoothness of the shopping mall, the urban antimatter of the *basti* (slum settlement) and the informational flows that now circulate in the 'cybermohalla' (wired communal district).

Due to their critical influence on this particular project, we make specific reference here to the collective interdisciplinary work of Sarai in New Delhi and the equally interdisciplinary civic activism of Collective Research Initiatives Trust (CRIT) in Mumbai (Sarai 2007, CRIT 2007). Sarai is a research network launched in 2001 and based at the Centre for the Study of Developing societies in New Delhi that brings together academics, media practitioners, activists and artists engaging with urban public culture. As Monica Narula explains it:

> The Sarai initiative interprets this sense of the word Sarai to mean a very public space where different intellectual, creative, and activist energies can

intersect in an open and dynamic manner to give rise to an imaginative reconstitution of urban public culture, new/old media practice, research, and critical cultural intervention.

(2002: 405).

CRIT, in Mumbai, is a group bringing together architects, scholars, technicians and artists. CRIT 'was established in early 2003 with the aim of undertaking research, pedagogy and intervention on urban spaces and contemporary cultural practices in the Mumbai Metropolitan Region' (CRIT 2007). The web portals of these two collectives provide an ample indication of the innovative approaches that are now being applied to understanding, and intervening in, the changing nature of Indian cities.

Writing for Sarai, Gyan Prakash asserts that the increasing recognition of urban India as a conflictual terrain for sociology represents an important shift from a temporally-defined conception of modernity (i.e through the discourse of 'development') towards a spatially-constructed view (that focuses on geometric and sociological relations of proximate existence) (Prakash 2002). For Prakash, the major implication of such a re-evaluation of social perspective is the abandonment of a historical race towards progress in which certain citizens, groups and communities were seen as being ahead, but sharing the same destination, in favour of model describing a multi-polar struggle between the various actors over the urban environment that is perpetual, shifting and open-ended. In this sense, it is the stated intention of Sarai to remain 'alert to the city as a locus of imaginary engagements, a body of distinct practices, a compendium of different ways of knowing, and as a field of power, strategies of survival and resistance' (Sarai 2002). This recasting of the 'urban milieu' in Foucauldian terms is a far cry from the high modernism that was given formal expression in the planning of New Delhi or Chandigarh in the last century.

Kong and Law (2002) observe that most commentators have been relatively slow to acknowledge the extent to which urban landscapes, including public space and the built environment, are politically contested social spaces. Further, Kong and Law note that it is only recently that the impact of culture and cultural change has begun to figure in the discussion on patterns of urban development to the extent that it arguably should (ibid.). In this respect, what has been achieved to date by a more critical form of urbanism in South Asia has been the opening up of a human vantage point that allows us to see the processes of urbanisation as necessarily partial, divisive and contested. That is not to say that this is a case of modernity versus the masses, since the remaking of Indian cities is as much the product of local desires as it is the subject of local resistance. To put it simply, but without oversimplification, this is a political contest being fought out on a number of fronts (and by an array of disparate militias). In recognising this, the recent work on Indian cities is comparatively rich and is further strengthened by its tendency to treat Indian cities and their transformations as *sui generis* rather than immature replicas of European or North American urban blueprints (Banerjee-Guha 2002, Patel and Thorner 1995a, 1995b, et al.). At the same time, government planners have been less innovative in this regard, and successive attempts to remake India's cities in the guise of 'world cities' thus continue unabated (Gugler 2004, Newman and Thornley 2005).

Ashis Nandy has made the influential observation that the popular Indian cinema promulgates a lower middle-class sensibility that is synonymous with the urban slum. He claims that:

> popular cinema is low-brow, modernizing India in all its complexity, sophistry, naivete, and vulgarity . . . [it] may be what the middle class, left to itself, might have done to itself and to India, but it is also the disowned self of modern India returning in a fantastic or monstrous form to haunt modern India.
>
> (1997: 7)

In this sense, the popular cinema is taken as a projection of both the lumpen past and the newfound social aspirations of the lower middle classes. The parallel with the slum thus becomes apt because

> the more numerous lower middle class exposed to modern media, pan-Indian politics and the global market . . . is the class that has closest links with the slum and lives with the fear of slipping into a slum or never getting out of it.
>
> (Ibid.: 5)

The slum settlement is the dark underside of modern India, an 'unintended city' that feeds off the planned spaces of the modernizing elite, bleeding their civic vision of its rationality (Sen 1975, 2001).

The slum is much more, however, than a useful metaphor or an aesthetic insult. It has long been the dominating feature of the urban conditions extant in the sub-continent, where the imbalance between the need for cheap labour and the deficit of affordable living space have placed the Indian middle class in an intimate but traumatic relationship with the proximity of the urban slum and its denizens. The slum is on everyone's doorstep and it is palpably not quiescent. Rather, it is a rau-cous multi-sensorial contagion preventing the emergence of a modern urban land-scape in which there is a mutually constituted separation of citizens on the basis of economic utility. At the same time, the slum is symptomatic of the ferment of dem-ocratic mobilisation and mutual oppressions, of internal migrations and social change. All of this radical newness is thus a direct threat to the older feudal certain-ties of caste purity. The slum then, is the enemy of both past and future, its recalci-trant impermanence marking a perpetual dissatisfaction with the present. Perhaps most importantly, it is widely seen by the upper middle classes as the habitat of those primeval 'others' always ready to congregate into the unruly mob that threat-ens to overrun the planned city and its more genteel patrons. A spatial politics of urban India is thus far from being simply an architectural matter. As Radhika Subramaniam notes:

> crowds, whether cast as the teeming millions of a growing population, as the citizens of the largest democracy, as the violent mobs stoked to communal

hatred, or even as a source of annoying fascination for the tourist, occupy centre stage in any account of India. They inevitably govern any discussion of its cities.

(2002: 8)

In recent years, the middle classes have consistently sought to escape from the spatial relationship which has placed them in proximity to the urban slum, a process that has resonance with the socio-spatial segregation of cities around the world, particularly in places where economic equalities and cultural disjunctures manifest in ways that the upper and middle classes perceive as threatening. In much of the developing world, malls and other spaces of retail leisure operate as exclusivist public space. As well as providing locales for the performance of hybridised global modernities, these steel and glass architectures are notable for their emphasis on cleanliness and order, secured from the unruly world outside of these fortresses of consumption (Tomic, Trumper and Dattwyler 2006, Kuppinger 2005, Erkip 2003, Abaza 2001, Dodson 2000). In India, this urban form has been sanctioned by the technocrats of liberalisation and the dreams of commercial developers.

That is not to say that the affluent no longer require the services of the slum dwellers. Even in an era in which India's cities are being remade for a post-industrial knowledge economy, there is still no Indian city that could function without its slum-dwelling workforce. However, the patterns of redevelopment that are seeing the mushrooming of new gated residential colonies at exactly the points where the rapidly expanding flyovers touch down from their vantage point above the crowded city do appear to demonstrate a newfound capacity to finally push the slum out of sight (Paul, Shetty and Krishnan 2005). The willingness to do so has long existed, of course, but it has taken a decade of liberalisation and 50 years of independence to legitimate the spatial politics within which such a social divorce has become formally permissible. It is at precisely this point that both the shopping mall and the multiplex have become synonymous with progress. The multiplex as the venue for a new consuming Indian public must be considered, therefore, alongside the other spaces towards which it is configured, that is as an intrinsic component of the leisure infrastructure of this new urban ecology of enclaves. In counterpoint, it must also be considered alongside the spaces against which it is configured: the bazaar, the pavement and the urban slum. Correspondingly, the story of multiplex theatres in India cannot be easily separated from both the ideological forces and physical works that have led to their construction and which determine their use and value.

In light of such developments, Partha Chatterjee (2004) has been prompted to ask 'Are Indian Cities becoming bourgeois at last?'. He phrases this question within the theoretical logic of a contest between 'civil' and 'political' society that he has been developing over the last ten years. These two definitions do not indicate different categorisations of Indian society as a whole so much as an attempt to situate two broad, but competing, viewpoints that provide an illustration of the inherently political terrain of Indian society in an era of mass mobilisation and social change. The Hegelian concept of civil society, according to Chatterjee, is best used in India 'to describe those institutions of modern associational life set up by nationalist elites in the era of colonial modernity' (1998: 61). These institutions, which, it can be argued, emanate from the first urban associations formed under colonialism

> embody the desire of this elite to replicate in its own society the forms as well as substance of Western modernity. It is a desire for a new ethical life in society, one that confirms to the virtues of the enlightenment and of bourgeois freedom.
>
> (1998:61)

By contrast, the much larger, less coherent and unashamedly populist political society 'is built around the framework of modern political associations such as political parties' (1998: 64). This untidy brawl, where both the modern and the traditional are invoked in a politics of association that offends the sensibilities of civil society, and which threatens its ideological hegemony, can be seen to represent 'a site of strategic maneuvers, resistance, and appropriation by different groups and classes, many of those contests remaining unresolved even in the present phase of the postcolonial state' (ibid.).

Chatterjee's overall argument is that the story of post-colonial India can be seen as a social history where the civil society that emerged within the native elites during the colonial period was able to adopt the governing structures and mores of colonial society during the course of the nineteenth and twentieth centuries. This dominance, however, has been widely and increasingly contested during the last three decades by the rise of a political society that is the logical outcome of the democratic experiment in India. Chatterjee furthers argues that in the present phase of this contest, the globalisation of capital is 'heightening the opposition between modernity and democracy, and thus between civil and political societies' (1998: 65). In his recent writings, Chatterjee (2004) pays particular attention to how this process is currently being played out in urban space. Chatterjee describes the programmes of urban renewal and gentrification now being undertaken in Indian cities as part of a concerted counterattack by civil society through which it seeks to reclaim its dominance over the public sphere and roll back the advances made by plebeian groups under the auspices of political society since the beginning of the 1970s. This has taken the form of renewed efforts to clear slum settlements and pavement vendors from the centre of Indian cities. In consolidating the ground that is being gained, there is also a massive effort underway to construct new global cities over the top of the old Indian and Indo-British ones:

> The idea of the new post-industrial globalised metropolis began to circulate in India sometime in the 1990s. Bangalore was the city that was said to be the most likely to fit the bill, but Hyderabad announced its claim too. I suspect, however, that the idea of what a city should be and look like has now been deeply influenced by this post-industrial global image everywhere amongst the urban middle classes in India. The atmosphere produced by liberalisation has had something to do with it. Far more influential has been the intensified circulation of images of global cities through cinema, television, and the

internet as well as through the Indian middle classes' far greater access to international travel.

(Chatterjee 2004: 144)

It is of considerable importance, then, that the role played by both ideas and images has to be incorporated within any critical account of urban renewal. That is not to diminish in the slightest the importance of concrete and corporate finance, but to emphasise that the image has itself always been a notable feature of Indian urban culture. In every corner of every Indian town and city, mass produced posters, hand-painted hoardings and lavishly decorated vehicles have been making their own statements about modernity for decades. Thus, images are not primarily decorative; they are an intrinsic part of the city itself. In the present moment, the adoption and rapid spread of the very particular aesthetics of American corporate capitalism is beginning to re-saturate this already crowded public debate with a new public consciousness. New streams of imagery that are seeking to take the tides of Indian urbanism in new directions have been introduced. Chatterjee, at least, sees this turbulence as already producing demonstrable effects on the physical architecture of Indian cities. Naturally enough, it is also implicated in the reshaping of India's 'public culture' in the wider sense of the term employed influentially during the 1990s by Arjun Appadurai and Carol Breckenridge (Appadurai 1996, Breckenridge 1995). An intrinsic component of this formulation is that the 'imagination is itself a social fact' and that the circulation of images is rapidly transforming the world in the form of globalisation (Appadurai 1996, 2001).

In this context, it is particularly important to emphasise that a cultural turn in the sociology of India as a whole is taking place during an era of unprecedented market prosperity arising from the steady, but cyclical, rise (and transfer) of consumer capitalism on the Asian mainland. In India specifically, its critical focus, therefore, must necessarily include an account of the emergence of a globalising and more affluent, but highly disparate, society where the grand narratives of independence and nationhood are increasingly required to make accommodations with local and international interlocutors. At this stage, there continue to be significant unanswered questions surrounding the nature of the political societies that will emerge in this new India. These are questions that require serious attention and which have implications for scholars of all disciplines, whether they are primarily concerned with India or otherwise. At a broader level, unravelling the processes of social transformation at work in the reshaping of Indian cities may prove potentially decisive for understanding the forces of social production worldwide during the so-called 'Asian Century'. As Ackbar Abbas notes:

The urban concepts useful for thinking the Asian city are likely to be the concepts crucial for an understanding of urbanism today . . . because it seems likely that that is where some of the more radical urban and cultural experiments of the twenty-first century will be taking place. Asian cities are the most problematic. Transformed at unprecedented speed by new forms of capital, politics, media and technology, the Asian City today threatens to outpace our understanding of it.

(2005: 607)

For those who continue to focus on India specifically, the corporate populism expressed through the form of the multiplex represents a direct challenge to the classic anthropological understanding of India as culturally rich but economically backward. As such, there is an obvious need to augment, revise and extend an earlier focus on the clash of pre-modern traditions and industrial society with a less teleological analytical framework more amenable to understanding the contemporary emergence of cultures of demand (of which traditionalism is one product amongst many). Of course, it is and will always be crucially important that India is a multicultural society – in the sense that it possesses not one but a number of public cultures that are constitutive of Indian society. At the same time, few would argue that the structuring logics of the dharmic order remain impervious to the impact of political contest. India's public cultures can thus be clearly seen today in instances and occurrences where they are mutually distinct and at variance with each other. For this reason, no account of social change in India will be wasting its formative years establishing why the cultural is politically significant. Instead, what is required is an understanding not only of the 'conditions of the peasantry' and the science of economic development, but also of what Chatterjee now calls the 'politics of the governed' in an era where the many constituent parts of Indian society are grappling with the lived experience of imperfect modernity, economic liberalisation, ZEE TV and the seductive fantasy of 'Soft Power'.

The Indian multiplex in situ

Situating the multiplex as a research object in the Indian context has taken us on a circular journey from popular culture to cultural industry to urban environment to political society and, hence, back to popular culture. Similarly, we have undertaken another loop through international formats, contests over local neighbourhoods and the globalised circulation of ideas and images. This does not, very clearly, make culture, and certainly not Western culture, a foundational determinate of the globalisation process, but it undeniably foregrounds the necessity of a cultural approach that extends far beyond the functional formalism of aesthetics. Public culture is a social domain. It is a discursive site through which social meanings are produced, but it is also a physical environment where actions are undertaken. For both these reasons, the recent phenomenon of the multiplex cinema in India demonstrates the necessity, and the utility, of an integrated approach to the symbolic and the material in researching social change. Accordingly, the wider purpose of this particular study is to locate the discursive structures of social change in the physical and imagined spaces inhabited by Indians today. In that sense, this constitutes an attempt to consider both the mythic and prosaic experiences of public culture and to demonstrate the social significance of pubic leisure in relation to the critical scholarship on the urban environment that is now emerging along a broad front.

The following study is the result of two years of work, during which time we spent many months in the field conducting interviews, surveys and collecting empirical evidence concerning the multiplex. Bearing in mind the unsatisfactory nature of extrapolating a set of findings from a single metropolitan context, this book incorporates research conducted in several major metros (Bangalore, Delhi, Mumbai, Kolkata) as well as in the 'second-tier' cities of Panaji and Baroda. At time of writing, we remain keenly aware that the story of the multiplex is very much a story in progress, with rapid expansion and industrial change outstripping the pace at which this book could be produced. Similarly, we also remain keenly aware that this account can only be a preliminary sketch conducted at the national level, and that valuable, more detailed accounts of each particular location are likely to follow later.

As foreign scholars, we make no attempt to imitate a local perspective on the changes that are now taking place in metropolitan India. However, at the same time, we remain critically aware that the stakes of this game are extremely high for the very large numbers of people who will be living out their lives in these urban environments during the twenty-first century. So while it is true that nothing is so far away in today's world as to encourage complacency, it is undeniably the case that the remaking of the neighbourhoods that we discuss in this book will have negligible impacts upon us personally. That said, we make no claims to dispassionate objectivity either. This book simply represents the panorama on view from the front steps of the Indian multiplex as we saw it in the early part of 2007. In order to paint that picture, we first turn to the specific history of the Indian cinema hall, however contested, contingent, divisive, interrupted and incomplete any public history of India must necessarily be.

2   From cinema hall to multiplex

A public history

Lawrence Liang argues that there cannot be a 'distinct account of cinema or cinematic spaces, which is not at the same time an account of the history of the city, of the experiences of modernity and of the conflicts that define the very occupation of these spaces' (2005: 366). S. V. Srinivas (2000a, 2000b) also seeks to illustrate how the interior space of the cinema hall in India has historically been the site of political contest. This awareness of the contestation of space therefore becomes essential for understanding the social dynamics of the cinema in India. Building upon these insights, this chapter provides a brief account of the public history of cinema as it has unfolded within the context of urban India. As it is presented here, this history broadly corresponds to the typical periodisation of Indian film history, and of modern India itself, that has emerged through the films histories written by Barnouw and Krishnaswamy (1963, 1980), Chakravarty (1993), Prasad (1998), Mishra (2002) and others.

In this narrative, the story of Indian cinema begins with the successful emergence of an indigenous cinema in India amidst colonial suppression and nationalist aspiration. The subsequent era of independence and nation building is taken to embody a golden age of Bombay cinema that was fashioned by, but also opposed by, the golden age of Nehruvian socialism. The third period is seen to correspond with the economic crisis, political struggle and public anger during the 1970s that was contemporaneous with the government of Indira Gandhi and the dominance of Amitabh Bachchan as the foremost star of the Indian screen. The following decade is seen as one of repetition, stagnation and neglect in the film industry, prior to the ushering in of an era of economic liberalisation after 1991 that has seen the media industries expand rapidly due to new technologies, economic globalisation and media de-regulation. This latter period has witnessed the return to dominance of middle-class romance in (and with) the cinema – this time in an explicitly consumerist form.

Colonial rule, civic order and the birth of the cinema 'crowd'

Indian cities during the early twentieth century were characterised by the complex spatial politics of the colonial order. In the major Presidency cities (Calcutta,

Bombay and Madras), where British economic power was concentrated, the urban landscape was organised around a central district reserved for Europeans and their servants, with a number of native suburbs radiating away from this core, many of which were organised around a particular ethnic or social group, although there were also some highly mixed neighbourhoods along with some tied to related occupations or trades. The spatial relationship of these social groups to each other was defined by a number of factors: 1) the rank of that community in the social order established by Company, and later Crown, colonialism 2) the role played by that community in the economic life of the city 3) the date from which that community came to occupy space in the city 4) the social standing of the group in relation to the caste system in that historical epoch. In all but the first aspect, this made the principles of spatial organisation in the Presidency cities similar to traditional Indian cities. However, if we take into account the military and economic dominance of the British, it is clear that the British were able to determine all but the last aspect (i.e. caste) in the ordering of their Indian capitals. As such, communities identified by the British as natural interlocutors, such as the Anglo-Indians in particular, but also the casteless Parsis in Bombay, came to occupy metropolitan spaces with a value disproportionate to their social standing in the wider community at that time (Luhrmann 1996, Caplan 2001). That is not to say that various other social groups were not capable of gaining entrance to valuable real estate by occupying a pivotal economic role and thus establishing themselves as an intrinsic part of the terrain of the colonial cities. The Marwaris prominence in central Calcutta provides a significant example of the strategic colonisation of an Indo-British city by an established trading caste (Hardgrove 2002).

Needless to say, the management of the colonial city required a trade-off between the needs of its various inhabitants. This did not lead, during the late nineteenth century, to the widespread extension of civic authority, as was the case in Britain itself. The rapid growth of the Presidency cities and the increasing recognition of the importance of sanitation and urban planning did, however, lead to the establishment of more limited civic authorities and regular, albeit typically ad hoc, attempts to regulate the colonial urban landscape. Often such initiatives would arise from the insecurities or prejudices of the white population, but the more established and affluent sectors of the Indian population also increasingly agitated for the sustained intervention of urban authorities in the so-called 'native districts'. As such, the management of metropolitan life in colonial India was fitfully extended beyond the narrow self-interest of the Europeans (Dossal 1991). The colonial cities were thus bifurcated in the first instance by a power line between colonisers and colonised as well as being subject to markedly decreasing civic investment and organisation in their traverse from centre to periphery. Accordingly, the legacy of an urban mentality in which the majority of the population inhabited districts that typically arose with little or no formal planning, and which sustained themselves in an environment of scant civic provision and regulation, was to leave an indelible stamp on the mindset of urban India.

The first moving picture shows came to Indian cities in 1896, just a few months after the first shows in Europe and America. At this time, the British Raj was at the height of its power, although anti-colonial nationalism was also emerging as a powerful political force. The early years of the cinema in India were thus accompanied by the catalytic events (such as the abortive partition of Bengal in 1905, the Great War in 1914–1918, the passing of the Rowlatt Act and the subsequent massacre at Amritsar in 1919, followed closely by the *khilafat* agitation) which were to lead eventually to the independence and partition of the patchwork of territories assembled under British paramountcy. As such, the advent of moving pictures, and their subsequent growth in popularity as a mass medium, took place against the backdrop of increasing mass mobilisation against colonial occupation and a very public contest for the metropolitan spaces of an India already in the throes of urbanisation and political change. Initially, the exhibition of film reels in India consisted of imported material from Europe and America screened for a predominantly European audience in a small number of exclusive metropolitan picture places in the central spaces of the Presidency cities. The first cinema halls, commonly known as 'film theatres' or 'picture palaces' at that time, were constructed in the districts where the European population either resided or conducted their business affairs.

Even at this early stage a national chain of theatres that would dominate the film business in India was conceived and pursued. According to Barnouw and Krishnaswamy's historical account, it was in Calcutta that: 'J. F. Madan built the Elphinstone Picture Palace, the first of many Madan Film Theatres, in 1907. During the 1910s he expanded rapidly and by the end of the decade had thirty-seven theatres' (Barnouw and Krishnaswamy, 1980: 6). As the film medium evolved rapidly in the early years of the twentieth century from an ocular curiosity into a widely accessible narrative form, Indian film artists such as D. G. Phalke launched an increasingly popular indigenous film production industry. The first Indian films, notably Phalke's *Raja Harishandra* (1913) but also Calcutta-based Ganguly's *England Returned* (1913), were notable successes with the urban Indians who saw them. A growing demand for Indian productions provided the basis for nascent film industries to develop in British India's Bombay, Bengal and Madras Presidencies. As such, the 'number of theatres in India increased from about 150 in 1923 to about 265 in 1927' (ibid.: 38). It was during this period of expansion that the market for film exhibition steadily expanded beyond the consumption of European and American films by European and native elite audiences to encompass a more socially diverse audience in the bigger cities.

Given the rise of anti-colonial feeling, the government of India in the twilight years of the British Raj had little interest in the development of a leisure industry predicated upon public assembly and accessible to the lower social orders. The primary interest of the government was therefore in controlling the construction and programmes of cinema halls in order to prevent the inculcation of seditious ideas, whether they resulted from American or Indian movies. Accordingly, the censorship of films in India was instituted as early as 1918 with the Indian Cinematograph Act. Censorship of the cinema sought to prevent the degradation of the image of Caucasians arising from the exposure of the natives to Hollywood films (that were seen to present white woman as promiscuous and thus threaten the moral superiority of the white race) and to restrict the ability of Indian filmmakers to make films which sympathised with the growing nationalist movement (Prasad 1998: 78). Indian films were forbidden to ferment unrest or criticise colonial rule. As Stephen Hughes observes, the colonial authorities in urban India were particularly adverse to the 'idea of crowds of Indian working-class men gathering for film shows in close proximity to important government institutions' (2000: 49). Given the location of those institutions, we could take this to indicate European-dominated districts generally, and, as Hughes also notes, it remains significant that the earlier construction of theatres for upmarket audiences in those self-same districts had not raised similar concerns (ibid.: 50).

It is worth recognising that this kind of paranoia surrounding new forms of mass culture, and their social impact, was also being felt at home by European elites in the wake of socialist agitation. However, in the case of British India, a colonial government which was rapidly losing legitimacy had even more cause to experience trepidation about the growth of a modern public culture. When it came to the emergence of a popular Indian cinema, it was not simply the presumed psychological effects, or the ideological efficacy of the medium, that concerned colonial officials. Rather, it was the combination of these effects with the degree of mass participation required to make the exhibition of films profitable in a market where tickets had to be priced from just a few annas (a fraction of a rupee) which concerned officials. For the authorities, the rapid turnover of large crowds that was intrinsic to mass exhibition implied

> The daily collecting of crowds in the street . . . at regular intervals before a film show and then, after being emotionally galvanised through the collective experience of film-watching, exiting together on to the streets again, [this] made the police authorities particularly concerned. The colonial government of India had long recognised crowds, especially those of religious processions and at dramatic performances, as a potentially uncontrollable threat to the political and social order. The very notion of collective gatherings, even at places of public entertainment, carried assumed connotations of riotous mobs and revolutionary masses.
>
> (Hughes, 2000: 49–50)

In 1927, the government of India conducted a major enquiry into the cinema industry. The resulting Report of the Indian Cinematograph Committee (ICC) is the most extensive and best-known account of the early years of the medium in India. A significant part of the rationale for this enquiry was a (failed) attempt to build support for a mandated quota of 'Empire Films' to counter the impact of American dominance of the world film market after the First World War (see Jaikumar 2006). In the process of surveying the state of the industry in India, however, the ICC report recorded invaluable information about the early exhibition industry. The following extended quote is an edited selection from Barnouw and Krishnaswamy's distillation of matters pertaining to theatrical exhibition in the three-volume report:

> Most theatres apparently had two or more showings per day; one theatre gave twelve a day during melas [fairs] . . . prices were usually in three or more classes,

often from 2 or 3 annas to 2 rupees. In cities the top price might be 3 rupees, for 'box' or 'sofa' seats. In the lesser cinemas, the lowest price might be 1 anna, for 'ground' seats. In an Assam theatre the 393 tickets sold for one performance were for 350 ground seats, 40 bench seats, 3 chair seats; this was a normal distribution . . . some of the mofussil theatres were described by witnesses as being in sorry state:

The lowest class of spectator has to squat on the ground and the benches and chairs in the other classes are in wretched condition and infested by bugs. There is no proper ventilation and most of the theatres are merely corrugated tin sheds.

The city of Bombay had 20 cinemas, Calcutta 13, Madras 9, Delhi 6, Poona 6. A number of other cities had three or four. Exhibitors testified to many problems with local authority: 'The police, the custom, the postal, telegraph, municipal and a host of other people have to be admitted free to avoid trouble'. Women filmgoers were scarce in the south and in mainly Muslim areas of the north, but were increasingly evident in most cities . . . Shortcomings of Indian films were often mentioned. But what emerged most unmistakeably was the growing preference for Indian films in spite of these shortcomings . . . In 1918, in Bombay, only one theatre had specialised in Indian films. By 1927 more than half of the twenty theatres showed Indian films at least part of the time. Exhibitors catering especially to a European and Westernised clientele – there were nine such theatres in Bombay – generally felt is essential to stick to Western films. One such exhibitor had shifted for only one week to a Phalke film:

The type of people who like Indian pictures, their way of living is quite different and generally they are people who chew betel leaves . . . let me give you an example. I did show an Indian picture at my Western theatre, Lanka Dahan, and I made 18,000 rupees in one week. But it ruined my theatre altogether . . . I had to disinfect the hall and at the same time I had to convince my audience I had disinfected it . . . Till that time I went on losing money.

(1980: 46–48, emphasis not in original)

The ICC report is of great interest because it catches the cinema in India during the transition from being a pastime of the colonial elite in the 1910s to being India's foremost mass media by the 1940s, a process greatly accelerated by the coming of sound in the early 1930s. However, despite the growth in the popularity of cinema and its dominance of the exhibition sector, Madan Theatres (which by this time was operating 126 theatres from Lahore to Ceylon, Rangoon and Singapore) collapsed abruptly between 1931 and 1933 due to the worldwide economic crisis, profit leakage and the cost of re-equipping for sound (Barnouw and Krishnaswamy 1980: 64–67). From this point, the exhibition business became the domain of independent entrepreneurs – a development that would remain critical to the political economy of the Indian cinema for many decades to come.

In thinking about the implications of the cinema hall as a public space in India, it is crucial to recognise that the cinema hall was a thoroughly modern addition to public life, not simply in terms of its technological apparatus, but in its re-ordering of social space. In a context where 'respectable' women may not have appeared in public at all, and where temples, residential areas and water sources were often subject to exclusive access by certain caste, faith and class groups, the gathering together of a diverse public within a single social space appears to have represented a radical departure from existing social norms. At the same time, however, the space inside cinema halls was always regulated by different classes of seating, typically ranging from 'floor class' to 'bench class' to 'chair class'. The adoption of a sex-segregated seating option was also introduced within weeks of the first showings at Watson's Hotel (Barnouw and Krishnaswamy 1980: 5). On this basis, Binod Agrawal (1984: 189) argues that the organisation of the public within the cinema hall in India can be productively related to the Vedic treatise of the *Natyashastra* since different classes of seating indicated the preferred location of different social groups in relation to the Hindu social order. However, the case for the particularity to India for such arrangements is not strong since social segregation within the space of cinema halls on the basis of class and/or race has been a constituent feature of the public history of cinema in a number of other countries (Maltby et al. 2003, Bowles and Huggett 2004).

By the end of the 1940s, British rule had ended in India and their direct regulation of urban life was over, even though their imprimatur remains upon the urban landscape of India to this day. The British colonial authorities, however, were not the only critics of the cinema and its public. In a written contribution to the ICC in 1927, Mahtama Gandhi denounced cinema as 'a sinful technology', although writing for his journal, *Harijan*, he also conceded that: 'If I began to organise picketing in respect of them (the evil of cinema), I should lose my caste, my Mahatmaship' (see Jeffrey 2008). Jawaharlal Nehru was also critical of popular cinema, albeit for different reasons, believing it to be a waste of resources for a country where poverty was so widespread. India's first Prime Minister believed that the technology should be used for bringing the message of national development to rural India, rather than squandered on escapism for the urban masses. It is perhaps unsurprising then, that anxieties about the behaviour of cinema audiences and of public safety in cinema halls were to continue long after the defeat and departure of the British Raj.

Entertaining the post-colonial public

The social conditions within which cinema in the subcontinent operated were to change dramatically with the end of colonial rule and the August 1947 partition of British India into the Indian Union and Pakistan. Although the cinema had enjoyed an enormous boom in popularity and in production capacity during the last years of the Raj, the division of the subcontinent had powerful effects upon the film industry. In Punjab, partition brought film production to a halt as personnel and capital relocated to Bombay, where the Punjabis have subsequently become an evermore significant presence in the film industry (Dwyer and Patel 2002: 82, Das 2006). In Bengal, partition cost the Calcutta industry a major part of its audience as Eastern Bengal became part of Pakistan and many leading figures from the industry also made the move to Bombay. Although South Indian cinema developed steadily in

the years after independence, the Bombay Hindi-language cinema was the undisputed film capital of South Asia for the first two decades after independence. This
period has been referred to as the 'Golden Age of Hindi Cinema' (Kasbekar 1996:
402, Gokulsing and Dissanayake 1998: 16, Thoraval 2000: 49–51).

The first post-independence government, led by Jawaharlal Nehru and the
Congress party until 1964, faced considerable challenges in its early years. Not least
of these challenges was the traumatic violence that accompanied partition, and its
aftershocks, in addition to the precarious economic situation that it inherited.
Despite these obstacles, the government under Nehru quickly laid down the foun-
dations of modern India through a series of rapid moves towards a universal franchise, the absorption of the numerous Princely states and the reorganisation of
India's administrative territories along primarily linguistic lines. In economic policy, Nehru was personally committed to a centrally-planned socialist approach,
which led to the creation of the Planning Commission (PC) in 1950. At the same
time, however, he was also inclined to compromise with regional interests, a private
sector lobby and a smaller group supporting Gandhi's pastoral ideals, all contained
inside the Congress system. Furthermore, the support of India's small industrialist
class and the co-operation of the British companies who were still in the process of
a phased withdrawal from their command role in the Indian economy throughout
Nehru's tenure were essential to avoid an economic crisis in the first decade of independence.

As a countervailing force, the Communist Party of India enjoyed wide-scale support in the countryside, particularly in the eastern districts, in the early post-colonial
era. The communists demanded that the post-colonial government address the
crippling rural poverty that afflicted millions. Needless to say, the landlords and
rural elites also looked to the government to protect their interests in the rural economy. In all these matters, and whatever his own personal sympathies and his public
rhetoric may have appeared to favour, Nehru consistently sought to hammer out
compromises between the various interest groups. It was on this basis, therefore,
that India came to adopt a variant of the mixed-economy model with government-
led attempts in the public sector to increase industrial output being accompanied by
the creation of favourable conditions for the private sector to contribute to the
industrialisation of the country. Despite the necessity of political compromise at
many levels, the dominant sentiment of the new Government of India was, in ideological terms, an anti-colonial strand of high modernism. India was to be directed
towards industrial mechanisation, a production-led economy and a more progressive society engendered by the diffusion of a socialist conscience amongst the urban
middle classes, the extension of formal education and a particular focus upon the
rural districts.

The selective emulation of a European enlightenment model, drawing upon
both liberal and socialist agendas, was accompanied by the rhetorics of cultural par-
ticularism and revivalism that had emerged during the anti-colonial struggle. Thus,
a modern technological future was presented as a return to the former glories of
ancient Indian civilisation rather than as a continuation of foreign socio-economic
paradigms. This paradigm also had the effect of relocating the emotive political

charge of cultural nationalism into the safer terrain of the more distant past, as opposed to the traumatic immediate past of Partition. However, this mode of cultural politics was antagonistic to the contemporary popular culture of the period, seeing the commercial Indian film as a crass and hybrid cultural form unsuitable for the national-building project envisaged through the government's didactic project of modernity (Chakravarty 1993: 55–79). Accordingly, the post-colonial government increased its powers of censorship over the film industry, placing a ban on the construction of new film theatres and, at one stage, limiting the import of raw film stock. Taxation of the industry also increased dramatically in the 1950s (Chakravarty 1993: 63, Armes 1987: 118). Charges were frequently made against the cinema as an agent of Westernisation and a polluting source of Western morality (Barnouw and Krishnaswamy 1980: 137). Nonetheless, leading film producers such as Mehboob Khan sought to express the zeitgeist of national liberation and to employ the cinema in both the symbolic reinvention of indigenous cultural narratives and in the imaginings of social reform. Thus the 'social film', which, by independence, had largely supplanted the 'mythological' and 'stunt' films of the earlier years, articulated both the 'need to maintain indigenous realities against the fascination for Western cultural behaviour' as well as a 'critique of Indian society . . . setting up an agenda for change' (Vasudevan 2000a: 133).

Despite the overwhelming importance given both to heavy industry and to formal planning in India's national development in the Nehruvian era, there was a considerable delay in efforts to set up institutions or legislation to regulate the growth or structure of urban areas. It is generally recognised that the First Five Year Plan (1951–1956) focused on industrialisation and the developmental effort in rural India at the expense of the urban centres (see Mohan 2005: 53). The development of an effective urbanisation strategy was also sidelined by the many pressing national issues, such as managing the economic and democratic transitions, conflicts with Pakistan and the institution of the governing structures of federalism. Nonetheless, for the purpose of planning the further development of the national capital, the Delhi Development (Provisional) Authority (DDA) was set up in 1955, becoming a permanent body two years later. The deliberations undertaken by that body provided the first desperately needed model for post-colonial urban planning in Indian cities. It has been argued, however, that the DDA largely serves to inaugurate many of the mistakes that would go on to be made elsewhere, of which a failure to account for the housing needs of the labouring classes was perhaps the most obvious omission (Baviskar 2003, Chaplin 1999, Kumar 2000, Legg 2006).

Since the other major urban centres were located within specific states, the development authorities that were subsequently set up for them were not generally empowered to act independently of the wider state government. While the benefits of co-ordinating metropolitan development along with the smaller cities and towns and the rural hinterland statewide cannot be denied, it was also the case that the municipal bodies in the major cities suffered from a lack of regulatory authority on matters specific to their own domain. The practical application of urban management was further complicated by the fact that although urban management fell with the jurisdiction of the newly formed states, it was resourced on the basis of economic plans formulated at the centre. The rollout of the democratic system in 1952, and the increasing desire of elected politicians to respond to grassroots demand for urban interventions in their own electorates, further ensured that the urban environment was ultimately co-managed between local, state and central bodies.

Within these competing jurisdictions, it is relatively unsurprising that planning was slow, and that the application of the master plans that had emerged by the end of Nehruvian era was fitful at best. Aside from the bureaucratic hurdles and the competing demands of the rural districts where the majority of the population was to be found, it is also important to recognise the inherent difficulties of managing the rapid urbanisation of the Indian population in the early independence period. This was a feature of India's human geography with many different causes. At one level, educated Indians were relocating to occupy previously European districts and managerial occupations. At another level, there was the urgent need to resettle millions of refugees of all classes after Partition, along with the shortfall in the administrative capacity to legally manage the property vacated by the departing British and by those who had fled to Pakistan. Furthermore, these processes of semi-managed resettlement were taking place amongst a wider acceleration of migration from rural areas into both the major cities and the mofussil towns, particularly in the north of the country.

The steady shift of a significant part of the economy from the east to the west of the country throughout the 1950s and 1960s instigated a further population shift. As such, whilst the classic Indian films of the period, like Mehboob's *Mother India* (1957), celebrated the continuity of the Indian village, they were being watched for the most part by the ever greater numbers of Indians who had left the villages for the urban areas. Unable to absorb new migrants within their existing residential capacity, but increasingly dependent upon them as an integral component of economic growth, the metropolitan authorities entered into a protracted struggle over the growth of shanty towns and their encroachment upon unattended public spaces (Mukhija 2001). If housing and public amenities were unable to keep pace with the urbanisation of the Indian population, then places of assembly and entertainment were also in scant supply. Given that the cinema in India was, and still is, a primarily urban pastime, the steadily increasing pressure upon limited urban infrastructure had an important bearing upon the composition of the movie audience in the early post-colonial period. It is worth noting that, despite already having one of the world's most prolific film outputs in terms of production, there was a chronic undersupply of theatres in comparison to the vast size of the audience.

In the first two decades after independence there was (as there still is) a shortage of entertainment capacity in Indian cities. For the large populations of new citizens living in the cheek-by-jowl conditions of the semi-permanent shanty towns that arose after the 1950s there was, in addition, an unhealthy scarcity of access to both personal and public space in general. The more itinerant pavement dwellers occupied the public space of the city even more visibly, and they too constituted a growing audience for the cinema hall – an audience with a relatively low spending capacity and few other entertainment choices. These were social conditions that gave an increased significance to the limited resources for public entertainment that were available to the urban population, for which the cinema was already the dominant mode of urban leisure.

The public debates after 1947 on cinema halls, as S. V. Srinivas (2000a) relates, were centred upon the discomfort of middle-class Indian viewers with the public behaviour of the lower social orders within theatres, as well as concerns regarding the potential for contacts between 'respectable' Indian women and thoroughly 'unrespectable' men that were being made possible by the institution of cinema. By contrast with the slum dwellers and pavement dwellers, upper middle-class viewers had more living space, if not by Western standards, and more access to other forms of leisure practice than their fellow citizens. Nonetheless, the omnibus nature of the Indian *masala* film was designed to appeal to a wide and differentiated audience, and films remained in high demand amongst the middle classes in the decades before television. Both the economic logic of film exhibition as a mass medium and the scarcity of public leisure space meant that people of all classes were regularly brought together by the instrument of cinema during this period. Both the lower and upper middle classes, if they wanted to enjoy the rich products of the Indian cinema, had to rub shoulders with the working poor.

Given the shortage of screen capacity, the producers, directors and exhibitors in the film industry had to cater to this widely divergent audience in a single format, which in turn had implications for the idiosyncrasies of Indian film style. Since these operating conditions were also contemporaneous with the formal realisation of the nation-building project, it is perhaps unsurprising that the Indian cinema of the period has been frequently cited as an important site in the formation of national consciousness and of the democratic project in India. In terms of the products of the golden age of Indian cinema, scholars such as Ashish Rajadhyaksha point to the inclusive narrative address of the Indian film and the gradual, and fitful, construction of an Indian film spectator as a ready parallel with the search for an 'Indian' citizen (Rajadhyaksha 2000). In specific relation to the social practice of attending a film screening, Srinivas offers the following as representative of similar democratic claims that have been made for the cinema hall itself:

> The Cinema Hall was the first performance centre in which all Tamils sat under the same roof. The basis of the seating is not on the hierarchic position of the patron but essentially on his purchasing power. If he cannot afford paying the higher rate, he has either to keep away from the performance or be with 'all and sundry'.
>
> (Sivathamby in Srinivas 2000a)

Despite his earlier parallel of the cinema audience with the Hindu social order, Agrawal also observes that 'often desperate viewers must buy tickets of higher classes. But in the dark who knows who he is sitting next to? Money is the only factor in deciding who will watch in which class' (1984: 190). In this light, there is certainly the potential for arguing that the requirement of cinema as an industrial medium for a mass, rather than select, audience might well have given rise to a sense of commonality amongst patrons in the Nehruvian era. This reading opens up the possibility of a mutual entitlement to public participation and the occupation of public space that transcended prior social structures. The cinema could be compared in this regard with some of the other public spaces offered by modernity, such as railway stations, whose logic was directed at a mass public arranged by capitalist mobility, rather than the maintenance of feudal spatial practices.

Srinivas (2000a), however, points out that the utopian dimensions of the cinema hall appear in practice to have been widely contested in India during the 1950s. Commentaries, typically complaints, written by middle-class viewers to film journals illustrate the fact that despite suggestions 'that the cinema had tremendous democratic potential in a context where distinctions of caste have played a crucial role in determining access to public places', it was equally clear that 'the conflictual relations between the middle class public and other audience groups is central to understanding the public sphere of cinema' in the Indian context (Srinivas 2000a). Srinivas recounts how middle-class cinemagoers in Andhra Pradesh in the 1950s lamented the chaotic nature of cinema hall management. The failure to ensure orderly systems of booking, queuing and seating meant that 'it was not possible for the respectable viewer to avoid coming into contact with an unruly mass' and these 'respectable' viewers were as often as not caught up in the brutal reprisals by police which took place when the lower classes of the audience got out of hand (Srinivas 2000a). Srinivas emphasises, therefore, that while the cinema hall may have permitted new forms of social proximity in a certain sense, its democratising effect must be reconciled with the fact that:

> There is now a growing body of evidence indicating that although members of lower castes were allowed to enter cinema halls, theatre managements ensured that caste and class hierarchies were reinforced within them . . . [therefore] It is important to note that the cinema hall was one of the sites for the struggle for political rights as far as the lower caste-class viewers were concerned.
>
> (Srinivas 2000a)

Here the cinema hall emerges as more complex site of democratic engagement. There is some evidence of a general acceptance of the parity of spectators based upon purchasing power, which is itself highly significant as an organising principle for the cinema hall, as opposed to other areas of public activity. The hierarchical principle of wealth, markedly different from that of purity, was widely accepted in cinemas worldwide and enforced in Indian theatres by ticket prices, theatre management and police officers stationed with the hall. However, such social arrangements in the cinema hall remained a largely consensual arrangement in the context of a large crowd and could become rapidly destabilised. Even in the absence of disorder, the letters of complaint researched by Srinivas provide evidence of the obvious discomfort of middle-class commentators with occupying the same social space as the lower social orders. The whistling, cheering and general demeanour of the floor class was commonly seen to disturb the ability of their betters to watch the programme in an appropriately detached manner, simultaneously denying middle-class spectators the opportunity to conveniently ignore the new social arrangements taking place in the dark of the theatre.

Beyond the dimension of the cinema hall as a complex model of class relations, and as a site of political struggle, the gendered dimensions of cinema as public space also receive a high degree of attention in the complaints published in the Telugu film journal, *Roopvani*, and analysed by Srinivas. Although, none of these writings were produced by women, a large proportion of them deal 'with problems faced by female audiences and [emphasise] the need to strictly segregate male and female audiences' (Srinivas 2000a). The accounts presented are of intolerable instances of 'feeling', 'pressing hands', 'posing for' and 'looking at' women by men in the cinema as well as in the queues and toilet facilities. According to Srinivas, these accounts provide a further indication

> of what the middle class audience found anxiety inducing about cinema halls [and] draw attention to the larger problem of managing an assembly of diverse groups of people, some of whom were perceived to have tremendous disruptive potential and some others deserving special protection.
>
> (Srinivas 2000a)

Each of these groups is clearly identified in the readers' letters analysed by Srinivas; it is groupings of lower-class men who had 'tremendous disruptive potential' and middle-class women who deserved 'special protection'. As such 'the demand for the strict separation of women was simultaneous with the call for separating the diverse classes of viewers' (Srinivas 2000a).

The construction of the female viewer is therefore primarily one of a 'respectable' woman made vulnerable by proximity to men of lower social status. There are, however, other complaints of a sexual nature which arise in Srinivas' work, where segregation was demanded not simply for the protection of demure female citizens from inferior males, but also for 'preventing what some readers called 'romances' (the English word is used) in cinema halls, particularly in the highest priced seats . . . One reader wondered if the 'Box' class was exclusively meant for this purpose' (Srinivas 2000a). Thus, although there are obvious differences between the discourse on cinema halls fashioned by the colonial administration and post-colonial debates on audience behaviours, the two obvious elements of continuity are the spectre of an unruly mob and the perception of threats to female honour and public propriety. In relation to the notion of cinema as a democratic social practice, however, what Srinivas sees as most significant is that:

> Despite the listing of problems caused by lower classes and difficulties or threats faced by women, this section of the audience was not asked to stay away from cinema halls. There was a tacit recognition of the 'right' of both women and the lower class audiences to be present at the cinema hall.
>
> (Srinivas 2000a)

In the reading provided by Srinivas, the institution of cinema continues to be seen as a democratic institution – not simply as an inherently universalising practice, but more convincingly as a site of ongoing contest based upon a principle of universal franchise. In making this argument, Srinivas draws a parallel between the public space within the cinema hall and the Habermasian public sphere of India itself, where the contest between bourgeois civil society and plebeian political societies mobilised by urbanisation and enfranchisement is seen as the logical outcome of democracy in India. In sharing the same place of exhibition, the audience does indeed represent a social undertaking enacted in a single space. This singularity of purpose, however, becomes internally differentiated in the process of describing the audience as a mass public segregated by complex spatial arrangements around their object of mutual interest and in relation to each other. Finally, the competing notions of the appropriate decorum for public assembly and the suitable forms of expression for appreciating the film itself indicate that the audience in that era was not only spatially differentiated, but was also in conflict within itself over the proper ritual function of the cinema experience. In locating the cinema during the 1950s as a manifestation of political society in this way, the audience takes on a more variegated form in relation to its democratic function. These differing dimensions of the social space of the cinema hall thus constituted the political dynamics that continued to dominate the public history of the cinema in India into the crisis era of the 1970s.

Rise of the angry young men

The erosion of consensual politics after the death of Nehru, the Naxalite peasant uprisings in 1970, the Bangladesh war in 1971, the worldwide economic crisis after 1973, the rising tide of both population levels and perceived corruption, the failure of the early planning regimes to achieve economic lift-off – there were many contributing factors to the deepening sense of crisis that culminated in Indira Gandhi's suspension of democracy and imposition of the 'Emergency' period of 1975–1977 and its aftermath. Throughout this period the rate of urbanisation continued to grow exponentially. The city of Calcutta (now Kolkata) achieved international notoriety for urban squalor and the collapse of civic order resulting from its economic decline, the massive inflow of refugees from the rural crisis throughout the east and the cyclone, civil war and India-Pakistan conflict that afflicted nearby Bangladesh in rapid succession in 1970–1971. The 1970s were characterised by decreasing rates of growth, to which the government responded with increased regulation and nationalisation. Although government intervention managed to alleviate some aspects of the economic crisis, the overall effect was to further stymie productivity and further entrench corruption. For the cinema business, the economic depression as a threat to profits was offset by the lack of any real leisure alternative for the urban population. The introduction of the Urban Land (Ceiling and Regulation) Act in 1976, however, did have major implications for the cinema business since it made the acquisition and disbursement of land for commercial uses subject to stringent legislation (Shrinivas 1991).

The increasingly crowded urban landscape and the disaffection of large segments of the population during this period had a considerable impact upon

Figures 2.1 and 2.2 Firmament of India's Democracy? Auditorium and seating in a traditional cinema hall in Bangalore. (Adrian Athique)

the cinema. The development of the political contest in the cinema, at this stage, followed a general pattern where the cinema hall became increasingly dominated by the young men of India's urban underclass at the expense of the middle-class spectator. The proletarianisation of the movie audience, the politicisation of subaltern groups and the zeitgeist of the Emergency all exacerbated the extant anxieties of middle-class citizens about the cinema hall. The middle classes thus became increasingly unwilling to enter into social situations where they could be confronted with the caste-, class- and gender-inflected presence of the 'lumpen class of men who lived and still live on the streets of the cities' (Inden, 1999: 53). Ravi Vasudevan has documented how cinemas in New Delhi experienced a downturn in status (rather than ticket sales) during this period, since 'cinemas were no longer attracting families and women audiences, always considered crucial to the cinema's social legitimacy' (2003). Instead cinemas increasingly catered to a 'mobile 'bachelor' population . . . a restless, transient population hustling for goods and attracted to a cinema of sensation and distraction' (Vasudevan, 2003).

Since the demographics of the cinema hall became dominated by young men of the lower social orders, the industry adjusted its themes accordingly. The major theatrical successes of the period, from *Zanjeer* (1973) to *Coolie* (1981), demonstrate how the romantic hero of the 1960s was rapidly supplanted from the early 1970s until the end of the 1980s by the 'Angry Young Man' personified by Amitabh Bachchan (Kazmi 1999, Mazumdar 2000). Bachchan's status as India's biggest star throughout this period provided a significant degree of continuity as he repeatedly preformed his role as an avenging vigilante from the margins of society, taking on the criminal and the corrupt in the name of the poor and dispossessed. According to Fareeduddin Kazmi:

> in Bombay nearly one-third of the population lived in slums or on pavements, with minimum civic amenities; they were displaced from their original social milieu, without being integrated into the city. Even this animal-like existence was not secure; their slums were treated as illegal occupation and they had to pay a fine every month. While they lived in constant fear of eviction from or demolition of their urban hutments, they could expect no support from the official-legal machinery. It is this context that Amitabh Bachchan's persona as an angry young man should be understood. Bachchan in his films is always one of the oppressed . . . In all these films the hero, although he belongs to the subordinate classes, rises to equal his exploiters. His image is of one who can give justice to his class while the police cannot. He protects them from official tyrannies like the demolition of their hutments (consider the innumerable scenes where the demolition of slums is stopped by the hero in the nick of time) and he functions as a private adjudicator dispensing instant justice.
>
> (1999: 139)

Themes of socially marginalised vigilantes targeting a corrupt society were hugely popular amongst the urban underclass, and these films were also able to tap into the frustration of the lower middle classes' suffering from urban overcrowding and economic stagnation. However, these were much more difficult themes for the upper middle classes to assimilate than the romantic and introspective heroes of the preceding decades. Just as the cinema came to represent, as Ashis Nandy (1999) puts it, a 'slum's eye view of politics', the cinema hall itself, particularly after dark, began to be associated with gangs of young 'rowdy-sheeters' and was therefore increasingly seen as an unsuitable place for middle-class families. Vivek Dhareshwar and R. Srivatsan, in their analysis of the figure of the rowdy-sheeter, note that

> in the middle class imagination, the 'rowdy' inhabits the dark zone of the city, trafficking in illegal, immoral activities; a zone that is invariably in need of law and order, and always threatening to spread to the safer, cleaner habitat of the city.
>
> (1996: 202)

The founding definition of the rowdy is taken from a metropolitan police record that is used for 'petty' offences including 'breach of the peace', 'mischief', 'intimidation', 'public nuisance' or 'persons who habitually tease women or girls by passing indecent remarks or otherwise' (ibid.: 205). The wider signifier of the rowdy in circulation amongst the middle classes is of a lower-class male with a history of 'eve-teasing', that is, of harassing and intimidating women. Dhareshwar and Srivatsan note that 'a rowdy is almost never an upper-caste Hindu. He is either a Scheduled Caste, Backward Class, or Muslim, all belonging to a socio-economic (non-) class which by definition resides in a *basti* or slum' (ibid.: 208).

By this time, cinema in the south of the country had become dominated by the local-language industries as opposed to the Hindi films from Bombay. Thus, in Tamil Nadu and Andhra Pradesh the dynamics of the cinema hall as public space were increasingly shaped by the close links that emerged between the film world and regional politics – with fans clubs linked to major stars-turned-politicians and grass-roots political activists staking a major claim upon the cinema hall as a site of proletarian politics (see Pandian 1992, Dickey 1993, Srinivas 2000b). The importance of the cinema as political terrain in urban India was thus more evident during the 1970s and 1980s than in the early independence years. Arguably, this was an era of gains for the disadvantaged in urban society. Despite authoritarian measures taken to clear slums during the Emergency, these was a gradual recognition of the importance of these populations to the economic life of the cities and subsequent attempts to hammer out a compromise between the legal and illegal domains of urban life. As Partha Chatterjee describes,

> Populations of the urban poor had to be pacified and even cared for, partly because they provided the necessary labor and services to the city's economy and partly because if they were not cared for at all, they could endanger the safety and well-being of all citizens.
>
> (2004: 135)

While the changing nature of Indian politics, and particularly the growth of regional parties, led to the emergence of sectors of the disadvantaged populations as strategic vote-banks to be cultivated, some of the lower middle-class groups were also able to prosper in the wake of legislation that protected areas of the economy for small traders. Given the intense urban overcrowding and the difficulties of alleviating shortages of both finance and available space for new housing and infrastructure, these gains did not dramatically improve the immediate living conditions of these groups, but they did provide a degree of disposable income to be spent on leisure. Furthermore, recognising the social (and electoral) benefit of guaranteeing access to the cinema for the urban population, various state governments instigated legislation fixing ticket rates at an affordable level as well as requiring cinema halls to offer a set capacity (typically three rows) of seating at extremely low rates for the poorest. However, lower ticket prices also diminished the profits of exhibitors, which led to decreasing interest in the maintenance of the cinemas, with the physical deterioration of many urban cinemas highly apparent by the end of the 1980s.

For the more privileged sections of society, aside from the numerically tiny elite, these measures represented further gains for others which symbolically refuted their sense of entitlement over setting the norms for public culture and which practically diminished their access to urban leisure facilities. It would be an exaggeration to say that there were no theatres that continued to enjoy middle-class patronage during the 1980s, but it does appear to be the case that middle-class audiences had mostly vacated the central public spaces for theatres located within specifically middle-class colonies or suburbs (see Vasudevan 2003). Even here, the encroachment of itinerant settlements on open grounds further encouraged a sense of siege. Something that served to mitigate their declining participation in the cinema was the slow growth of television ownership amongst the upper middle classes and the advent of the VCR, which was taken up enthusiastically by these groups throughout the 1980s (Friedberg 2000). As such, reflecting on the 1980s for *India Today*, Madhu Jain observed that this was a decade in which 'the gentile class had retreated to the comfort of television and video', leaving cinema halls to 'the children of the mean streets' (Jain, 1990: 46).

The liberalisation era and the multiplex

The final, and therefore contemporary, period in the public history of the Indian cinema is the era of economic liberalisation in India, the push for a consumerist society and the return of the middle-class romance as the dominant theme of the Indian cinema. At the economic level, the era of liberalisation consists of policies that de-regulate areas that were previously heavily controlled by the state through a licensing system, policies that favour private investment, including foreign investment, as well as major revisions to the policy of import substitution in favour of an export-oriented approach. Initiated, originally in response to the growing frustration amongst India's economic managers about the pace of change during the 1980s, the wider economic crises that arose with the collapse of the socialist world economy and an acute balance of payments crisis in 1991, the popular image of the contemporary era is that of a switch from a socialist to a free-market society. The identification of this new era in the public imagination of India should not imply that the pugilist terrain of the Indian cinema in the previous phase has been entirely overwritten by the new types of films and the new social values that have emerged since 1991. It is fair to say, however, that the 1990s and 2000s have constituted a moment in public culture within which the old logics of the all-India movie have been severely truncated by new technologies, a changing regulatory environment and new ways of imagining India.

These factors have all contributed towards a new economic logic for film exhibition that has made the multiplex cinema a viable proposition in India. Thus, there appears to be a ready parallel between the liberalisation of the economy and the return to prominence of romantic films of the kind currently associated with directors such as Yash Chopra and Karan Johar. In these glossy productions, the new superstar of Hindi cinema, Shah Rukh Khan, along with the various children of 1970s films stars, has been playing out a celebration of consumer affluence, cultural nationalism and international leisure travel over the past decade. These are themes which have proved massively popular with South Asian expatriate audiences overseas (whom, due to relaxed foreign currency controls, have now become a valuable source of income for the film industry) and with a broad range of the domestic middle classes. Even the formerly angry Amitabh Bachchan has been re-born (in films such as *Kabhi Khushi Kabhie Gham* (2000)) as the benign patriarch of a comfortable Punjabi elite mixing international wealth with Hindu revivalism and middlebrow sentimentalism. Thus, for Ronald Inden, the commercial Indian cinema of the 1990s has publicly addressed an explicit desire by the Indian middle classes to 'reclaim the cinema as a vehicle for representing themselves not only to themselves but to the nation and the world' (1999: 64). This shift in the imagination of the Indian cinema finds a ready parallel in the contemporaneous remaking of urban space, where

> Government policy, at the level of the states and even the municipalities, has been directly affected by the urgent pressure to connect with the global economy and attract foreign investment. The result has been, one the one hand, greater assertion by organisations of middle class citizens of their right to unhindered access to public spaces and thoroughfares and to a clean and healthy urban environment. On the other hand, government policy has rapidly turned away from the idea of helping the poor to subsist within the city and is instead paying the greatest attention to improving infrastructure in order to create conditions for the import of high technology and the new service industries. Thus, manufacturing industries are being moved out beyond the city limits; squatters and encroachers are being evicted; property and tenancy laws are being re-written to enable market forces to rapidly convert the congested and dilapidated sections of the old city into high-value commercial and residential districts.

(Chatterjee 2004: 144)

It is in this context, and in a marked contrast to the downshifting trends in the exhibition sector over the previous two decades, that the multiplex has appeared in India's urban landscape. The multiplex cinema hall in India was instigated in the upmarket Saket district of New Delhi in 1997 through a tie-up between a local family-run exhibition concern, Priya Exhibitors Ltd., and Village Roadshow Ltd., a multi-national concern based in Australia. The site, PVR Anupam, was the result of a refurbishment of a large, old theatre into a multi-screen site modelled on the international standard of a multiplex facility – what has since been dubbed by the industry a 'retrofit'. According to PVR, the site 'was an instant success on account of its strategic location and first mover advantage' (PVR Cinemas 2006). Located in a suburban commercial district with manned security gates at its access points and surrounded by national and international retail franchise outlets, including McDonalds, Pizza Hut, Barista, Nirulas, Subway, Moti Mahal, Planet M, Lee and Reebok, PVR Anupam has proved highly popular with an upper middle-class crowd and has been one of Delhi's most profitable cinemas over the last ten years. The success of PVR Anupam prompted a number of other players to reconsider the opportunities in India's exhibition sector, where thousands of small, independent single-screen theatres were still largely catering to entrenched lower-class audiences. During the last five years in particular, investors have rushed to jump on the multiplex bandwagon, and in the process the entire landscape of film exhibition in India has been radically transformed.

The newfound willingness of the more affluent segments of the population to abandon their televisions and to patronise a facility like PVR Anupam indicated a rejuvenated market for upscale projects modelled on the format of the multiplex. These additions to the urban landscape have been appreciated by middle-class citizens seeking a better standard and wider choice of entertainment than that provided by the older large-capacity halls. Due to its smaller auditoriums, higher admission prices and its rationale of providing an entertainment menu, the multiplex has certainly had major implications for the film industry. In the first place, the multiplex has served to elevate the box office value of the middle-class public and therefore to underscore the pre-eminence of the contemporary aspirational mode of middle-class melodrama and the values that it espouses. At the same time, however, the multiplex has also provided a venue for niche middle class-oriented films in a range of styles not previously viable with the old mass public as well as ceding a much greater toehold for Hollywood films in the Indian market. It is upon this basis that Aparna Sharma claims that:

> Once in place, the multiplex developed a counter to the unitary propensity of the single screen hall, founded on exclusion, perpetuating homogeneity and cultivating committed audience segments. While single screen cinemas identify themselves with films of particular kinds, say the Hindi *masala* and blockbuster, the English, or the porn movie, the multiplex has capitalised on an inclusive tendency to motivate and assemble diverse audiences.

> (Sharma 2003)

Figure 2.3 PVR Cinemas at Saket in South Delhi. India's first multiplex since 1997. (Adrian Athique)

Figure 2.4 The Natraj, a single-screen cinema hall in Baroda, Gujarat, opened in 1970. (Adrian Athique)

This 'inclusive' tendency is predicated on a diversity of content arising at the expense of a more socially diverse audience. This is an outcome not only welcomed, but publicised, by the multiplex operators who know that the absence of the cheap crowd is a prerequisite for attracting the kind of patrons they desire. As with Srinivas' account of the earlier historical period, Ronald Inden has been able to demonstrate the sensibilities being associated with the multiplex through the use of public letters written to contemporary film journals:

> The addition of Movie Time Cinema (at Malad West) to the many, new, compact and highly-sophisticated cinemas in Mumbai's suburbs is welcome indeed. The tickets may be priced higher, at RS 75 or thereabouts, but the ticket rates are deliberately priced to keep unwanted elements away. These theatres cater to family audiences and the bubble-gum crowd and offer a variety of snacks and viewing comforts, even hygienic toilets. The fact that they are situated in the suburbs and screen the latest big films, is a major plus point.
>
> (in Inden 1999: 62)

The multiplex in India has thus been widely seen as responding to a latent demand amongst the upper middle classes for sufficiently sanitised and controlled public space where the behaviour of patrons corresponds with middle-class norms and where the overwhelming numerical superiority of the mob is mitigated. The multiplex has been marketed in India with specific regard to the long-standing middle-class anxieties that have arisen around the cinema hall. When the longevity of these concerns is taken into account, we have to take them seriously as indicative of an inherent difficulty faced by the cinema in a diverse society. Rather than simply decrying the advent of top-end facilities as exclusionary, it is important to remain acutely sensitive to both the gendering of public spaces and the critical shortage of leisure environments in India's cities. If the multiplex is finally providing a secure and socially acceptable space for middle-class women of all ages to enjoy out-of-home entertainment, then that can only be of social benefit. However, a critical response to these developments could diagnose these new operating conditions negatively as the beginning of more entrenched narrowcast taste cultures separating the haves and have-nots in the new Indian economy and a fragmenting public. Similarly, it is also worth questioning what degree of access the vast majority women in India outside of the upper middle classes are gaining to either the multiplex or the traditional cinema hall. Whatever side is taken, it seems irrefutable that the multiplex cinema in India must be understood as part of a sustained attempt to create appropriate public spaces for theatrical exhibition for the middle-class family.

As part of the wider public history of urban leisure, multiplex theatres are undertakings that reflect an era in which the more affluent groups in society have generally been the perceived beneficiaries of policies and planning decisions designed to re-order India's urban environments. In this respect, the story of the multiplex in urban India has been as much a story of suburbanisation as it has previously been in Singapore, albeit representing a shift of white-collar rather than blue-collar populations. Correspondingly, the Indian multiplex might be seen as more akin to the American experience in this regard, despite the obvious fact that the multiplex in India to date has associated itself with an exclusive nature that stands in direct contrast to the markedly proletarian habitat of the American multiplex. What unites all three narratives, however, is the demonstrable relationship between multiplexing and suburbanisation. In the first four decades after independence, Indian cities have generally been seen as having failed to privilege Fordist relations as the organising principle of urban space over the existing terrain established by the colonial past and the feudal caste order. This spatial and temporal disjuncture across the metropolitan landscape indicates the inherent limitations of a labour-intensive, service-oriented society that had adopted the functions, but not the form of industrial society. There is no doubt, however, that in the contemporary period the urban landscape is being transformed by a newly-dominant ideological programme favouring a consumption-led economy, as Leela Fernandes notes:

> At a surface level, this process appears to embody a conventional pattern of gentrification. Exorbitant real estate prices in south Mumbai, the heart of the city, have pushed middle-class individuals into suburban areas. The result has been the production of new and distinctive forms of suburban cultural and social communities. In what are now considered upmarket suburbs, neighbourhoods in areas such as Bandra and other western suburbs have witnessed the growth of upmarket restaurants, shopping enterprises and movie theatres.
>
> (2004: 2419)

It is not sufficient, therefore, to understand the multiplex simply as a place for watching films, nor as a stand-alone activity. In this sense, what is notable about the rise of the wider leisure economy is also indicative of the changing geography of cinema in urban India. The cinema halls of the previous eras were first centrally-located elite habitats. They subsequently became popular facilities constructed in relation to the areas of the cities where mass crowds gathered, such as around railway stations and markets. By contrast, in this latest phase, the multiplexes have for the most part been constructed in the suburbs situated along the route of the new flyovers and arterial routes that are re-shaping Indian cities. Of course, this implies that these sites must be reached by private rather than public transport. This spatial distribution therefore serves to further augment the segmentation of the film-going public. As Sharma has also noted:

> While the masses take to cinema readily, given their financial capacity and lack of identification with the plush appearance, products and services at the multiplex – in any case targeted at the socially and economically mobile sections – this numerically significant chunk of audience has remained confined to the outer edges of the multiplex experience. And it is unlikely that the dynamics of the multiplex in its present avatar will manage to secure their participation.

> Spatially too, multiplexes can mostly be spotted in affluent neighbourhoods, within the easy reach and concentration of young audiences.
>
> (Sharma 2003)

In the context of urban India, it is obvious that the new leisure economy has not enjoyed access to a blank slate. The flyovers, malls and multiplexes have all required the acquisition of large areas of land in the most crowded environments to be found in one of the world's most densely populated countries. It would be disingenuous to ignore the marginalised populations that have been forcibly relocated to make way for the rash of infrastructure projects in Delhi, Mumbai and elsewhere. One outcome of this is 'the growing "physical" distance between the poor and the privileged in India. The poverty and deprivation in the country is so great that those who have moved up the income scale seek to barricade themselves from its pervasive presence' (Varma, 1998: 203). As such, while the overall shortage of cinemas in India, and their different clientele, appears to suggest the continuance of the older cinema circuit along with its new, upmarket cousin, it is also the case that the patrons of this two-tier infrastructure are becoming not only economically, but also spatially, separated.

While this segregating effect can be cast as symptomatic of the processes of globalisation, the significance of the multiplexes in India in this regard should be related in the first place to the internal tensions inherent in the long-standing, uneven development of India in socio-economic terms, as well to the legacy of feudal and colonialist spatialities. Leela Fernandes notes that: 'The expansion of such socio-cultural spaces for the changing lifestyles of the middle classes in liberalising India rests on the creation of a new urban aesthetics of class purity' (2004: 2420). While the concept of purity has some relationship to the cleanliness desired by suburban multiplex patrons in Britain, it is important to recognise that it has very particular connotations in the Indian social imagination, significantly shaping popular attitudes towards fellow citizens as well as to the environment itself in ways that both exacerbate and transcend class society (see Sharan 2002, Mawdsley 2004). At the same time, it is equally apparent that the multiplex is also indicative of the impact of global economic trends on the urban landscape (Gandelsonas 2005, Koolhaas 2005).

The process of dislocation between the consuming classes and the rump of the Indian population is thus commensurate, and intimately entwined, with the liberal economic policies and urban redevelopment agendas currently being pursued by the Indian government. In that sense, local histories do not exist in isolation from global histories, rather they exist in both complementary and contradictory interactions within the lived environment, variously reinforcing and refuting the ideological power of the forces of conservatism and modernisation. On both counts, it may be pertinent in the light of the present history of the multiplex for film scholars to revisit and even reconsider their claims made upon the cinema hall and its occupants as the site of a nascent democratic principle. By contrast, the story of the multiplex to date appears to provides greater support for Partha Chatterjee's prediction that, frustrated with the burden of development and the politicisation of the masses,

Figure 2.5 Queue at Sagar cinema hall in Central Bangalore, February 2007. (Adrian Athique)

Figure 2.6 Queue at INOX multiplex in Panaji, December 2006. (Adrian Athique)

'The elite will form its own community – a spatially bound interpersonally networked subculture . . . [with] segregated and exclusive space for shops, restaurants, arts and entertainment aimed at this clientele' (Chatterjee, 2004, 144–145).

A legacy of public history

From the account given here, we can clearly see the antecedents of the multiplex in the history of the cinema crowd and the conflicts that have been constituted within and around the cinema hall. Taking these factors into account, we begin to see how the multiplex has been consciously deployed in India in order to solve the problem of the cinema from a particular set of perspectives. It is apparent that the (re)appearance of cinema as an extension of environmentally-regulated retail leisure has been predisposed by a series of ideological motives (and social anxieties) deeply ingrained amongst the middle classes pertaining to the suitable composition of the audience and the appropriate ritual purpose of the cinema experience. At the same time, it is important to recognise that the ground for spatial segregation has long been laid. Indeed, it was one of the intrinsic principles in the formal organisation of the colonial city and, in the post-socialist era, it is relatively unsurprising to see its revival in the commercially-oriented urban redevelopment agendas being pursued under the instrument of the Jawaharlal Nehru National Urban Renewal Mission (JNNURM). This reclamation of public space is enacted through the production of new, exclusive forms of social space under the rubric of 'urban renewal'. In the specific case of the multiplex, this process should be further seen as part of (and a response to) the history of social contest within (and outside) the cinema hall.

The 20-year lag between the debut of the true multiplex and its adoption in India is also proving to be a significant factor in the shaping of the Indian multiplex, not least because it brings with it to India particular histories, technologies and rationales and the terminologies that go with them. However, while the proponents of the Indian multiplex have enjoyed the benefits of adopting a tested international formula, they have also been required to accommodate or overwrite the particular nature of the Indian cinema and its idiosyncratic commercial culture, aesthetic mobilisations and modes of operation. So whilst it remains useful to analyse the multiplex in terms of impact, it is also the case that the status of the multiplex cinema in India is determined in a large part by a public history that has predetermined its arrival. The multiplex is also, of course, further subject to the existing tensions within the market itself. As such, the following chapter seeks to situate the multiplex within the specific industrial context of the Indian cinema.

3   Film exhibition and the economic logic of the multiplex

Historically, the Indian film industry has been located within the domain of India's unorganised, or informal, economy. The reasons for this are manifold, from its emergence in the late colonial period to the economic and cultural prerogatives which guided successive post-independence governments. The term 'unorganised', of course, is somewhat misleading, given the great complexity of the informal economy in India, which continues to dwarf the state-owned and corporate concerns that are generally referred to as the 'organised' sector (see Harriss-White 2003). Given the considerable co-ordination required by cinema as an industrial mass-medium, it is perhaps more suitable to use the term 'disorganised', implying a dispersal of organisation, rather than a lack of it. In that sense, the Indian film industry is most obviously 'disorganised' when compared with the paradigm of formally integrated capital interests and operating procedures set by the film industry of the United States. In Hollywood, just a handful of players control the entire product chain from production through to worldwide exhibition via various media formats, as well as a range of ancillary products. By contrast, the disorganised industry in India has instead been characterised by the dispersal of working capital and assets amongst large numbers of small, independent operators who, despite their common interest in the successful exploitation of cinematic culture, lack formal association with each other.

Although Hollywood-style studios did come into existence in Bombay, Kolhapur and Calcutta during the colonial era, their operating interests remained in production and did not extend to the distribution and exhibition sectors. The collapse of Madan Theatres in the 1930s led to an overwhelmingly fragmented system of distribution and exhibition throughout India, and this pattern was to be repeated in the production sector a decade later. In the context of the wartime economy of the 1940s and the imminent departure of the British, the funds for the rapid expansion of Indian film production primarily came from outside of the industry, and from non-institutional sources of finance. Businessmen with large sums of cash which they wished to place beyond the reach of British taxation began to offer large sums to finance film making. Before very long, these new independent producers had managed to lure the major stars and directors away from the studios, which promptly collapsed (Barnouw and Krishnaswamy 1980: 121). Consequently, from the 1940s onwards, the vast majority of films in India were made as one-off productions intended to recoup all their costs in one go, as opposed to offsetting risks by producing a clutch of films at any one time as in the studio system.

This structural adjustment to industry practices during the 1940s had cultural implications since it resulted in the formalisation of the *masala* film, a super-genre, a three-hour spectacular providing something for everyone: comedy, romance, action, family drama and numerous songs. This proved to be the best way to max-imise audience share in an increasingly anarchic industry with extremely narrow profit margins and considerable overproduction. Due to intense competition, the vast majority of Indian films throughout the post-independence period have failed to break even, leading to the general assumption that many productions are simply money-laundering vehicles for independent financiers (see Pendakur 2003, Athique 2008a). For those who have been seeking to make a production profitable in its own right, the over-reliance on a narrow and expensive star system, along with unofficial and high-interest sources of production finance, has compounded the imperative for each film to succeed with a large proportion of the mass audience, perpetuating a risky one-size-fits-all approach over several decades.

Beyond the highly fragmented production sector, the informal organisation of commercial interests has led to a distinctly dispersed and mutually competitive working structure at the levels of distribution and exhibition in India. Most films are sold by independent producers to various distributors in different regions at either a flat rate, on a percentage basis or as a pre-sale with a proportion of the expected box office gross upfront. There are no all-India distributors. Instead there are a large number of independent distributors who compete for film rights at various levels. At the top are Indian territories (traditionally Bombay and West, Delhi/Uttar Pradesh, East, South and North) that are now augmented by a num-ber of overseas territories. Below those territories are the A centres, B centres and C centres. These categories are calculated roughly along two vectors. The first is from the major metropolitan centres to the second-tier cities and ultimately the regional (mofusil) towns. The second vector is from the higher-value cinemas in upmarket districts to rundown halls in poorer neighbourhoods. It is usual that in the course of its theatrical life a major feature will pass through a number of different distributors across the different segments of the market, while lower-budget productions may target the B or C centres exclusively. Most distributors do not own any cinemas of their own, but instead bid for rights to a film in particular territories and then pay either a fixed sum in rental to the owners of each hall or take a percentage share of gross profits.

The exhibition sector has also been overwhelmingly disorganised for a number of reasons. In the first place, the demand for cinema grew at such a rate through the 1940s that the boom in theatre construction was considered to be a significant waste of resources by the wartime government, who duly banned it. A chronic shortage of theatres in per capita terms was compounded after independence by continuing restrictions on the construction of new cinema halls (Chakravarty 1993: 58). This greatly strengthened the hands of existing exhibitors who were able to rent their theatres to distributors at higher rates as a glut in production driven by illicit capital ran up against a lack of screen capacity, beyond which was an ever-growing and enthusiastic audience for moving pictures. According to Valentina Vitali, 'By controlling the few exhibition outlets' exhibitors were able to 'impose whatever fees they wish' (2004). Amongst the exhibitors themselves, the consolidation of cinema chains was prevented by lack of working capital as well as ceilings subsequently imposed at state and federal levels upon urban land holdings (see Shrinivas 1991).

Since independence, the Government of India has also traditionally seen cinema as a useful source of revenue. At the regional level, the state governments were empowered to increase the entertainment tax levied on cinema tickets from pre-war levels of around 12.5 per cent, leading to entertainment taxes as high as 75 per cent of the ticket price in some areas (see Mittal 1995). This encouraged the widespread misreporting of attendance figures by exhibitors as well as the spreading of the tax burden through further rental hikes charged on distributors (KPMG 2005). For this reason, the feedback of box office data and profits back up the chain has been extremely unreliable throughout the post-colonial history of the Indian cinema. While the levels of entertainment tax levied in the various states have fluctuated over the years, and currently appear to be on a downturn, they still remain at very high levels in some states. Historically, this is particularly evident in northern India, where taxes on cinema tickets commonly run at 50 per cent or more. By contrast, the regional politics of the southern states since the 1960s, and the close relationship between political parties and local film stars, have led to the official encouragement of the local-language film industries that now dominate the market in the South. Accordingly, entertainment taxes are consistently lower in South India, which may serve to explain why two-thirds of the nation's cinemas are to be found there, despite the southern region being home to only 22 per cent of the national population (India Infoline 2006).

At the all-India level, the high rates of taxation being applied to profits made from the exhibition of films, accompanied by the difficulty in gaining clearance for the construction of new theatres, has greatly held back the growth of screen capacity in India – making it to date one of the least-resourced nations worldwide in terms of screens per capita (UNESCO 1999). Although the high degree of underscreening suggests room for growth, the difficulty in gaining clearance for constructing theatres has been compounded over the past two decades by endemic media piracy, which has allowed increasing numbers of patrons, largely from the middle classes, to watch films outside of the theatres. The wider economic malaise of the 1980s also led to price stagnation, declining profits and dwindling investment in exhibition infrastructure. In order to understand the multiplex phenomenon of the last decade, which appears to overturn the prevailing conditions of the market, it is important to recognise a number of key factors which contribute to the economic logic that is driving the multiplex boom.

The new leisure economy

The multiplex has been just one of the major changes in the Indian leisure economy brought about by the staged liberalisation of the national economy over the last 15 years. Contemporaneous developments have included the rapid expansion of private cable and satellite television, personal computing and mobile telephony, as well as vibrant growth in the marketing and services sectors (Butcher 2003, Mazzarella 2003). The commercial application of new media technologies and the swift arrival of large, vertically-integrated media combines from abroad has prompted a wide-ranging review of the anarchic conditions of mass independent production which have existed since the 1940s. On the one hand, since international players have only been partially successful in expanding the market for dubbed US imports in existing theatres, media multi-nationals such as Fox have begun to provide finance for local production. On the other hand, in recognition of the growing importance of the media sector as part of a services-oriented economic paradigm, the Government of India bestowed official industry status upon the film industry in 2000, thus opening the way for access to domestic institutional finance. For local producers able to access them, these new sources of investment capital, both domestic and foreign, along with the liberalisation of export controls, have provided both the means and the economic rationale for increased integration. As such, some of the major producers have been making serious efforts to co-ordinate their activities as production houses with the marketing and distribution of their films. This new trend towards integrated operations amongst the top echelon of the industry is being presented as a corporatisation of the film business, with a number of what were previously essentially family firms operating in various niche roles instead raising funds on the stock market and diversifying their interests across the industry (Price Waterhouse Coopers 2006, Moullier 2007).

Corporatisation in the media sector is an important context for understanding the multiplex. In a marked departure from the disaggregated form of the established exhibition sector, the multiplex phenomenon over the past ten years has been dominated by just a handful of players who are building the first truly national exhibition chains since the demise of Madan Theatres some 70 years ago. Currently, the five leading operators are PVR Cinemas Ltd., Adlabs Films Ltd., Shringar Cinemas Ltd., INOX Leisure Ltd. and FUN Multiplex Pvt. Each of these companies has diverse origins that we explore here in brief. At the same time, they all share some key characteristics, operational practices and business outlooks established in opposition to the traditional working model of film exhibition in India. Significantly, with the exception of the most recent entrant, FUN Multiplex Pvt., (which is part of media mogul Subhash Chandra's business empire), all of these companies have attracted major institutional and public investment from outside of the entertainment sector. At the time of writing, these five companies operate two-thirds of India's multiplexes and they are all engaged in massive programmes of expansion.

PVR cinemas

PVR, the operators of India's first multiplex at Saket in New Delhi, was originally incorporated in 1995 as Priya Village Roadshow, a joint venture between Priya Exhibitors Private Ltd. and Australian exhibition chain Village Roadshow Ltd. Priya Exhibitors Private Ltd. acquired the stake formerly held by Village

Table 3.1 Shareholding Pattern PVR Cinemas Ltd. 2006

Foreign institutional investors		
Fid Funds (Mauritius) Ltd	2287737	10.00%
T Rowe Price New Asia Fund	1000000	4.37%
Matthews International Funds A/C Matthews India	464890	2.03%
Citigroup Global Markets Mauritius Private Limited	286353	1.25%
Total	**4038980**	**17.65%**
Promoters		
Bijli Investments Pvt Ltd	4920068	21.51%
Priya Exhibitors Pvt Ltd	4330000	18.93%
Total	**9250068**	**40.43**
Corporate bodies		
Sonata Investments Limited	800000	3.50%
Total	**800000**	**3.50%**
Mutual funds		
The Western India Trustee And Executor Co Ltd (India Advantage Fund-1)	4253208	18.59%
Uti-Opportunities Fund	1139247	4.98%
Fidelity Trustee Company Private Limited	525495	2.30%
HSBC Midcap Equity Fund	276016	1.21%
Total	**6193966**	**27.07%**

Source: Adapted from PVR Cinemas 2006

Roadshow Ltd. in 2002 when the latter contracted its overseas operations (PVR Cinemas 2006a). PVR subsequently received 380 million rupees in investment from the private equity interest India Advantage Fund in March 2003, laying the ground for further expansion. A successful public offering was also made in March 2006, raising further funds (PVR Cinemas 2006b). PVR is currently India's largest multiplex cinema operator in terms of screen capacity, with 62 screens in 16 cinemas as of April 2006 (PVR Cinemas 2006a).

PVR does not own any of the multiplexes that it operates, holding the majority through lease agreements and offering the remainder as franchises. PVR currently has a further nine sites under construction and/or fitting, which are expected to become operational during 2007. There are further plans and agreements for 28 additional sites, which will bring the screen capacity of PVR to 250 screens. The majority of these new sites will be in the north-west: Punjab (nine), Gujarat (two), Rajasthan (one), Uttaranchal (two), Uttar Pradesh (three), Delhi (one) and Haryana (one). Other sites are also planned in Jharkand (two), Chattisgarh (one), Karnataka (two), Tamil Nadu (one) and Andhra Pradesh (one) (PVR Cinemas 2006c, 2006d). In 2005, PVR cinemas acquired a subsidiary company, PVR Pictures Ltd., which handles distribution of Indian films within territories where its theatres are located (primarily Delhi-Haryana-Uttar Pradesh) as well as nationwide distribution of imported, mostly American, features. Another 100 per cent subsidiary of PVR Cinemas is CR Retail Malls (India) Pvt. Ltd., which has been constituted to pursue the development of a seven-screen multiplex at The Phoenix Mills compound in Mumbai (PVR Cinemas 2006c).

Adlabs Films Ltd.

Adlabs Films Ltd. was founded in Mumbai as a film processing laboratory in 1978 by Manmohan Shetty and Vasanji Mamania. The company currently holds about 70 per cent of the film processing market in Western India. Adlabs entered into film exhibition in 2000, and opened its first multiplex at Wadala, Mumbai in March 2001. Adlabs made an initial public offering in December 2000, raising 528 rupees million for its expansion plans. Adlabs also moved into film production through its wholly-owned subsidiary, Entertainment One, in 2002 and in the following year launched a 50/50 joint venture with Mukta Arts (Mukta Adlabs Digital Exhibition Limited (MADEL)) to promote digital distribution and exhibition technologies. In October 2005, the land investment arm of the Reliance Anil Dhirubhai Ambani Group (Reliance – ADA Group) acquired a 50.16 per cent stake in Adlabs Films Limited for a price of 3.6 billion rupees, buying out Vasanji Mamania's stake in the company. Manmohan Shetty was retained as the managing director and chairman

Table 3.2 Shareholding pattern Adlabs Films Ltd. 2006

Public Shareholding – Institutions		
Foreign Institutional Investors (7)	4,996,344	12.55%
Mutual Funds/ UTI (9)	1,719,221	4.32%
Total (16)	**6,715,565**	**16.87%**
Public Shareholding – Non-Institutional		
Bodies Corporate (598)	919,250	2.31%
Individual Shareholders Up To 1 Lakh (14752)	2,203,101	5.54%
Individual Shareholders Above 1 Lakh (7)	601,122	1.51%
Non-Resident Indians – Repatriate (66)	46,787	0.12%
NRI – Non-Repatriate (20)	21,668	0.05%
Clearing Members (138)	109,384	0.27%
Market Maker (80)	37,389	0.09%
Directors (2)	7,291,334	18.32%
Total (15664)	**11,230,185**	**28.22%**
Promoters		
Reliance Land Private Limited	20,600,000	51.76%
Reliance Capital Limited	1,255,000	3.15%
Total	**21,855,000**	**54.91%**

Source: Adapted from Adlabs Films Ltd. 2006

of the company, which is now positioning itself with new interests all the way along the cinema chain, from production through to exhibition, as well as cross-media interests in television and radio (Adlabs Films 2006a).

Adlabs currently operates multiplex 11 sites with 42 screens and a seating capacity of 12,742. Seven of those sites are located in Maharashtra: Mumbai (four), Nasik (one), Indore (one) and Pune (one). Three sites are located in Uttar Pradesh: Meerut (one) and Ghaziabad (two). A number of Adlabs sites are owned by companies which are joint ventures or subsidiaries of Adlabs Films Limited. Other multiplexes are held under lease agreements with the lease model likely to serve as the basis for future sites. Adlabs has signed a large number of such leases for further multiplexes and current projections are for a further 110 screens and 32,000 seats over the next three years. Adlabs is concentrating on second-tier cities or B centres in tax exemption states, which are regarded as either an untapped (i.e. underscreened) or unregulated sector (i.e. both high levels of piracy and under-reported box office from local theatres) with high potentials for profit capture. Sites are also proposed in select A centres in other states. Three-quarters of the projected new Adlabs sites will be in the north and west regions (Adlabs Films 2006b).

Shringar Cinemas Ltd.

Shringar Cinemas Ltd. was incorporated in 1999. The beginnings of the Shringar Group of companies, however, reach back to the 1950s, when a partnership firm between Gobindram and Vasudev Naoomal Shroff began financing Bollywood films. In 1975, Shyam and Balakrishna Shroff launched Shringar Films, which subsequently became one of India's biggest film distributors. From 1995, Shringar Films began offering programme management to theatre owners. In 1997, Shringar Films began managing some film theatres. Shringar moved into the multiplex business in partnership with Adlabs in 2002 with the opening of Fame Adlabs in Mumbai, followed by the subsequent development of its own multiplexes under the Fame brand. A public share offering in Shringar was made in April 2005. In July 2005, Temasek holdings (an investment arm of the Singapore government) acquired a 14.9 per cent stake in Shringar (Shringar Cinemas 2006a, 2006b, 2006c).

Shringar Cinemas operates theatres on a ten-year lease model. There are currently six Fame Multiplexes with a total of 27 screens and 7,501 seats. Five of the six sites are in Maharashtra (Mumbai (three), Nasik (one) and Pune (one)) and the other is in West Bengal (Kolkata). Shringar plans to pursue a rapid expansion of its business through further lease agreements and through Shringar's management model, where it will offer programming, procedures and staffing to theatre owners. Shringar also has plans to move into the food court business through a new subsidiary, Oxford Multiplex Cinemas Pvt Ltd. The 31 new sites currently being proposed will be a mixture of new multiplex facilities, retrofits and single-screen theatres. Two-thirds of these sites will be dispersed nationwide, whilst one-third will be concentrated in Shringar's home market in Maharashtra (Shringar Cinemas 2006a, Fame Cinemas 2006).

Table 3.3 Shareholding pattern Shringar Cinemas Ltd. 2006.

Public Shareholding – Institutions		
Foreign Institutional Investors (3)	3,588,133	11.3669%
Mutual Funds (2)	1,462,262	4.6323%
Total	**5,050,395**	**15.9992%**
Public Shareholding – Non-Institutional		
Bodies Corporate (757)	2,452,450	7.7692%
Individual Shareholders Up To 1 Lakh (14,192)	5,736,110	18.1715%
Individual Shareholders Above 1 Lakh (35)	822,118	2.6044%
Non-Resident Indians (119)	2,360,270	7.4771%
Clearing Members (52)	71,340	0.226%
IPO Drop (1)	2,065	0.0065%
Total	**11,442,288**	**36.2547%**
Promoters		
South Yaraa Holdings	15,057,760	47.7017%
Shyam Shroff	1	0.0000%
Balkrishna Shroff	14,001	0.0444%
Shravan Shroff	1	0.0000%
Aditya Shroff	1	0.0000%
Rita Shroff	1	0.0000%
Total	**15,071,765**	**47.7461%**

Source: Shringar Cinemas Ltd.

INOX Leisure Ltd.

INOX Leisure Limited is unlike the other major multiplex company in that its origins do not lie in the entertainment sector. Operating since May 2002, INOX Leisure Ltd. is a diversification venture of the INOX group into entertainment. Also, it is a subsidiary of Gujarat Fluorochemicals Ltd. INOX currently operates 12 multiplex theatres across India. With no particular home territory, INOX promotes itself as the most national of the multiplex chains and has pursued a wide distribution of theatres from the outset. As such, INOX is currently the only player of significance in the eastern regions (INOX Leisure 2006a). INOX currently operates at 12 sites on 44 screens with 13,267 seats. The INOX sites in operation are in Mumbai, Baroda and Pune (Maharashtra), Panaji (Goa), Kolkata and Darjeeling (West Bengal), Kota and Jaipur (Rajasthan), Indore and Nagpur (Madhya Pradesh) and Bangalore (Karnataka) (INOX Leisure 2006b).

INOX owns a number of its major sites outright, but as the company expands, new additions are all expected to be undertaken on a lease basis. A further 11 new sites currently under construction and/or fitting are expected to come online by 2008 (INOX Leisure 2006c). INOX is now planning to enter into a partnership with leading retailer The Pantaloon Group. This alliance is intended to pursue the development of 51 malls nationwide, 35 of which will contain multiplex facilities.

Table 3.4 Shareholding pattern INOX Leisure Ltd. 2006

Public Shareholding – Institutions		
Foreign Institutional Investors (15)	6,712,018	11.19%
Mutual Funds (17)	3,675,108	6.13%
Financial Institutions / Banks (5)	113,193	0.19%
Total	**10,500,319**	**17.5%**
Public Shareholding – Non-Institutional		
Bodies Corporate (741)	2,011,829	3.35%
Individual Shareholders Up To 1 Lakh (41,215)	3,470,037	5.78%
Individual Shareholders Above 1 Lakh (22)	3,748,667	6.25%
Trusts (10)	505,713	0.84%
Non-Resident Indians (236)	141,996	0.24%
Clearing Members (81)	21,439	0.04%
Total	**9,899,681**	**16.5%**
Promoters		
Gujurat Flourochemicals Ltd.	39,600,000	66.0%
Total	**39,600,000**	**66.0%**

Source: Adapted from INOX Leisure Ltd.

INOX has also signed a term sheet with Calcutta Cine Private Limited (CCPL) and its shareholders for acquisition and merger of CCPL with INOX. The acquisition of CCPL will contribute up to eight more multiplexes in eastern India, mostly in West Bengal (INOX Leisure 2006a, 2006c).

FUN Cinemas

The FUN Cinemas brand, operated by FUN Multiplex Pvt., which came into being in April 2005, is the most recent entrant amongst the major players. FUN Multiplex is a division of E-City Ventures, which represents the entertainment and retail interests of the Essel Group (E-City Ventures 2006). The Essel Group, which started out in 1982 as a packaging company (and remains a world leader in this area), famously diversified into media in 1992, when chairman Subhash Chandra launched ZEE television, India's first satellite channel (Essel Group 2006). During periods of both partnership and competition with Rupert Murdoch's STAR, ZEE has been a giant of India's television boom during the deregulation era. ZEE TV now operates a suite of regional, national and international television channels (ZEE Television 2006). Essel had made earlier forays into the leisure economy with a number of theme parks, starting with Essel World in Mumbai in 1988 (Essel World 2007). E-City Ventures, launched in 1999, is composed of five divisions: E-City entertainment (developing and running shopping malls under the FUN Republic brand since 2001), E-City Films (distributing films since 2001), E-City Digital Cinemas (rolling out digital distribution and exhibition technology on lease, profit-share or theatre-hire basis in B centres since 2004), E-City Property Management Services (offering management expertise to private shopping mall owners) and, finally, FUN Multiplex.

The first three FUN Cinemas were opened as part of the FUN Republic 'family entertainment centres' built by E-City Ventures (Ahmedabad in June 2001, Andheri (Mumbai) in August 2003 and Chandigarh in November 2003). In this model the cinemas were operated as part of a mall package that also included eating, shopping and gaming. Following the setting-up of FUN Multiplex as a separate division in 2005, FUN Cinemas have launched four sites in New Delhi as well as opening in Jaipur (Rajasthan) and Ghaziabad (Uttar Pradesh). FUN Multiplex offers a choice of lease, profit-share and franchise-operation models to private mall owners (including sister concern FUN Republic) for the operation of FUN Cinemas at those sites. As of September 2006, FUN Cinemas was operating a total of 32 screens at nine locations. FUN Multiplex anticipates that it will be operating 180 screens nationwide by the end of 2008, with agreements signed with the operators of 35 malls (FUN Cinemas 2006).

The corporatisation of film exhibition

When we look at the structure and interests of these companies, a trend towards the increasing integration of different areas of film-related activity, and across the media sector more widely, is highly apparent. This, of course, would be supported by the history of the multiplex in other parts of the world. To recap the Indian field briefly: PVR has its roots in the exhibition sector but is now expanding into distribution and mall development. Adlabs is a film-processing concern that is also preparing for the shift to digital cinema through its move into exhibition, with its purchase by Reliance adding a suite of further interests in radio, telecommunications and elsewhere. Shringar has moved from being a distribution business to having new ambitions in production, distribution and exhibition (not to mention its plans for food courts). INOX is also handling film distribution. FUN Cinemas is just one piece of Subhash Chandra's multi-media empire, which includes film production, television, shopping malls and theme parks.

The rise of the multiplex in India is clearly part of the wider story of the rise of media conglomerates within the entertainment industry (or at least within its premium markets). With the exception of FUN cinemas, the financial backing of the multiplex operators is also indicative of the entry of external capital into the exhibition sector since the status of the film industry was revised in 2000. The FUN Cinemas story is slightly different as the Essel Group had previously diversified from plastic tubing into commercial television with the launch of ZEE TV in the early 1990s (Essel Group 2007, ZEE Television 2007). The links between the multiplex companies and the wider economy are also apparent when we take into account smaller regional players with ambitions in the multiplex business. Wave Cinemas in Uttar Pradesh is owned by the Chadha Group, which has a background in industries such as sugar and paper but has now moved into property development along with the operation of multiplexes (Wave Cinemas 2006, Chadha Group

2007). Cinemax, with a dozen sites in Mumbai, is a subsidiary of a residential property development concern, the Kanakia Group, another logical tie-up if you consider the upward push a nearby multiplex gives to the price of apartments (Cinemax 2006).

It is also pertinent to note that the multiplex operators form a distinct segment of the theatrical industry. Indeed, they do not see themselves as part of the existing industry, but rather as an industry in their own right. They have formed their own consultative industry body, rather than join existing exhibitors associations, and very few of the management staff in these firms have been drawn from the older theatrical industry. The majority of senior operations personnel have a background in the top-end of the hospitality industry, typically luxury hotels, although some have also come from retail and television. As such, both the self-image and the outward image of the multiplex industry is light years away from the model of operations formerly associated with India's disorganised entertainment sector and described as 'briefcase in a darkened restaurant' and 'assets buried in the backyard'. As Alok Tandon, Chief Operations Officer (COO) at INOX, explains:

> When we talk about standalone cinemas we talk about single family-owned cinema halls, dilapidated structures, not doing well, dirty places. And, again, what also happens is that as they pass down from generation to generation, there are many people who stake claim over that place. And hence, the vision is not there and naturally we would not come and be in those places. Now that is the scenario, the story of most of the single screen cinema halls in India. With the coming of corporates and especially the making of multiplexes: number one, it gives you a broad canvas in terms of you've got more money with you, you've got trained staff with you, you've got people who are only working for that particular business. For example, in a cinema hall, that business was a part of the entire family's other things that they used to do. In olden times people used to just, if they had money, they used to make a cinema hall. Just as a statement. Yes. I own a cinema hall. Now what is happening with more corporatisation is there are professionals coming in who are running this business.
>
> (interview 04/01/2007)

The multiplex chains are thus very conscious of both corporate image and brand value and, in light of the negative conceptions surrounding the older exhibition industry, they are at pains to emphasise the transparency of their operations, with a corporate model requiring the public declaration of shareholdings and profits. The value generated by more transparent operations goes further, with the computerisation of their working practice providing for the collection of significant volumes of box office and point of sale data which can be passed back up the production chain. According to Tushar Dhingra, COO at Adlabs Films Ltd., computerisation means that:

> You know what is the transaction size. You get to know what do they eat, what do they like, when do they come, how often do they come. How early do they

come for the cinema? And where do they book it? Do they book it from box office, or do they book it from internet or do they book it by telephone. A very important thing.

(interview 08/01/2007)

This kind of information, previously located in the owners of cinema halls but now available as a readily transferable dataset, is of great value to the industry as a whole, as Alok Tandon relates:

> every morning we send an SMS to distributors telling them how many seats were sold yesterday for this movie . . . Every morning they come to know how many tickets at INOX were sold for their movie . . . The producers, the distributors, even our competitors, they all know that working with INOX means they you are working with a really clean corporate. Absolutely 100 per cent.
>
> (interview 04/01/2007)

This degree of box office reporting is a major departure from the historical relations between exhibitors and distributors, and the emphasis given to transparency overall by the multiplex operators can be seen as both the cause and the effect of attracting the significant inflows of institutional finance from outside of the existing entertainment industry. That is not to say that the adoption of corporate processes is a matter of industrial collegiality or altruism. There are important competitive advantages to be gained from corporatisation in the exhibition sector, not only over existing theatres, but also in relation to distributors and producers. From the perspective of PVR Cinemas, Ashish Shukla identifies that:

> The advantages of becoming a national chain would be that you get economies of scale when you go to negotiate your film hire, which would be a big one, if you have a leveraging ability for marketing, then that is another advantage that comes . . . And in terms of market control, to a certain extent, in terms of if you are a percentage in double digits of the market, then you are able to do that. And, if one was to look at backward integration, and forward integration, of the business, then there are lot of new avenues that open up which obviously betters the profitability in each destination. It creates a model which is recession-proof. Gives you the ability to run the business more efficiently and effectively.
>
> (interview 20/03/2007)

Alok Tandon at INOX and Tushar Dhingra at Adlabs both concur that achieving scale at the level of exhibition leads to a stronger negotiating position with distributors over film rights and percentages (interviews 04/01/2007 and 08/01/2007). Tandon also believes that achieving scale offers the potential to serve a customer base amongst an increasingly mobile professional population:

> The advantage for me is that if a patron has gone to INOX in a particular city and if he is travelling and he goes to city B and he wants to see a movie, and if there is an INOX over there, he is likely to come to me.
>
> (Ibid.)

While the growth of the corporate model in the multiplex companies and its benefits seem relatively self-evident, it nonetheless remains critically important to consider the various factors that have encouraged various heavy industry companies
and private equity funds, as well as Subhash Chandra and the Singapore government, to enter the cinema business in India at this particular time. Alok Tandon is
candid on this point:

> Gujarat Fluorochemicals was purely a gas company making refrigerants, and
> when we wanted to diversify we took the help of MacKinsey. They told us to
> get into entertainment and especially multiplexes in particular. Now that is the
> reason that we entered this entire multiplex business.

> (Ibid.)

However, Snehhal Chitneni, the General Manager, Corporate Communications,
at INOX is also quick to point out that: 'the environment was just right', because the
'state governments had just introduced a number of tax incentives' (interview
04/01/2007). In this sense, it is not only the advice of investment experts, but also
the guiding hand of government that has been a relevant factor in generating the
multiplex boom.

Entertainment tax exemptions

In terms of the wider economic picture, the various states of India have increasingly
been required to compete for central funding and to attract greater foreign investment (Saez 2002). With varying degrees of success, therefore, the state governments
have enacted policies designed to make their jurisdictions attractive to incoming
investment. For its part, the interest of foreign capital in India rests not only upon
acquiring cheap English-speaking labour for back-office operations, but also upon
the potential for a numerically-large middle class to become consumers of goods
and services. As such, the policies adopted by urban authorities in Indian cities are
increasingly inflected with an entrepreneurial orientation, reflected physically in
the spatial transformation of urban environments towards the needs of investment
capital and towards those able to actively participate in a lifestyle centred upon
rising consumption. At the same time, the government has been keen to placate the
middle classes who have become increasingly assertive during the post-1991 era
of liberalisation. As such, in their desire to foster prestige commercial development
projects, a significant number of the economically-important Indian states,
including Maharashtra, Punjab, Gujarat, Haryana and West Bengal, elected
to give entertainment tax exemptions specifically to multiplex theatres after
2002. As Shriram Krishnan, the Chief Financial Officer for Shringar Cinemas,
explains:

> First of all we were facing a movie-going problem. It was a mixture of enter-
> tainment tax laws; I mean entertainment tax in Bombay which is your prime
> movie industry market. Entertainment tax rates were at one hundred percent

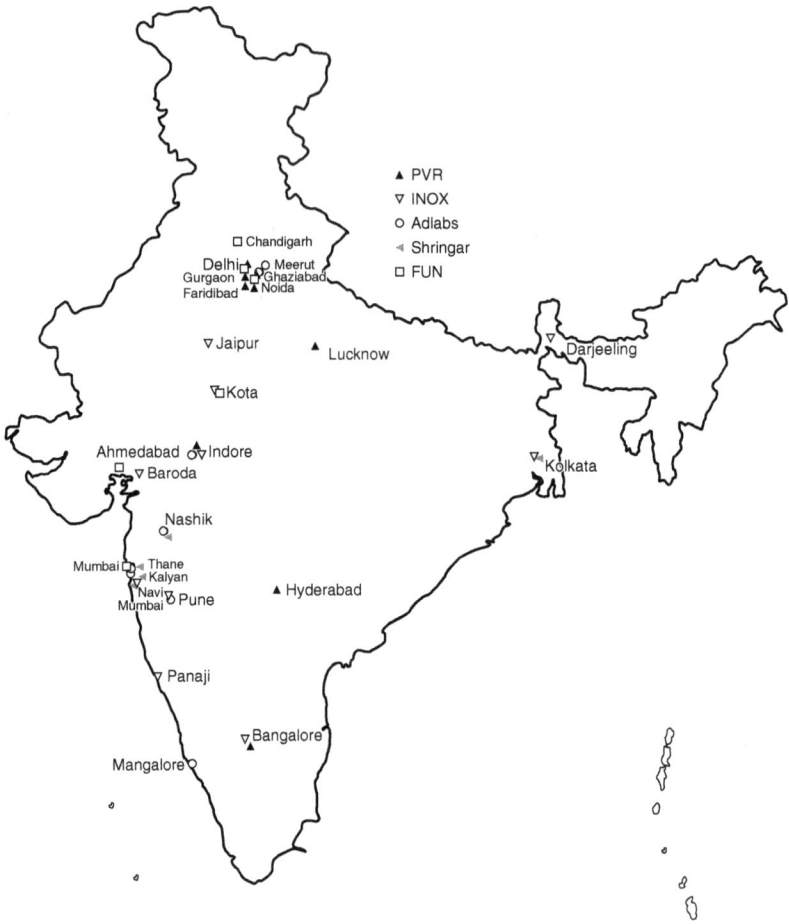

Map 3.1 Existing multiplex cinema sites of the five major chains, September 2006.

of the net ticket price. So if the whole thing was a hundred, fifty rupees was all you had to pay the distributor, the exhibitor and to take care of your overheads. Then, at that time, there was really a decline, satellite television had just started taking off in this country, and that was encouraging people to stay at home and watch satellite television. That's when cable came in, and India is known for piracy. So people could watch the movies they wanted on the same Saturday the movie got released in the cinema halls. So you know, all this happened and then what happened is the government came up and said 'Okay. Here are entertainment tax sops where you won't have to pay entertainment tax for five years, in the case of larger multiplexes for ten years'. So that really got the industry going. People got interested when they knew that they didn't have to pay entertainment tax. When we started setting up multiplexes, people started coming back to the theatres. So that what is really, for me, it has promoted that growth.

(interview 20/01/2007)

Further decisions by a number of states to allow multiplexes to operate with dynamic ticket prices outside of the fixed tariffs and low-price seating quotas set for regular theatres have paved the way for admission prices four to six times the average cost of a ticket to a regular theatre. Coupled with a low- or even zero-level of taxation during the initial five-year exemption window, the multiplex currently has numerous advantages over the old cinemas. Anand Moorthy, Corporate Brand Manager at FUN Multiplex, explains the differential tax regimes applied to the multiplexes and the traditional theatres:

> There are two kinds of entertainment tax modules that exist in India. One is the single screen taxation module and one is the multiplex taxation module . . . Single screen basically for a hundred rupee ticket, two dollar ticket say, so out of a hundred rupee ticket, thirty percent goes to the taxes. The distributor takes a share depending on the content. The first week share is fifty percent normally. The second week share is forty, and thirty is the third week collection. That is how it goes traditionally. So for a single screen guy who gets a hundred rupees, fifty percent, fifty rupees goes in the first week to the distributor. So that leaves him with fifty bucks. And out of the hundred, thirty percent goes to the entertainment tax. So fifty and thirty and the single screen guy only has twenty. So has got to play with twenty rupee revenue for his costs, so the deductions are big, but for his maintenance and running the show his costs are very low. So that's how they are sustaining, but for multiplexes the exemptions are for the first five years, presently [and] if I collect a hundred rupees, I give to the distributor. That's my first cost. Other than that, there is a service tax also, which is two percent. That is also applicable to the single screens. We are also paying that service tax. So I pay distributor cost and service tax, that's it. Other than that, the rest is the money that I earn. But if you see my actual overhead costs, my people, my infrastructure, my land. Accounting for that my profits will not necessarily be better than single screen. So, yes, on capital terms we have an advantage, but when you calculate the operating costs, both the single screen and myself have to achieve a particular number to break even.

(interview 06/01/2007)

Since the majority of entertainment tax exemptions are time-limited, the multiplex operators typically adopt a project outlook where sites are projected to break even in terms of capital investment costs within the initial tax exemption window. Beyond this, however, the continuance of a friendly tax regime remains a key factor in the long-term profitability of multiplexes. Income revenues will be reduced considerably if multiplexes become subject to levels of taxation similar to the older theatrical infrastructure, and the expiry of many of the initial exemption periods from

2007 onwards already makes this an important issue for operators. The overarching question here is whether the states will be willing to continue giving up their revenues once the initial investment has been attracted, particularly in light of the increased agitation amongst traditional cinemas that continue to pay high taxes and remain subject to price fixing. Traditional theatres in Maharashtra held strikes in 2003 and 2004 over 55 per cent entertainment tax rates as well as legislation that prevented the owners of 100 derelict halls from selling them on for redevelopment. At that time, all of the multiplexes in the state enjoyed tax exemptions and the right to set their own prices. As such, this kind of disparity between the treatment of low-end and high-end theatrical sectors may prove hard to sustain politically. In this case, the state government agreed to reduce the overall level of entertainment tax on single-screens to 45 per cent of the ticket price, which hardly satisfied the demands of the Cinema Owners Association (BBC Online 19/03/2004).

For the multiplex operators, there are two countervailing factors to be considered in relation to the future course of entertainment tax. On the one hand, their higher ticket prices and more transparent accountancy make them a more logical target for effective taxation than the single screens. On the other hand, if their expansion plans are successful, their sheer size may well give them the kind of leverage over regulators that will facilitate the negotiation of an ongoing favourable tax regime. This is the kind of critical mass that the disorganised theatrical industry has traditionally lacked in India. At present, however, uncertainty continues in this area. Whilst Anand Moorthy at FUN notes that: 'Today we do not know if exemptions will go on. There is a lobby happening' (interview 06/01/2007), Alok Tandon at INOX is more positive: 'The tax structure will come down in all the states. It is just a matter of time before the taxes are reduced' (interview 04/01/2007). Indeed, there are some signs that this may already be happening in some states, with Haryana reducing entertainment tax from 50 per cent to 30 per cent in 2006. Shriram Krishnan at Shringar is sceptical, however, that the current tax holidays can simply be extended through industry pressure: 'At some point they will need it. Otherwise how can we have the infrastructure?' (interview 20/01/2007).

The argument for lower levels of entertainment tax overall is put by Alok Tandon of INOX:

> Look at states where tax structure has been reduced. There also, the footfalls are increased. People have become much more transparent in reporting their figures to the government. Classic example is a place like Haryana, in Haryana the tax was very, very high. It has been reduced three or four times … What we see is that the collections that are less tax are much more than when the rate of tax was very high.
>
> (interview 04/01/2007)

Anand Moorthy at FUN also notes that: 'the government got tax collection of about ten percent more last year. So that is one way to look at it. The government is also benefiting by giving us tax exemptions' (interview 06/01/2007). This a view supported by Tushar Dhingra at Adlabs:

Table 3.5 Entertainment tax exemption regimes for multiplex cinemas

State or city	Entertainment tax rates	Entertainment tax exemptions for multiplex cinemas				
		Year 1	Year 2	Year 3	Year 4	Year 5
Mumbai	45%	100%	100%	100%	75%	75%
Delhi	30%	—	—	—	—	—
Kolkata	30%	100%	100%	100%	100%	—
Bhopal/Indore/ Jabalpur	60%	100%	100%	100%	75%	50%
Maharashtra	45%	100%	100%	100%	75%	75%
Uttar Pradesh	60%	100%	100%	100%	100%	100%
Punjab	50%	100%	100%	100%	100%	100%
Haryana	30%	—	—	—	—	—
Madhya Pradesh	50%	100%	100%	100%	75%	75%
Rajasthan	30%	100%	100%	90%	80%	—
Karnataka	40%	—	—	—	—	—
Andhra Pradesh	20%	—	—	—	—	—
Tamil Nadu	15%	—	—	—	—	—

Source: Adapted from: India Infoline 2006

I think entertainment tax, the basic fundamental root comes from the socialism society of India, saying that this is not something good to do and the rich should be taxed. It started from there and it was fairly high. And what multiplexes or corporates have done is created transparency in terms of reporting to the producers, to the government. So that there is no tax evasion. And governments have understood that and they are welcoming that and they are being supportive towards it. There are certain states which are yet to wake up to that. But, yes, it is a work in progress.

(interview 08/01/2007).

Whilst all of the major multiplexes operators identify entertainment tax exemptions as a major driver for investment in the industry and a factor in their choices of location, they also make the case that their operations are in for the long haul, and that their investors are not simply availing themselves of tax holidays, since the business has to be viable in the first place if they are to realise returns. Ashish Shukla at PVR therefore cautions that tax exemptions are an important factor driving growth, but not the only one:

Tax benefit is not the only reason to be looked at because you have to have the business to have the tax benefit. So the way that we look at it is that it has to be something where there is propensity in the consumer to come. I mean in places like Bihar the propensity of watching is very, very bad. So one is that you will have to spend extra efforts to cultivate a market. Then after cultivation you have to make your business . . . Karnataka is still not a tax free state, but Bangalore is doing the best overall with seventy percent plus occupancy.

(interview 20/03/2007)

Shringar Cinemas takes a similar position on adopting strategies that balance access to tax exemptions with the ongoing importance of traditional A centres:

> You see, fifty-six percent of my sites are in entertainment tax exempt areas. Except for Tamil Nadu. Our focus has been Tamil Nadu because Tamil Nadu has one of the best audiences in terms of occupancy percentages . . . Karnataka, the tax exemption policy is not very favourable, but we have to balance these things out because there are big audiences.
>
> (Shriram Krishnan, interview 20/01/2007)

When talking of the Shringar expansion programme, Krishnan is also keen to point out the importance of a strategic vision that goes beyond the tax exemption era:

> We are very conscious that we are going to be focusing on cities where there is going to be migrancy population, because that is what is going to take us to the next level of growth, after the entertainment tax holidays are over.
>
> (Ibid.)

In order to adequately contextualise what is at stake in the ongoing debate over entertainment tax, it is important to recognise the scale of the impact made by the multiplexes in the ten years of their existence, not just upon the exhibition sector, but also at the levels of production and distribution. Tushar Dhingra at Adlabs, speaking for the multiplex industry overall, emphasises the contribution being made by the multiplexes to the Indian film industry: 'Today, we are three to four percent of the number of screens available, but we are sixty percent of revenues to the film makers . . . And that has really helped the production sector (interview 08/01/2007). Similarly, Shriram Krishnan at Shringar, the multiplex company with the longest pedigree in the film industry overall, says:

> When I look at my distribution business, I see at least twenty eight to thirty per-cent of my revenues coming in from multiplexes now . . . I think it has really helped our industry, although it has a killed a few single screens . . . From a dis-tributors perspective, they have seen their overall revenue go up. So for them I think it is a sunrise business. They are seeing how much a print will realise, and then they realise that putting a print in a multiplex brings in much more rev-enue than putting a print in a single screen even though they have large capac-ity. So I think only for large movies is it a tough decision whether you put them in thousand-seaters or three hundred-seaters. But for the normal run of movies, it really makes sense to actually play them in multiplexes.
>
> (interview 20/01/2007)

At the level of taxation, if the multiplexes continue to increase their share of the overall box office, it seems equally clear that they will become a major source of rev-enue for state governments, even if overall entertainment tax rates are reduced. This will be due to their higher admission prices and the much greater ease of collection compared to the thousands of older theatres. Thus, if the guiding hands of state governments have encouraged the multiplex boom to date through friendly tax policies, they have undoubtedly done so with an awareness of their own long-term advantage arising from the corporatisation of film exhibition. On this basis alone, it is obvious that the multiplex phenomenon has major economic implications for the entire film industry, including implications for financiers, producers, directors, distributors, exhibitors and, of course, consumers.

The consuming class

Aside from their shared investment in the multiplex format and in the corporate model, it is salient to point out a further strong correlation between the thinking of the major players in their targeting of a particular audience demographic. Adlabs describes its customers as occupying the 'middle and upper income strata'. The Adlabs moviegoer is thus a 'Discerning customer looking for quality as well good value for money', who is also described as 'Aspirational – wants the best for himself / herself & family'. Adlabs further claims that 'Young Upwardly mobile people with high disposable income constitute a substantial percentage of our patron profile' (Adlabs Films 2006c). Similarly, INOX targets an upper–middle-class audience in 'upscale' locations 'in high-traffic, commercial areas, or in the midst of affluent residential areas' (INOX Leisure 2006e):

> We have got a higher average ticket price. Now that means that the patron that comes to me is a big spender and hence our main reason of having a plex, when we decide on a locality or decide on a place, is either we go for a central business district or an affluent residential area. That's to do with the fact that our pricing is always high. I want people who can pay me more for the ticket. Then they spend more money inside on my concession counters and when they come out, as I am part of a big mall in most places, they spend money in the mall also. So that's what I look at. I look at affluent spenders.
>
> (Alok Tandon, interview 04/01/2007)

The major multiplexes host regular promotions and star premieres to create buzz and compete for market share. They also target the upmarket audience with a suite of luxury seating classes. For example, the standard 'Classic' seating classes at PVR cinemas are augmented at selected sites by 'Cinema Europa' and 'Gold Class' auditoriums. Cinema Europa facilities include 'preferential' access to the Europa lounge bar and restaurant, while Gold Class auditoriums offer reclining armchair seating and in-seat waitress service (PVR Cinemas 2006e). Although they actively target a family audience, as with multiplex operators worldwide, the high socio-economic status of the ideal consumer type for the Indian multiplex is typically combined with the long-standing pattern of cinema as a generally youthful pastime. To support their focus on this demographic, Shringar Cinemas quotes National Council of Applied Economic Research (NCAER) figures that claim that two-thirds of the Indian population is below 35 years, and that the 'Urban growth rate

Figure 3.1   Forecourt of the Crown Plaza mall, Faridabad, home to one of 11 PVR Cinemas sites in the National Capital Region. (Adrian Athique)

Figure 3.2   Gold Class auditorium at the 11-screen PVR Cinemas in Bangalore, currently India's largest multiplex. (Adrian Athique)

for 15–24 years and 25–59 years is growing by 35% and 41% respectively' due to a 'young population moving to metros for education and work' (Shringar Cinemas 2006). In numerical terms, Shringar estimates that there are '82mn Urban Indians between 20–30 years growing 6.4% per cent~ p.a.' (ibid.).

Aside from a youthful demographic, which is also true of the traditional theatres, it is the elite nature of the audience claimed by the multiplexes that probably accounts for their much greater share of advertising revenues compared to regular theatres. According to India Infoline: 'Multiplexes charge anywhere between Rs5000 to Rs12000 for one-minute film per week. On the other hand, conventional theatres even in A+ category cities charge anywhere between Rs600 to Rs7500' (India Infoline 2006: 13). PVR, for example, offers a description of its audience to advertisers which suggests a mixed-sex, educated, car-owning family audience in the upper-middle income range. PVR also attributes its customers with an affluent, adventurous and out-of-doors behavioural profile of the type increasingly favoured by the marketing industry, which has recognised that the means to consume must be augmented (or even predetermined) by the will to consume (PVR Cinemas 2005). Clearly, the imagined community of the multiplex crowd constructs a vastly different customer from the lower class, and primarily male, audience that has dominated the cinema since the 1970s.

The lifestyling of the multiplex is extremely important, not just for attracting advertisers, but for persuading the more affluent customers, who now enjoy ready access to an unprecedented range of domestic audiovisual entertainment, to pursue out-of-home entertainment. For this group, the pulling power of a multiplex is not simply content-based, but is derived instead from ambience. As INOX puts it: 'To more than 3000 cinemagoers who walk into each of our multiplexes every day, INOX is a lifestyle statement rather than just any cinema hall' (INOX Leisure 2006e). According to Manmohan Shetty, Chairman of Adlabs:

> It is a matter of societal pride that we are now seeing new multiplex markets like Mulund emerging on the scene. It means that more and more people now are upwardly mobile and are aspiring for better standards in life. R Adlabs meets the rising aspirations of the people; it is not just a multiplex that screens films but a value added entertainment destination where various leisure activities are blended together to give an enhanced experience to the consumers.
>
> (Adlabs Films 2006e)

Much is made in the marketing and investment literature on the multiplex phenomenon, whether produced by the operators themselves or by financial advisors, of the importance of the growing wealth and numbers of the Indian middle class to the projected growth of the entertainment sector. (KPMG 2005, D'Essence 2006, India Infoline 2005, Price Waterhouse Coopers 2006, Singhal 2006). According to INOX:

> The demographic of movie audiences has expanded dramatically over the last few years as well, with a larger percentage of the population having entered

higher income brackets. In 2001–2002, the consuming class stood at 54.6 million households – today, it has grown to 90.9 million.

(INOX Leisure 2006a)

Although speculation on the economic potential of India's middle classes as a consumer market has taken place over decades, this kind of claim has become increasingly influential over the last decade. Indeed, these claims have been a major factor driving investment into India. The particular definition of the 'consuming class' referred to here originated in a 1994 report from the NCAER entitled 'The Consumer Classes'. This large-scale survey, undertaken in support of liberalisation measures sought to ascertain the consuming power of the Indian middle class, and to reclassify Indian society upon that basis. Thus the middle classes, situated between the tiny elite and the utterly destitute, were classified under three bands: 'consumers', 'climbers' and 'aspirants' (Varma 1998: 171).

This attempt to quantify and re-categorise the middle classes in India is indicative of a programme to create a new Indian middle class. According to Leela Fernandes, this 'culturally constructed' imagined community is intended to embody 'a cultural standard associated with the globalising Indian nation' which 'proponents of liberalisation have sought to deploy . . . as an idealised standard that other groups can aspire to' (2004: 2418). One of the better-known of these proponents is Gurcharan Das, a former chief executive of Proctor and Gamble India, whose book *India Unbound* (2002) makes a powerful case for rebuilding Indian economy and society around the industriousness and aspirations of the middle classes. According to Das,

> When half the population is middle class, its politics will change, its worldview will be different, its poor will be fewer, and society will have greater means to look after them. Thus to focus on the middle class is to focus on prosperity.
>
> (2002: 351)

In support of this view, the consuming classes are seen as having more than doubled over the past decade. A useful illustration of this perceived expansion can be found in the KPMG report entitled 'The Indian Entertainment Industry: Focus 2010 – From Dreams To Reality' (KPMG 2005).

Given their desired patron profile, the continued growth of a consuming class in India is highly significant to the future of the multiplex. It is the predictions of both the scale and the rapid growth of the segment of the Indian population possessing the means to consume that are central to the economic logic behind the multiplex boom. The multiplex operators are counting on the continued growth of the IT sector, with rising salaries in the services industries in particular being seen as a factor that will continue to drive the further expansion of the industry over the next ten years. In historical terms, the middle-class audience in India has either not been large enough or not been sufficiently concentrated anywhere outside of the old Presidency cities to constitute an easily exploitable high-value theatrical market. The selective economic growth of the liberalisation era post-1991, however, has

Table 3.6 Class mobility in terms of consumption within the Indian economy

The classes ($ income per annum)	1994–95 (million households)	1999–00 (million households)	2005–06 estimate (million households)
Rich ($4600 pa and above)	1	3	6
Consuming ($970–4600 pa)	29	66	75
Climbers ($470–970 pa)	48	66	78
Aspirants ($340–470 pa)	48	32	33
Destitutes (less than $340 pa)	32	24	17

Source: Adapted from KPMG 2005

increasingly favoured the educated urban upper middle class, increasing both their income and their aspirations in real terms. Nonetheless, despite the emergence of this long-desired upmarket audience, the capacity of the film industry to exploit it effectively might well have been held back by long-standing government regulations and the entrenchment of lower-class groups in the moth-eaten traditional theatrical sector. The deployment of the multiplex has overcome this hurdle by responding directly to the increased spending capacity of the new middle classes, as well as to their ongoing suburbanisation resulting from the rapid growth in personal credit, car ownership and the subsequent property boom. The multiplex format has provided a logical and attractive option for the film industry to cater exclusively to smaller, more affluent social groups. This is an endeavour for which the numbers have finally added up, this time not in bums on seats, but in rupees:

> Multiplexes have numerous benefits for the few: exhibitors and distributors earn more per film because of higher ticket prices; by breaking the one-film-per-week model, and shuffling the number and timings of shows of particular films, investment is made to yield the highest possible revenue; a certain kind of niche film . . . now becomes commercially viable; by exhibiting six or seven films per week, the chances of a loss to individual exhibitors is minimised; and socially, by targeting and catering to a niche audience, the multiplex becomes an extension of the home theatre, where the rich can watch films in the privacy of their own class.
>
> (Deshpande 2005: 192)

Naturally, the more obvious questions that arise at this point mostly surround both the projected growth and geographic dispersal of this new consuming class. In the first place, is such a group really big enough, or sufficiently concentrated, outside the A centres? How robust are these categorisations and how readily do these income categories translate into readily disposable incomes of the kind targeted by the multiplexes? Even if there is the capacity for expenditure, is there the necessary culture of consumption and, specifically, rising demand for cinema? In the first place, the euphoria surrounding the Indian middle class has to be understood as a consciously designed marketing phenomenon designed to attract inward investment. This is because the interest of foreign capital in India rests not only upon acquiring cheap English-speaking labour for back-office operations, but also upon the potential for a populous middle class to become consumers of goods and services. In his study of India's advertising industry in the liberalisation era, William Mazzarella provides the cautionary observation that the 'conjuncture of the meeting between foreign corporate executives and Indian marketing and advertising professionals in the wake of the 1991 reforms . . . encouraged vastly inflated estimates of the numerical size of this Indian middle class' (Mazzarella 2003: 272).

Pavan Varma's book *The Great Indian Middle Class* (1998) provides a counterpoint to Gurcharan Das's celebration of aspiration and India's newfound potential in the global knowledge economy. Varma instead describes the Indian middle classes as economically parasitic and socially indifferent and further claims that, just as it was their corruption that undermined the welfare state in post-colonial India, their current attempt to secede from the rest of Indian society in a rush towards narcissistic consumerism will undermine rather than underpin India's social and economic progress. Given his critical stance towards the advance of the consuming classes, Varma is also keen to point out that the flood of consumer goods into India during the 1990s was met by indifferent sales, and that those who believed that the liberalised Indian economy would employ the middle class as its 'engine for growth' need to recognise that 'the power of the engine was hardly in conformity with the wishful thinking of the enthusiasts', concluding that the Indian middle class does exist, 'but it is the middle class of a poor country' (1998: 171–172).

In the ten years since Varma's rebuttal, however, the growth of consumerism in India has been very considerable, even if it has not matched the original blue-sky predictions. So in that sense, the pessimism of Varma's account, and his reminder that the vast majority of Indian society remains poor, does not entirely negate the massive increase in car ownership apparent in Indian cities or the boom in soft industries such as telecoms and the visual media and the growing availability of mobile phones and televisions that has gone with them. Thus, the exuberance in the projections made by those with an economic interest in selling the new middle class is somewhat offset by the fact that even a vastly reduced estimate of the Indian middle class would probably still constitute a larger total than the overall population of many developed countries. Nonetheless, even liberalisation guru Gurcharan Das is quick to concede the uneven distribution of this new wealth:

> If we assume the NCAER's historical middle-class growth rate of the past fifteen years, then half of India will turn middle class between 2020 and 2040. To be sure there will be huge disparities. Much of west and south India will turn middle class by 2020, but the backward states like Bihar, Uttar Pradesh, and Orissa wont get there before 2040. Disparities are obviously bad, but vigorous migration helps to ameliorate them and creates pressure for the backward states to catch up.
>
> (Das 2002: 352)

More disturbingly, Das believes that the future of India can be determined in a large part by drawing a line between Kanpur and Madras, with the area east of the line likely to remain in an increasingly subordinate position (ibid.: 287). A wide variety of professional forecasters also agree that liberalisation has exacerbated spatial inequality and regional inequalities in terms of both broader patterns of invest- ments and quality of life (World Bank 2005, Gajwani, Kanbur and Zhang 2006). Returning to the definition, rather than the dispersal, of the consuming classes in India, it is also worth noting that the households currently classified by KPMG as 'aspirants', and even some of those classed as 'climbers', would fall below the official World Bank poverty classification of a \$2 per day income. Indeed, when you allow for the fact that the World Bank classification accounts for per capita income and the KPMG projection for household income, even most of the 'consuming class' would be poverty-stricken by international standards (see Datt and Ravallion 2002, Deaton 2003a, 2003b, Sen and Himanshu. 2004a, 2004b).

This relative poverty of the Indian middle classes may be slightly offset by pur- chasing power parity (PPP) measures, but there is certainly a half-full, half-empty element to the middle class debate that needs to be recognised here. A recent Asian Development Bank report suggested that while India is indeed amongst the largest economies in the world in PPP terms, on a per capita basis for Asia, only the very poorest countries (i.e. Nepal, Bangladesh, Cambodia and Laos) are worse off (Asian Development Bank 2007). Nonetheless, there is undeniably an important qualita- tive dimension to be considered here. In terms of the classification of the consum- ing classes, the numerical veracity of the KPMG predictions is possibly less important overall than the scale of value that the NCAER categorisations attribute to India's population under the terms of the New Economy. The degree to which a social scale in this form is being understood and assimilated by Indians in their worldview and in their everyday life is critical to the success of the new India in ways that transcend the ongoing dispute over the actual numbers involved.

At a more functional level, the geographic spread of the major multiplex chains to date certainly tells us something about where the consuming classes are believed to be found in India today. This is because the business model of the multiplex is expressly based upon the location and acquisition of what are assumed to be rising disposable incomes. FUN Cinemas, for example, describes its multiplexes 'as epi- centers of affluent New Economy suburbs', a view supported by Tushar Dhingra at Adlabs: 'What multiplexes are doing is creating an avenue for the New Economy that is coming in' (interview 08/01/2007). We can also see that the capital origins of the multiplex chains clearly lie in the north and west and that their markets to date favour these regions – especially Maharashtra, Gujarat and the National Capital Region (NCR) around Delhi. It is equally significant that, outside of these favoured areas, the multiplex operators have overwhelmingly pursued sites in major cities that are traditional A centres, such as Kolkata, Hyderabad and Bangalore.

The geography of the new leisure economy

In this chapter, we have detailed how the advent of the multiplex has been an inte- gral part of major changes afoot in the industrial organisation of leisure is India. In particular, we have demonstrated how the rapid spread of the multiplex has been officially encouraged over the last five years by the tax exemptions and deregulated pricings facilitated by state governments. In terms of the consumer profile targeted by the multiplexes seeking a market for multiplexes, we have further demonstrated that it is the growth of spending power amongst an (as yet unascertained) proportion of the Indian population, and the shift towards a consumption-led economy, that is providing the operational rationale for the multiplex operators. Subsidiary factors encouraging the multiplex boom include the general shortage of family-friendly cinemas in Indian cities as well as generational change, with the 1970s baby boom increasingly impacting upon the economy and bolstering the youthful demographic associated with cinema patrons. In order to exploit these favourable conditions for investment in new cinematic infrastructure, the entry of institutional capital into the exhibition sector from outside the traditional entertainment industry has been essential.

One of the effects of this investment has been the radical departure from the operating model of the traditional exhibition sector, with the multiplex emerging as the flagship of a new theatrical industry that combines corporate ambitions with increasing structural integration across the film industry and, more widely, the leisure economy. The following chapter seeks to further situate the multiplex within the New Economy paradigm, where India's regulatory authorities have been inclined to look favourably upon the development of new leisure infrastructure for the urban middle class. Along with the corporatisation of the media sector, what has also been made very clear from the shareholdings and the location choices of the multiplex companies is that there is a strong relationship between the multiplexes, urban redevelopment and what is now being called 'organised retail'. As such, there is a strong connection between the multiplex industry and the real estate sector. As a crucial component of charting the emerging geography of the multiplex industry, it is the operating context of the multiplex in this regard to which we must now turn our attention.

4   India poised

Assessing the geography of opportunity

Chapter 3 served to indicate some of the critical linkages existing between the rise
of the multiplex, ongoing structural change in the leisure industries and the emerging focus of economic planning in India. Extending this discussion throughout the
course of this chapter, we describe how the multiplex industry intersects with the
contemporaneous phenomenon of organised retail and the attempts being made by
its proponents to re-write India's commercial culture. In turn, both the multiplex
and its host body, the shopping mall, must be further considered in light of their
intrinsic relationship to the shifting regulatory frameworks governing the management of urban lands and an exuberant property market in India's major cities. The
volatile economic conditions within these particular contexts exert important
effects upon the strategic planning of the multiplex operators. At one level, the
shopping mall craze has been a growth driver for the multiplexes, but at the same
time the rising cost of lands and the issues raised by a rapidly overheating market
both raise questions over the long-term viability of the mall-multiplex combine.
The spiralling costs in their most favoured markets and the oversaturation of previously successful catchments by copycat developers are providing the impetus for
ambitious expansion plans to take the multiplex to India's second-tier cities. In
effect, this entails shifting the terrain of commercial competition between multiplex
operators to the national level.

The mall-multiplex combine

In the accounts provided by Acland, Hubbard and Ravenscroft and others, we
have seen how the multiplex has almost invariably been deployed within the context of a wider re-organisation of the retail economy. Specifically, the history of the
multiplex has been very closely related to the ultimate architecture of late capital:
the shopping mall. In this respect, the Indian story also provides ample support for
this symbiosis between new formulas for the provision of leisure and new environments for retail activity. As Malcom Voyce (2007) observes, the spread of shopping
malls designed to serve India's growing consuming classes has been a major focus
for both foreign and domestic capital investors in India over the last five years. The
widespread adoption of the shopping mall format in India that is currently being
proposed, in opposition to the existing network of small family owned stores and

open markets, cannot have less than dramatic outcomes for the urban landscape, notwithstanding the major change in behaviours it will imply for the general population. As such, we discuss the wider project of malling India in greater depth later in this chapter. For now, it is important to recognise that the advent of shopping malls of increasing size and in ever larger numbers has major implications for the multiplex operators. There has been a very obvious possibility of cohabitation which has been taken up by the major multiplex chains. Accordingly, there has been a sequential shift in the ten-year lifespan of the multiplex industry from the construction of dedicated multiplexes towards in-house facilities located in shopping malls. According to Saurabh Varma, Vice President, Cinema Marketing and Promotions, at PVR:

> Post-Saket, there have been a lot of developments. One is the advent of malls, so the combination for just movies has changed into a combination of entertainment, shopping and eating. So, from just a movie going concept it has become a wholesome experience in today's world. Plus, there are a lot of other things as well; look at destinations, multiplexes has also brought in a big retail boom in the industry. So, wherever the multiplexes are open they have brought in big brands. The recent big combination is that of cinemas with a hyper mall.
> (Exchange4Media.com, interview)

The developers of residential colonies and shopping malls have been well aware of the pulling power of on-site cinemas for their clientele. Multiplex cinemas are said to increase footfalls in a shopping mall by 40 to 50 per cent (KPMG 2005: 65). As such, multiplex operators are now able to lease floor space in these developments at relatively low cost. Indeed, the receptiveness of mall developers to their presence has eliminated the need for them to invest in property assets, which are a major stumbling block for expansion given soaring property prices in the major metros. Anand Moorthy at FUN explains why the multiplex is such an attractive proposition to mall developers:

> Any mall that gets a multiplex, signs all the other retailers like this [clicks fingers]. Very fast. Because movies are driving business. So, I've got to say, if I am the marketing manager of Globus Store, which I was before, and I now want to enter in, to sign up a mall, because I cannot afford to have my own malls but I can have my own stores – it's a fashion garment destination – we cannot afford to have such big places, so my idea is to open up in malls. When a mall owner comes to sell his property to me, I will ask him 'So what does your mall have?' and if he says 'I have FUN Cinemas', then I will sign up then and there. Or any other multiplex, because I know that by default the footfall will be rapid and that is good for my business. The crowd is the game, the footfalls is the game.
> (interview 06/01/2007)

We see here a change in the meaning of the crowd and its relationship to retail. The formation of crowds that go with the cinema, which have for so long been such a source of public anxiety, have now become a readily exchangeable commodity between different forms of retail activity. As such activity is reconstructed as the dominant form of leisure, a new form of ambience needs to be created. The mall provides this new form of public space: a sensual environment that is sanitised, secure, carefully planned, selectively accessed and privately operated. To facilitate this process, the value-making components of the old crowd, from a commercial viewpoint, have been distilled and relocated away from the rowdy elements, the unprofitable masses and the dysfunctional nature of Indian city streets, where the sheer density of human traffic makes affluent customers difficult to reach and modern marketing techniques almost impossible to apply.

By bringing the shopping mall and multiplex together, the commercial logic of the mall-multiplex is predicated upon the trading of a high-value crowd between four major sets of interests. The first player is the mall developer who puts up the property and collects rents and needs to attract large numbers to his mall to justify profitable lease rates and attract advertising revenues. The second player is, through entering into a tie-in with the mall, the multiplex operator who circumvents the need for infrastructure investment, both by leasing operating space and by effectively transferring the lobby of the cinema to the mall as a whole. The multiplex operator also gains access to a public suited to the staged show times and small auditorium model of the multiplex format, which is designed to cater to a continuous, mobile, browsing audience rather than the mass in-and-out crowds formed at set intervals at the older cinema halls.

The demographic targeting of the consuming class by the multiplex operators also makes the in-mall model a natural choice, given that there is a presumption that the presence of patrons in these 'temples of consumption' is an indication of both their capacity and desire to consume (Fernandes, 2006). The third player in the typical mall mix is the retail chains, who also defray their start-up costs by moving into malls and who also benefit from the crowd-pulling power of the multiplex. It is this group who is ultimately required to pay the rents from which the developer draws profits. Finally, the fourth player is the food courts who service the mall crowd by indulging the passion of the Indian middle classes for dining out. Of course, in order to effectively share footfalls and browsing behaviours between the various players, the spatial arrangement of the mall needs to be carefully thought out. Shriram Krishnan, from Shringar Cinemas, explains where the multiplexes fit into the mix:

> The multiplexes take the top floors of the malls, or at the basement level, where no retailer wants to take up, every retailer wants to be at the ground or the first floor. So when you look at all that, they [multiplex operators] take the worst area and they get a very low rate, and then they pull consumers on their own . . . in India, you call multiplexes part of a mall, it is almost a day out experience where you shop, go to a food court and watch a movie, enjoy yourself, take the whole day and go . . . there are two suburbs next to each other where our properties are. In the first property which is almost like a stand alone multiplex, and the second is part of the second most successful mall in India which is InOrbit

mall . . . There we notice that on weekends it is really going to go up very high on its occupancy numbers, because of the mall effect. If you go to that mall on the weekend, that mall is packed. And if you look at Andheri, it goes the same pattern, but when there are no movies on the market, the Andheri suburb, which is a stand alone multiplex, actually goes down quite drastically, while the mall site numbers don't go down as much. So we see that it has got a tempering effect.

(interview 20/01/2007)

The experience of Shringar with placing their Fame brand in shopping malls has encouraged them to consider taking up a wider role within the mall model. Shringar and PVR Cinemas have both recently diversified into the operation of food courts. These are currently found in the malls where they are opening cinemas, but are located beyond the confines of their multiplex operations. Krishnan explains the thinking that has led to this expansion of their operating models in the mall environment:

> We thought that there is a direct synergy in that business. You see what is happening is typically the food court and the multiplexes are on the same levels. So what we see in the InOrbit mall in Malad, our F & B numbers were getting affected because the product offering was the same sometimes. So I think by having them both on the same level, we will take the whole floor. Then you are able to control who are the food operators who come onto that floor. And then you can ensure that there is a synergy. If they are offering pasta, you don't offer pasta. You offer something else. You explore other options. When these things complement each other then what you can do is do cross-offerings: watch a movie and get some food, buy something in the food court, come to the movies. So you can actually promote things together. And secondly, when you take the whole floor plan, you get it at a lower rate and then you re-lease it at a higher rate. It's a simple business model.

(Ibid.)

Beyond synergies at the shop-front level, it is also important to note the growing formal alliance between multiplex operators and organised retail developers, for example the tie-up between INOX and the Pantaloon Group. The purchase of a majority stake in Adlabs by Reliance is also notable, given that Reliance is a driving force in the development of supermarkets through their Reliance Fresh division. Another formal linkage is the case of FUN Cinemas, where sister companies FUN Republic and E-City Property Management own and operate shopping malls respectively. Anand Moorthy outlines some of the ways in which the mall-multiplex tie-up is conceived within that business:

> We had already thought of it, Fun Cinemas and Fun Multiplex, as two related businesses. So when we can't afford to have our own property or Fun Republic then instead we can put in Fun Cinemas elsewhere. So right now we are

Figure 4.1 The Metropolitan Mall, Gurgaon, home to PVR Cinemas, March 2007. (Adrian Athique)

Figure 4.2 The Pacific Mall, Ghaziabad, Uttar Pradesh, home to Adlabs Films, March 2007. (Adrian Athique)

present in Sigma Mall. Fun Cinemas is part of Sigma Mall because we don't own that property, but we have entered that place and put in exhibition centres there . . . The other business is Fun Republic in Bombay, where the mall is mine, the building, the land, the structure, the people, everything is mine and I am running the show. It is not possible for me to say that I will only go with the first model and never do the second model. I will not do this because it is equally important if I want to grow that I need to adapt to both of those situations . . . in Kolkata, there was land that we wanted to buy and we got it at our price. We are erecting our own mall. A huge mall in which we will be the exhibition centre and there will be other people who will be tenants. In Lucknow we've got a huge mall that will be four lakh square feet, Shopper's Stop. It's a tenanted site, shopping, food, hotel, banquet area, gaming place. Everything is rented out, cinema is like that. But it will be called Fun Republic, but Fun Cinemas will be part of that mall. Fun Cinemas will pay rent to Fun Republic, because ultimately it is a tenant. So it our own business but my business also has to support my other business.

(interview 06/01/2007)

This acute awareness amongst the multiplex operators of mutually supportive relationships between different areas of activity within the leisure and retail sectors arises from the corporate nature of their businesses. The major investments that have been made by their parent companies in the cinema business have led to the increasing capacity of the multiplex chains to formally align their trading interests with related concerns. In that sense, the mall-multiplex combine provides a visible example of the tie-ups that are now taking place within the leisure economy. Furthermore, given the close relationship between malls and multiplexes, the future of the shopping mall will directly affect the spread of multiplexes.

The malling of India

The availability of retail space within shopping malls is currently expanding at a rapid rate across urban India, from one million square feet in 2002 to 40 million by the end of 2007, with an additional 20 million square feet to be added the following year (Urs 2007). To put the size of India's retail sector in some perspective, current figures put the value of the retail activity at $320–350 billion and growing at 30 to 35 per cent per annum (Kumar 2007). To date, the retail economy in India (like the leisure economy) has largely been the domain of small business. Although the retail sector has not been associated with the less salubrious side of the informal economy in the way that the film industry has, its popular image has been constituted around the small family-owned *Kirana* stores that have traditionally served urban neighbourhoods. By contrast, the appearance of large-scale shopping mall projects and the considerable investments made in the production of national shopping brands and retail franchises during the liberalisation era have led to the fostering of a new terminology of 'organised retail'. The rise of organised retail, whose domain includes supermarkets, health and beauty stores, hypermarkets, discount stores, convenience stores and cash and carry outlets, represents a large-scale shift from small traders and diffuse multi-stage distribution practices towards bigger business with more integrated operations. As with the corporatisation of the film industry, organised retail results from the entry of large-scale investment capital into an area of the economy formerly operating at a disorganised level.

Currently, both domestic and international corporations are investing heavily in the retail sector with as many as 40 retail players projected to be involved in the medium term. Domestic investors currently constitute around 60–65 per cent of the total investment in retail chains, with major foreign chains such as Wal-Mart, Tescos, Marks & Spencers, and Carre Four all announcing their intention to deepen their involvement in the near future (*Business Standard* 2007). To give some sense of the entities involved in the organisation of the retail sector, the table below details the future investment plans of some of the most significant retail players.

As with the multiplexes, the pursuit of an organised retail sector has meant the construction of a new physical architecture in preference to the established environments of the old shopping districts and areas. Again, there are obvious parallels with the multiplex. To a significant extent, the love affair with the shopping mall also represents an infatuation with the lifestyles of affluent, developed nations and with international standards. Beyond this, however, it is also undeniably the case that the existing retail economy in India is inefficient in economic terms and that

Table 4.1 Organised retail operations in India as of April 2007.

Retailer	Brands	Market entry date	Number of stores
Future Group	Big Bazaar, Food Bazaar, Various	2002	331
Subhiksha	Subhiksha	1997	700
RPG	Spencer's Express, Spencer's Fresh, Spencer's Daily, Spencer's Hyper	1996	125
Reliance Retail	Reliance Fresh, Reliance Digital	2006	135
A V Birla Group	Trinetra	1986	124
Dairy Farm	Foodworld, Health & Glow	1999	97
Metro Group	Metro	2003	2
K Raheja	Hypercity	2005	1
Nilgiris	Nilgiris	1971	36
Margin Free	Margin Free	1994	250
Shoprite	Shoprite	2004	1
Trent	Star India Bazaar	2004	1
Home Stores India Limited	Sabka Bazaar, Sabka Bazaar Mini	2005	25
Wadhawan Food Retail	Spinach	2006	23
Modi Enterprises	Twenty Four seven	2004	4
Avenue Supermarkets	DMart	2005	6
Spar International	Spar International	2004	1

Source: Adapted from IGD 2007

Table 4.2 Future investment plans of organised retailers.

Retailer	Brand	Future plans
Aditya Birla Group		To invest anywhere between Rs 15,000 and Rs 20,000 crore (Rs 5,000 in first phase) on a hyper market chain
Bharti Group	Wal Mart	Possible Joint Venture with Wal-Mart, the World's largest retailer. Wholesale cash and carry business and logistics. Also Bharti has franchise agreement to operate Wal-Mart stores in India.
K. Raheja Group	Shopper's Stop, Hyper City	To add two million sq ft. of retail space and increase the number of stores to 18 by FY08
Landmark Group	Life Style, Max	To target top 15 Indian cities and take its turnover to Rs 5000 crore by FY07 with a planned investment of Rs 450 crore over the next three years
Pantaloon Retail	Pantaloon, Big Bazaar, Food Bazaar, Fashion Station	To increase retail space ten fold to 30 million sq ft from its existing 3.2 million sq ft; eyes a turnover of Rs 2,500 by June 2010
Rajan Raheja	Globus	To take one million sq retail space by 2011 and invest Rs. 300–400 crore
Reliance Retail	Reliance Fresh, Reliance Mart	To invest Rs 25,000 crore on rolling out 5,500 stores in 800 cities, 85 logistic centres and 1,600 farm supply hubs by 2010
RPG Retail	Spencer's, Music World	To increase the number of outlets to 1,900 over the next three years
Tata Group	Westside, Star India Bazaar, Landmark, Croma	Recently tied up with international retailer Woolworth to open a consumer durables chain (Croma); eyes Rs 2,500 crore turn-over by June 2010; will raise retail area for Trent (holding firm of Westside, Sitar India Bazaar and Landmark) to 1.25m sq ft by 2007–08

Source: IRNR News 2006, Kaul and Prashant 2007

this places limits upon the capacity of the population to access consumer goods. It is also a barrier to more effective use of point-of-sale taxation by government. The advocates of this model therefore claim that the organisation of retail will increase tax collection and lead to more efficient supply chain management and distribution networks, ultimately benefiting consumers and the Indian economy. For this reason, the rapid development of this sector has been officially encouraged as part of an attempt to fast-track consumption-led economic development.

However, there are many outstanding questions about the merits of a large-format retail model in the Indian context. It is impossible to overlook the potential impact of organised retail on the 11 million employees of the small-scale, unorganised retailers (including grocery stores, bedi/paan stalls, convenience stores and street vendors) that are currently dominant and account for seven per cent of India's total employment (Guruswamy 2005). It is not unreasonable to expect that the livelihoods of small-scale traders and the previously ubiquitous street vendors and hawkers will be devastated, resulting in large-scale job losses in a sector that currently employs around 40 million people. The impact to date of organised retail has been modest, however. Despite the high visibility enjoyed by the new retail infrastructure, the organised sector still accounts for around three per cent of the total retail economy (KPMG and FICCI 2005).

As with the multiplexes, the exuberant growth of the organised retail industry entails significant financial risks. Developers have large initial outlays in fixed assets for construction and outfitting and most cannot expect to break even for at least five to eight years (Bhupta 2005). It will only be in the next couple of years that we will begin to see whether the first generation of malls successfully reach their break-even point. Beyond this, their longer-term future would appear to be threatened by the continuing construction of newer competing facilities, thus raising the spectres of the greymalls and deadmalls of suburban America. For the retailers, the risks are arguably even greater. Despite the fact that the bigger malls are currently achieving footfalls of around one million per month, this does not automatically translate into parallel growth in actual sales. Not more than ten to 15 per cent of footfalls currently translate into actual sales (Pal 2005). It is the specialised retail stores that receive the lowest footfall-to-purchase conversion rates. In addition, mall developers cross-subsidise the low rates they charge their anchor tenants, such as multiplexes, by levying high rentals to other retailers (Pal 2005). Both these factors mean that the viability of the mall environment for lower-priority tenants in retail outlets is far less assured than it is for the multiplexes, with the further added dimension of their necessary investments in sales stock.

As early as 2004, even some of the heavyweight mall tenants, like McDonalds, were predicting that there would be insufficient demand in the near future to cope with the number of planned mall developments, primarily because of this low conversion rate of footfalls to purchases (Adiga 2004). As such, whilst the retailers may be sharing the crowds drawn by the multiplexes, they do not seem to be making sales proportionate to their overall rental contribution to the mall owners. Like the multiplex operators, retailers and food providers require significant volumes of sales to maintain their position within the mall. The developers, by contrast, need to extract sufficient rents to justify their lands costs and investments in infrastructure. To keep rents at a sufficiently high level, developers may be prepared to subsidise their anchor tenants (the multiplex), but ultimately this will have to be paid for by others (the retailers). The relative importance of all these players is reflected, therefore, in their share of the overall turnover of the shopping mall. While percentages vary between malls, depending on the combination of outlets, the daily turnover is generally divided between food and beverage (45 per cent), fashion retail (30 per cent) and entertainment (25 per cent) (Bhupta, 2005). This would appear to indicate that, for now at least, the value of the leisure economy outweighs that of the retail sector in the shopping mall environment, which raises the question of whether India's shopping malls are primarily entertainment centres rather than shopping destinations.

Rocketing real estate and the lease model

While there are formal synergies between multiplexes and malls at the operational level, the operational environment of both the leisure and retail sectors is

Table 4.3 Growth in foreign direct investment (FDI) in real estate as a proportion of total FDI.

Year	Investment ($US Billion)	FDI in residential property as percentage of total FDI
2003–04	2.70	4.5
2004–05	3.75	10.6
2005–06	5.46	16.0
2006–07* (projected)	8.00	26.5

Source: Adapted from ASSOCHAM 2006

increasingly conditioned by the broader real estate boom. In the five years up until 2007, estimates suggest that the real estate market grew by 30 per cent each year. Currently valued at $16 billion, some projections suggest this could rise to $60 billion by 2010 as a consequence of the perceived need for office, residential and retail space (ASSOCHAM 2006). Current shortages in these areas have encouraged investment by a diverse range of sources, such as large corporate houses, Non-Resident Indians (NRIs), global investment funds and the domestic middle class. Again, the growing influence of the stock market is reflected in the fact that initial public offerings (IPOs) have been important in raising capital for real estate investment. Regulatory changes, specifically the Indian government's decision to allow 100 per cent foreign direct investment (FDI) in the construction of business from March 2005, have allowed the entry of high-net worth individuals and institutional investment, including foreign property funds, which have become a major source of much of this growth (*Times of India* 2005).

Beyond the growth of commercial developments, a further aspect to the dynamics of the property boom is the massive scale of investments being made in residential properties. Residential investment is thus emerging as a key driver of India's economic growth, particularly in terms of FDI. For the most part, these residential developments take on the form of high-rise apartments that yield the greatest profits for developers on an acreage basis. For the multiplex operators and for mall developers, the new residential districts that are appearing as a result of these developments represent natural locations for new sites, given that the access to credit necessary for purchasing an apartment is a useful indictor of consuming capacity. Similarly, since many of these developments are located in areas that are not serviced by the old leisure and retail facilities, there is an obvious need for commercial hubs to service these developments. Indeed, these relationships between residential, retail and entertainment developments are often synergised at the planning stages. In some instances, they have been produced collectively by developers who build and operate all three components. Undoubtedly, much of the impetus behind the real estate boom in the future will come from the increased interest of global investment funds, many of them operating in joint ventures with Indian-based corporations.

This inward investment would not have occurred except for two significant ongoing transformations in the major metropolises: the redevelopment of inner city

Table 4.4 Current projections of major real estate investors, 2007.

Investment company	$US millions	Activities
Royal Indian Raj International	2,900	Has a Corporate Land Library of 44 major prime parcels of in the four land major cities of India; Bangalore, New Delhi, Mumbai and Kolkata. With the lands available for prestigious real estate developments.
Blackstone Group	1,000	Blackstone Group LP is a private equity fund. Currently has three interests in India, Emcure Pharmaceuticals Ltd, Ushodaya Enterprises Ltd and Intelenet Global Services. However, the firm expects to have a total of over $2 billion invested in the Indian market
Goldman	1,000	Goldman Sachs (NYSE: GS) is planning to invest USD300m in Century Group, a real estate developer based in Bangalore, India. The investment is expected to be made in a special purpose vehicle (SPV) being created by Century Group for a range of commercial properties in Bangalore. Goldman Sachs recently raised a USD4bn property fund with key focus on India and China. Century Group reportedly owns a land bank of around 2,000 acres and assets of nearly INR50bn. The company is also looking to acquire a further 3,000 acres of land over the next two years.
Emmar Properties	800	Emaar-MGF Land Private Limited, a joint venture company formed by Emaar Properties PJSC - the world's largest listed real estate company, and MGF Developments Limited of India
Sachs Pegasus Realty	150	Gulf-based Pegasus Realty is looking to invest real estate and hospitality. Their projected realty investments are in Pune, Hyderabad, Chennai and Coimbatore.
Citigroup Investors	125	Citigroup is a financial services company that has around 200 million customer accounts in more than 100 countries. Citigroup is the single largest foreign direct investor in the financial services industry in India
Lee Kim Tah Holdings	115	Singapore based company whose interests include property development and investment, construction and project management and retail management. In India, LKT Holdings are constructing the integrated township Siruseri IT Park, which will consist of 6,000 residential units, and associated infrastructure
Salim Group	100	Indonesian based company developing Kolkata West International City in Howrah district, which will spread over 390 acres of land and contain 6,900 dwelling units along with a host of other facilities. The Salim company Mahabharat Motors Manufacturing Pvt Ltd is also beginning to produce two-wheelers under the brand name, Arjun
Morgan Stanley	70	One of the world's largest Investment Banks and global financial services companies, with headquarters in New York. Interests in India include Delhi-based real estate firm Alpha G:Corp. Morgan Stanley has suggested that it may invest as much as US$1 billion in the next four to five years.
GE Commercial Finance Real Estate	63	One of the world's largest financial services companies, has invested in a newly formed fund – the India IT Parks Fund – sponsored by Asia's leading business space provider, Ascendas Pte Ltd. This fund is currently looking to invest in International Tech Park, Bangalore and the Vanenburg IT Park in Hyderabad.

Source: ASSOCHAM 2006, industry

areas and increased suburbanisation. Both of these have required changes in the zoning and usage of land. The commercial nature of development drive is encouraging the targeting of high-value districts and populations for renewal projects, whilst bypassing poorer ones. This selective redevelopment of India's urban centres, especially its larger metropolitans, is furthering an urban ecology of enclaves. In assessing the manner in which these processes are occurring, we can see that while ostensibly liberalisation has been concerned about the freeing up the private sector, the state has remained an important player. The control of land by the state has been a mechanism utilised for several decades to generate revenue by acquiring land with minimal compensation and subsequently selling it for large profits (Shaw 2004: 50). The use of this mechanism in the liberalisation era has been highly significant. Rather than using their powers over urban development to keep land prices down for the benefit of lowly-paid state servants, India's major metropolitan authorities have begun releasing and re-zoning land in order to fuel a boom in property development and speculation.

The large volumes of private sector investment into land banks, special economic zones (SEZs) and other kinds of commercial property are made possible by the reclamation of land on a scale almost unparalleled in the post-independence period. Much of the legitimacy for these actions has been derived from a discourse emphasising the need for India's cities to become world-class or global cities. For example, the 90,000 huts demolished in Mumbai in 2005 in fulfilment of Vision Mumbai was only the most public example of a programme to reduce the proportion of slum dwellers in that city down to around ten to 20 per cent of the population. Similarly, Delhi Chief Minister Sheila Dixit emphasises that the 2010 Commonwealth Games 'provides a wonderful opportunity to strengthen the city's infrastructure to make it a global city' (Dixit 2006). To this end, as many as 300,000 people were evicted from their homes in Delhi in the period between 2003 and 2006. It is estimated that as many as 280,000 could be evicted from alongside the banks of the Yamuna in preparation for the 2010 Commonwealth Games. In Kolkata, the Left Front's earliest attempts at projecting a pro-investor image through evictions, 1996–1997's so-called 'Operation Sunshine', appear minor in comparison to the recent clearances of informal housing around canals and railway tracks.

Throughout these metropolises, the redevelopment of inner city areas has been achieved by the renovation of old factory areas and mills and the relocation of clusters of industries into areas outside the central business districts. Perhaps the most iconic of these recent redevelopments is DLF's plans to redevelop a 38-acre site of the Swatantra Bharat Mills in inner city New Delhi, complementing the adjacent 25 acres the company already owns, which will be India's largest private sector land deal when completed. Nonetheless, despite the aggressive upheavals taking place in India's cities, the transformation of the inner parts of the metropolises remains fraught with difficulties. Thus, suburbanisation has arguably engendered more substantial opportunities for constructing new facilities for the consuming middle classes. Suburbanisation has typically been achieved through the acquisition of land on the peripheral areas of the major metropolises, and their subsequent conversion from farmland or peri-urban activities by private developers or builders (Bidwai 2007). Much of this land has subsequently been converted into residential complexes, shopping malls and SEZs. Beyond this furious drive to reshape privileged enclaves with the urban landscape into the mould of a global city, there is no doubt that India's cities remain in desperate need of renewal in the face of mass poverty, clogged infrastructure and shortages of housing.

While there is considerable debate about the forms that urban renewal should take, for its part the central government has earmarked a large amount of money for urban renewal under the Jawaharlal Nehru National Urban Renewal Mission (JNNURM). The JNNURM is providing $11.2 billion in funds to 63 cities throughout the country. The most contentious aspect of this programme is the fact that state governments must undertake mandatory reforms in order to qualify for the money which has been earmarked for upgrading their cities. Of the reforms that are required in order to qualify for central government assistance, repealing the Urban Land Ceiling Regulation Act (ULCRA), reforming Rent Control Laws, and rationalising Stamp Duty are the most contentious (Skeers 2006). The reasons that these acts of legislation emerged in the first place were to prevent the concentration of land ownership, restrict property speculation and protect the interests of (largely middle-class) urban tenants. Thus, whilst ostensibly designed to fund poverty alleviation through infrastructure development, the JNNURM appears more likely to set in place a series of structural changes that will make it easier for commercial developers to further their own interests in the transformation of urban space. Advocates argue that this will free up the land market and reduce prices, while detractors believe that the JNNURM will encourage irresponsible property speculation and further push the refashioning of the city towards providing more infrastructure for the consuming classes at the expense of the rest of the population.

In this respect, the arrival of the multiplex within India's metropolitan landscape is imbued with an inherently political dimension. Using Partha Chatterjee's conceptual framework of struggles between civil and political society, we can see how the changing balance of societal forces over time is affecting the interplay of economic policy and urban space. In this context we should recognise that an extended political contestation has contributed to the remaking of Indian cities during the liberalisation era. Accordingly, as with other transformations occurring in India's polity since deregulation began in 1991, reform towards more market-driven cities has been assiduously opposed, but its momentum has continued to grow. This process certainly has many supporters, particularly amongst the heterogeneous middle-class groups who have become increasingly assertive in prescribing the way that urban space should be, and is being, transformed. The various municipal authorities acting on behalf of such interests have typically justified development projects on the basis that they are seeking to improve the lived environment. Thus, environmentalism legitimates the construction of shopping malls and multiplexes in tandem with the clearing of slums and the removal of pavement dwellers and hawkers. Both the environmental and the economic outcomes of the current property boom are far from assured, however, and the social implications of the drive to commodify and purify India's urban spaces by these means are considerable.

Figure 4.3 DLF's 'Mall of India' currently under construction at Gurgaon in the National Capital Region. At over 32 acres, and an investment of 15,000 million rupees, this will be the largest retail facility in Asia. (Adrian Athique)

Figure 4.4 Redevelopment site for a mall-multiplex combine in the heart of Bangalore's Kempegowda Road, a central district hosting cinema halls since the colonial era, February 2007. (Adrian Athique)

The huge rush of investment into the real estate market has mixed implications for the fortunes of the multiplexes, which can potentially aid or impinge upon their profitability and expansion. In the first place, the large-scale investment in real estate creates an expansionary environment that benefits the multiplex since it gives them access to thousands of square metres of readily available retail space. Being housed within a mall allows multiplex operators the opportunity to participate in attracting, sharing and manipulating the high-value crowd. However, since multiplexes require large plots of land, soaring prices can considerably affect the cost of setting up a new site. Compounding this dynamic is the fact that multiplexes target high-value customers, which means they need to be located close to the most desirable real estate areas where appreciation is likely to be highest. If multiplex operators invest in purchasing the properties in which they operate, they face the prospect of locking up large amounts of money in fixed assets, with the resulting lack of liquidity stalling potential expansion to other sites. With this in mind, most of the major multiplex chains currently believe that the best way to take advantage of the booming consumer market without being hamstrung by soaring realty costs is to lease rather than buy the premises in which they will operate. Although leases tend to be reasonably long term, at anywhere between ten and twenty-five years, the multiplex companies see leasing as a flexible arrangement that is more responsive to changing circumstances and less risky in a quickly shifting market terrain than the pursuit of landholdings and fixed structures. Ashish Shukla, from PVR, notes that

> We are only into a leasing model . . . They are not owned lands, but assets are owned. So it would be that the land is somebody else's. And he has built up a shell. Everything is rigged up. So we've got long leases, twenty years, twenty-five years . . . It is like: what is it that you ultimately want to do? . . . because although finance is not a problem, but it should not be considered that it unlimited. So it is putting the money to the best use where you can do your business better. If I was to say, if I had ten bucks in my pocket, I can do ten sites in the lease model, whereas I could only do two sites in the old model. If I had ten bucks limited. So that is the kind of philosophy that we have.
>
> (interview 14/03/2007)

Whilst the lease model has allowed the multiplex chains to maintain the fluidity of their working capital and to avoid fixed assets, their ability to negotiate low-cost leases is working against a general trend that has seen rental costs rising throughout urban India. In particular, many single-screen operators who are leaseholders are finding their margins squeezed by increasing rents. In Bangalore, there are scores of unprofitable large single-screen theatres sitting empty that can no longer be leased by small operators on a profitable basis. Ironically, in cases where theatre owners have been allowed to sell out to redevelopers, several theatres have been (and are being) pulled down to make way for malls and multiplexes, either individually or in combination. Nevertheless, while there are some instances of multiplex operators acquiring some of these lands to develop their own sites, most multiplex chains are now choosing to lease sites that are owned and developed by private developers. Shriram Krishnan at Shringar Cinemas explains why owning land is not desirable in the present climate:

> A lease model is going to work for us. Obviously you still need money, as when you are taking on a lease your rental commitments are fixed and as a multiplex you are locked into it longer. But at this point in time what makes sense is a lease model. Once you become very efficient you can start picking up, cherry-picking a couple of sites where you would like to own the land. But for me it is always going to be, if you are buying land, once you have put up a theatre over there, your only avenues after that, either you break the building down or you use it as a warehouse. So there's not other uses once it is set up. Because of the high roof or column-less space. Just to get it squared up or put in more levels. So I think owning land in that sense is a little foolish, if I may use that word. There is real estate appreciation but the only solution for you to use it for something else is to break the building down and start again.
>
> (interview 20/01/2007)

Tashur Dhingra at Adlabs, concurs with Krishnan, claiming that: 'we feel that owning a fixed asset is not the most optimum method for a cinema company . . . because that is not our core competence. A real estate company should do that' (interview 08/01/2007). Of course, it is pertinent to our overall discussion that the majority share of Adlabs is owned by the land-investment arm of Reliance (Reliance Land Investments) in particular, so that has to be seen as an important context for such a comment. Dhingra remains slightly less certain, however, than most of his peers that the mall-multiplex combination will continue to dominate in the future, noting that

> there is another view that shopping and entertainment doesn't necessarily help being together, that after the market has developed a little you will have entertainment centres separate where you will have food and entertainment, and you will have shopping malls separate. [Up until now] it has worked both ways, there are destinations that are entertainment-led destinations and there are destinations that are not.
>
> (Ibid.)

However, it is undeniable that at this point in time, the massive oversupply of retail space is a boon for the multiplex industry. As Ashish Shukla at PVR observes:

> Anchor tenants have increased but developers have increased. So I think the supply is more than the demand is right now in terms of multiplex spaces. And I think everybody is getting wary about what kind of locations they go into . . . We are rejecting more sites than we are selecting today. So today I have got about fifteen new locations and I am thinking that maybe I will explore two.
>
> (interview 14/03/2007)

At the same time Shukla is also sceptical that these favourable conditions will continue indefinitely:

> You see, the rental market today, and the property price market, I think property prices will continue to go up. That's not going to stop, but with renters I think that there is a correction that is going to happen for sure. Because renting there is no way that you are going to make money at eighty five or a hundred bucks rental, which Bombay's asking for, or Bangalore is asking for. You can't possibly make money as far as single-screens are concerned. We see it day-in, day-out. So either we don't build more or we build at percentage revenue share. So I think that the model of real estate developers for anchor stores, including multiplexes, would change. And I think that they will move towards a percentage share of revenue over time.
>
> (Ibid.)

The rapid spread of the multiplex over the last ten years has been subject to a number of push factors. Of these, the tax exemptions and deregulated pricings facilitated by state governments have been highly significant in the initial phase, and as of now it appears to be the sudden surplus of retail space made available at low cost lease through the shopping mall boom that is the major contributory factor driving further expansion. In terms of the latter, the rezoning of urban lands released by declining industry (for example, in Mumbai and Kolkata) and the facilitation of suburban developments and satellite conurbations (as in Delhi, Kolkata and Bangalore) have been highly significant in providing attractive sites for multiplexes in and around the major metros. Increasing competition, however, in some metropolitan areas (such as Andheri in Mumbai or Ghaziabad in Uttar Pradesh) and the overheating of the property market driving up costs is now contributing towards making smaller cities more attractive sites for development, heralding the next phase of expansion.

Mapping the (uneven) geography of opportunity

The diversification away from the high-value and high-cost areas of the major metros potentially presents significant opportunities for multiplex operators. Naturally it implies more customers, but it also promises lower set-up costs and greater economies of scale across their business as a whole. In recognition of these potential gains, as well as the obvious risk of market saturation in existing locations, all of the major multiplex chains have extensive expansion plans in progress at the time of writing. The industry overall is set to triple in size between 2006 and 2009. The sites currently under construction or at the stage of agreement between the multiplex operators and property developers indicate that overall the northern and western regions will continue to be the most significant areas of operation, although the current phase of expansion will also encompass other regions where the multiplex chains have thus far not had any significant presence. The immediate challenge for the multiplex operators is to undertake a calculated assessment of the potentials and limitations of the new markets into which they are expanding since these will encompass sites in untested regions of the country, as well as many smaller and thus potentially riskier locations. Accordingly, the multiplex operators have a staged process of expansion in mind. This expansion is premised on the evolving potential for the growth of the market at the national level, particularly in regard to rising disposable incomes in the smaller cities.

The varied economic geography of India means that anyone interested in expanding throughout the country must look beyond a categorisation of simply metros versus the rest. As such, opinion still varies amongst the various operators about how they should balance the potential opportunities in new states and cities with further expansion in the areas that they have favoured to date. Tushar Dhingra explains the approach being adopted at Adlabs:

> India is culturally diverse. And there are certain parts of India which are on our priority list rather than others. But the way the economy is going, I think, we have a plan which rolls out fifty two cities of India to start off. We capture that and then we move to the second stage.
>
> (interview 08/01/2007)

In this respect, certain indicators are clearly important when trying to anticipate future markets, including the expansion of sectors of the New Economy, such as the Information Technology (IT), Information Technology Enabled Services (ITES) and Business Process Outsourcing (BPO), which operators see as a logical indicator for the consumer base they are aiming to capture. As Shriram Krishnan at Shringar cinemas notes:

> For me, the definition of second tier-cities is too wide and these places are not all the same. See, the places where you will see that multiplexing is going to spread quite rapidly are the places where IT is already settled, look at Kolkata, look at Chennai, Pune, Hyderabad; these are all locations where IT is going in a large way, Bangalore and Pune it has already worked, and there are other places where it is also going to grow more. So I think that these are the next level of growth places.
>
> (interview 20/01/2007)

Of course, the spread of IT and services industries are themselves highly differentiated throughout India, with the majority currently concentrated in Bangalore, Gurgaon/New Delhi/NOIDA, Mumbai/Navi Mumbai/Thane, Kolkata, Hyderabad/Secunderabad and Chennai. These industries are also now expanding into cities such as Ahmedabad, Jaipur, Coimbatore, Kochi, Trivandrum, Chandigarh, Mysore, Mangalore, Madurai and Bhubhaneswar (IBEF – PriceWaterhouseCoopers 2004). All of these locations have recently acquired multiplexes or have sites in the advanced stages of construction. Beyond the pursuit of up and coming IT hubs, the overall expansion of the retail sector is also having considerable impact upon the choices of location that are being made

Map 4.1 Expansion plans of the five major multiplex chains to 2009. (Adrian Athique)

elsewhere, given the close relationship between the shopping malls and multiplexes at the operational level. Given their shared interest in mapping the growth of disposable income, there is a natural correlation in the way that the expansion of both is being conceived.

One recent guide to industry thinking on the future expansion of retail and residential sectors can be found in a report by Jones, Lang, Lasalle and Meghraj (hereafter JLLM), India's biggest real estate services firm, entitled 'The Geography of Opportunity – The India 50' (JLLM 2007). This report develops a typology for categorising the growth potential of 50 of India's cities, driven by the factors typically cited by reports of this kind: favourable demographics, rapid urbanisation, a booming economy and a growing middle class. Like similar reports on the multi-plex industry, JLLM's understanding of the retail environment is underpinned by growth projections surrounding consumption habits as well as market characteristics. For this reason, the JLLM report has a positive bias, maintaining a strategic silence on some of the issues that might induce a potential investor to stay away from a locality, such as political instability or a lack of corporate transparency.

In terms of current investment, the two cities identified as 'Tier 1', Mumbai and Delhi-NCR, are by far the most significant locations in the market, together accounting for about 40 per cent of the total organised retail sector in India. Within these two cities, the localities being concentrated on are the Central Business Districts (CBDs) as well as particular growth clusters in the outer metropolitan areas. In the case of the NCR, the central 'high street' areas that will continue to prosper are Connaught Place, South Extension, Khan Market and Greater Kailash, while the outer metropolitan areas that are currently 'hot' are Gurgaon, Ghaziabad, Faridabad and greater NOIDA. Another location at the fringes of Delhi, Maneshar, is also projected to boom because of its location on the National Highway 8 (NH8), connecting the NCR to Jaipur. In the case of Mumbai, the inner city areas seeing intense real estate and retail activity are SBD Central and SBD North, while the rising outer metropolitan regions are Malad and Goregaon as well as Powai, Mulund, Navi Mumbai and Thane. Again, we see that these are all areas that have been targeted heavily by the multiplexes over the past five years.

The JLLM report recognises that the expansion of retail in Delhi and Mumbai is likely to be hampered in the future by the difficulties associated with rising costs and land procurement, and therefore suggests that a large proportion of future expansion may well come from those cities that are the next rung down in its hierarchy, being characterised as 'transitional cities'. These cities, which include Bangalore, Kolkata, Hyderabad, Pune, Ahmedabad and Chennai were projected to contribute up to one-third of the total organised retail by 2008. According to the report, these cities are likely to embrace malls and organised retail as strongly as the two Tier 1 cities because they have 'increasingly vibrant corporate sectors, high economic growth rates, above average incomes and large middle classes' whilst having the advantage of lower property construction and labour costs (ibid.: 21).

Another category on the JLLM typology is the 'high growth' cities that are comparatively small and underdeveloped at present but have potential factors which will accelerate their growth. These cities, Chandigarh, Ludhiana, Jaipur, Lucknow, Kochi, Baroda and Surat, are likely to be targets for retail and residential expansion in future because they are seen to have high incomes and strong brand awareness, including, in the case of the Punjabi city Ludhiana, the influence of an NRI population. These are all areas that figure strongly in the current expansion programme of the multiplexes. (For example, Baroda already has three multiplexes in operation and Punjabi cities are a major focus for all the expansion programmes currently underway.) Yet another category, which the JLLM report argues is 'emerging' cities, is seen to have some impetus for growth because of the development of call centres, outsourcing or other factors that are likely to add to consumer spending. There are also cities included in this category that are seen as being tourist

Table 4.5 The geography of opportunity emerging cities.

Indore	Amritsar	Calendar	Mangalore
Nasik	Bhubaneshwar	Agra	Vizag
Coimbatore	Kanpur	Nagpur	Goa
Allahabad	Mysore	Jamshedpur	Thiruvananthapuram

centres with a large turnover of visitors from the major metros. The report suggests that within three years these cities will become major targets of investment because they are characterised by 'growing incomes, rising aspirations, scarcity of branded stores and growing corporate activity' (ibid.: 23). The 16 emerging cities named by JLLM, many of which are currently acquiring multiplex cinemas, are listed below.

The final category on JLLM's 'Geography of Opportunity' listing is those cities that are (arguably somewhat optimistically) referred to as 'nascent cities'. These are mainly smaller cities or cities in the more impoverished states and regions which have seen much less retail development to date. They have low incomes and limited corporate activity. Meerut is something of an exception here given its proximity to the NCR. Interestingly, it is the only city on the list that currently has a multiplex run by a national chain.

The major emphasis throughout the JLLM report is the opportunities for organised retail to expand on the back of increased spending and consumption by the middle class, particularly that segment of it which the report refers to as India's 'vanguard consumers'. As we have seen, similar projections surrounding the social mores and spending habits of a pan-Indian consuming class are driving the expansion of multiplex operators into other parts of the country. While there are some disparities between the overall economic model of the retail sector and the specific needs of cinemas (such as the continuing value of the mass audience in A centres), there are nonetheless obvious parallels between JLLM's 'Geography of Opportunity' and the mapping of the multiplex industry expansions highlighted in Figure 4.9. These include the overwhelming importance of Mumbai and Delhi, and the overall dominance of western and north-west territories. This correlation is a natural one at many levels, because cinema, as with retail, is a secondary industry targeting existing disposable incomes. Therefore cinema and retail expansion tends to follow the growth of incomes rather than precede it, although it is arguably the case in India that the rapid expansion of such infrastructure is presently preceding wealth creation.

Table 4.6 The geography of opportunity-nascent cities.

Jodhpur	Patna	Varanasi	Meerut
Rajkot	Aurangabad	Bhopal	Sonipat
Vijaywada	Madurai	Ranchi	Guwahati
Jabalpur	Asansol	Dhanbad	Panipat
Kolhapur	Srinigar	Solapur	

It is logical, therefore, to see the expansion of multiplexes as part of the wider growth of economic activity at the national level. For this reason, the projected location of future multiplexes can offer us something of a snapshot of where economic growth is being identified or predicted. Taking the inverse view, the gaps in the planning of the multiplex chains provide some indication of the areas that are being left behind or sidelined by economic growth, including the so-called 'red corridor', where a Maoist insurgency stretches from Bihar down to Northern Andhra Pradesh in the east of the country. However, there are also some mitigating factors against using multiplexes to map the consuming class at the national level. One factor is the relative surplus of existing cinemas in the South and their integration with strong regional film industries there. This has delayed the entry of major operators from elsewhere in the country, despite the fact that the state of Tamil Nadu, for example, is relatively prosperous and has long been regarded as a strong cinema market.

At the national level, the current concentration of investment in certain geographic areas reflects the difficulties of nationwide commercial expansion in a country characterised by highly uneven levels of development. To compete in this environment, multiplex operators must continually strive to gain first-mover advantage over competitors by entering into markets which do not yet have multiplex saturation. At the same time, however, they must be aware of the pitfalls of entering into locations that may not have the economic, political and social conditions to sustain their operations. At the same time, lower costs serve to somewhat mitigate the risks. In this respect, Anand Moorthy of FUN Cinemas highlights the attractiveness of 'high growth' and 'emerging' cities:

> See, in India I think is important to move first. First-mover advantage is still existing. There is a large untapped market still existing in India. A lot of people, a lot of business houses, were only trying to focus on Bombay, Delhi, Chennai maybe, before. Now they are moving to Calcutta, they are going to Hyderabad, to Bangalore for sure. If you're not present in those three cities, you're not pan-India. So the smallest of examples, and this is not just to our business but for anybody's business as a matter of fact, if you have got a hundred bucks and you have three cities, Bombay, Chennai and Delhi functional, then Bombay would be fifty percent of that hundred bucks, of your total collections. But if you are opening in smaller cities, so your sites are moving from three to ten, then the Bombay percentage falls to thirty percent. So those other cities are taking that kind of chunk. So imagine from the investment perspective the Bombay that was giving me fifty Rupees is now giving me thirty, and is the costliest. So, ultimately the more money that I am pumping in here, my net profit is going to be lower. While net profits are getting higher in the smaller cities because the numbers are better than Bombay, the price is a little lower, but if you see collection wise then they are making more money than Bombay. So, yes, I think that moving to the smaller cities is making good sense. We are getting into it, and the owners of the other companies are also getting into cities like Kota, Agra.

(interview 06/01/2007)

Figures 4.5 and 4.6 Signage at Central Malls, Baroda (Vadodora) (above) and Bangalore (below), January 2007. (Adrian Athique)

In recognising the uneven distribution of wealth across the country, many multiplex operators believe that the expansion into smaller cities inevitably implies a different business model, one which accounts for the differences in purchasing power and costs found in different locations. The emerging market in the smaller cities appears to entail reducing admission prices by at least 30 per cent. As the major chains expand, they are therefore adopting cost-cutting measures, such as scaling down the grandiosity of facilities to suit local conditions for the B centres. This latter strategy could mean a greater emphasis on retrofitting older cinemas rather than erecting new purpose-built facilities. The countervailing tendency is that the expansion of malls throughout the smaller cities is currently providing a surplus of cheap lease space. Whichever option operators choose, the most significant factor in the expansion plans outside the existing sites is the presence or absence of significant numbers of suitable customers rather than the lack of available infrastructure.

This being the case, it is worth briefly returning to our discussion of the variance in the presence of the consuming classes in different parts of India. The lack of interest by the multiplex operators to date appears to suggest a lack of a significant consuming class in Bihar, Kashmir or the north-east. The capacity of the multiplex format to reach beyond the cities into local towns also remains very much in doubt, given that few of the rural areas have shared in the fruits of liberalisation. Similarly, it is clear that even within the metropolitan regions, large groups of people are unlikely to be able to afford the new leisure activities on offer, even if multiplex operators substantially reduce their ticket prices. Indeed, it is arguable that, notwithstanding the current optimism of large investors, the quantum of investment currently projected to flow into the retail, residential and leisure industries in the very near future will only be profitable if there is an unfeasibly large increase in the average purchasing power of consumers. This income growth would also need to be distributed much more evenly than has been the case thus far, and a more profligate consumer culture would also need to take root amongst a greater segment of the population. Multiplex operators are all too aware of these issues, as Shriram Krishnan from Shringar Cinemas suggests:

> I think there is a pricing limitation for multiplexes, when you go to the really local cities, and that to a certain extent will limit the growth for a while . . . we can keep talking about sort of low cost areas, combining low cost areas with low cost multiplexes but I don't think that there is enough growth potential. We keep looking at this. We have got a couple of properties in smaller centres and we struggle to move the average ticket price. People are more economical and they don't tend to spend in that way. I mean, in Bombay, a guy will spend around a dollar, but I don't think they will spend even a dollar. Let's say they will spend a quarter of a dollar. So that's the kind of difference. In my best property in Bombay people spend around forty-five to fifty bucks and in Nasik they spend around fifteen to twenty bucks. Everybody understands in multiplexing, the real moulah is in the top end.

(interview 20/01/2007)

Many of the multiplex operators and real estate investors discussed in this chapter have dwelt on the growth engine of the New Economy, such as the IT, ITES and BPO sectors. When we consider the overall context of future economic development of India, however, it is also important to consider other areas of the Indian economy, such as manufacturing, and the potential implications they also have for spreading purchasing power to other parts of the country. This is in light of the fact that many parts of India are considerably behind the major metropolises or the southern states when it comes to factors necessary for participation in the New Economy, such as high levels of education in English. Gujarat, for example, is a state that is fairly well industrialised but has comparatively poor levels of English-medium tertiary education. This inevitably makes it a relatively weak market for Hollywood films, for example, but it also has implications for the growth of the New Economy. At the same time, the industrial economy of Gujarat is clearly producing enough wealth to encourage the development of multiplexes, with the state capital, Ahmedabad, gaining a reputation as a city of multiplexes in recent years.

While there is comparatively little recent work examining the regional dimensions of the manufacturing industry, particularly compared to the voluminous writings appearing on the New Economy, there is certainly enough data to suggest that the Indian industrial economy in the post-liberalisation era is also highly regionally differentiated. In recent years, Chakravorty and Lall (2007) have found that post-liberalisation private sector investments are biased towards existing industrial areas and coastal districts to a much greater extent than was the case when the economy was driven by state industrial investments. Within these contours, Chakravorty and Lall identify patterns of 'intra-regional convergence' operating alongside 'inter-regional divergence'. Through these processes, many industries have moved out of metropolitan centres to areas on the periphery, but they contribute to operate within specific regions.

As such, we can identify areas where the growth outwards of economic activity from regional hubs is increasing the connections between metros and their hinterlands, driving the growth of satellite cities and hence improving economic integration (most obviously in the NCR and greater Mumbai). These areas have been the cradle of the multiplex industry in most respects. There are also rural areas that have successfully diversified into profitable cash crops and non-agricultural activities are increasingly integrated into the broader economy (of states such as Punjab and Haryana). Regional cities are growing in these areas, and malls and multiplexes are following this growth. However, vast areas of the country remain isolated from both the drivers and followers of economic growth. These areas are in the midst of deep agrarian distress (particularly in the central and eastern regions). These latter areas are also often characterised by poor levels of human capital, high levels of corruption and political instability. For all these reasons, these latter areas are being bypassed by the multiplex operators.

In the face of such overwhelming disparities in regional development patterns across the country, there has been an official recognition by government of the need to try and ensure a more spatially even growth pattern. One element of this recognition is the increased attention that various levels of government, private investors and donor agencies have given to improving the quality of India's transport infra-structure, including roads, railways and waterways (Wallack and Singh 2005). Indeed, it is noteworthy that many locations that now have multiplexes, such as Baroda, Jaipur and Indore, have grown precisely because they have been linked with larger cities via infrastructure such as the new Golden Quadrilateral road net-work, which links Delhi, Mumbai, Kolkata and Chennai. Many cities along the route of the NH8 between Delhi and Mumbai, the two largest centres of economic activity, have shown signs of growth, and the spread of multiplexes along this par-ticular stretch over the last three years is also a notable feature of the mapping in Figure 4.9.

Despite these gains, it is clear that either government infrastructure projects or private sector investment can only have a limited impact in spreading employment and purchasing power to less prosperous parts of the country in the immediate future. Similarly, the New Economy continues to be even more localised and unevenly dispersed than earlier heavy industry and manufacturing developments. For all these reasons, there will continue to be challenges for multiplex operators seeking to tap into hitherto untouched markets. It seems likely that many remote, neglected or otherwise 'difficult' areas will remain outside of the 'Geography of Opportunity' for some decades to come. The smaller cities, *mofussil* towns and rural areas are absent from the projections of even the most optimistic multiplex opera-tor at this time. On this basis, it is only logical to assume that, despite the all-India ambitions of the multiplex chains, the geography of the leisure economy in India will continue to be marked by uneven development for some years to come.

Recasting the geography of opportunity

While there is a widespread recognition of regional disparities in India, there remain political conflicts over how they should be resolved. This is particularly the case because, as we have previously noted, since the mid-1990s, the encouragement and regulation of private sector investment in many different industries has become the domain of the states to a much greater extent. The new post-liberalisation envi-ronment is described by one influential commentator in terms of 'competitive fed-eralism' (Saez 2002). This pits region against region and city against city, consistently favouring the most developed parts of the country. In this sense, the dif-ferent state-levied taxes and investment inducements have had a marked effect upon the choices made by multiplex operators to site their business in one state instead of another. However, pro-investment strategies are just one part of a much broader economic picture that the multiplex operators need to consider since the uneven nature of the Indian economy overall fundamentally affects the nature of their operating environment and the scale of their customer's purchasing power.

As we have noted, the symbiosis between the multiplex and the shopping mall is indicative of a merger between the leisure and retail economies at the organised level. At the same time, it is also indicative of the continuing separation between the organised and disorganised sectors in both areas. As such, it is important to be aware that multiplexes have much more in common with shopping malls in many respects than they do with traditional cinemas. It appears to be increasingly the case that the future of the multiplex at the all-India level will be closely tied to the fate of the shopping mall boom. In this respect, although there is now an established market for multiplexes in the big metros, and to a certain extent in second-tier sites like Pune, the cities that are 'emerging' or 'nascent' in the 'Geography of Opportunity' characterisation represent a far greater challenge. Despite the current excitement that surrounds these new facilities in such places, the long-term viability of the multiplex is unproven in these markets.

In charting the dispersal of multiplexes at the national level, we can see the impact of numerous factors. For multiplexes, the determinants of location choice include favourable tax and regulatory regimes and rising levels of disposable income. Other critical influences are the operational synergies with the wider retail economy, the availability of affordable property, the nationwide variance of population size, industrial activity and infrastructure development, as well as competition between states and between the multiplex operators themselves. While all the major chains are currently promoting the advantages of geographic diversification to investors, there are many tangible obstacles to their expansion plans that we have taken note of here, in particular, the macro-economic differences between cities, states and regions. At the next level to be addressed, there are also variances between neighbourhoods within any given city that are equally, if not more, important to the strategic vision of the multiplex.

5 Location and lifestyle

The infrastructure of urban leisure

Ravi Vasudevan suggests that we pay regard to the institution of the Indian cinema 'as a form of regular, normalized public congregation, sometimes assuming great symbolic functions', but at the same time we need to keep in mind that the cinema hall is also an 'everyday space: composed of the hall, its internal organization of foyer, auditorium, seating and the projected film, [with a] public presence, as in its façade, advertisements, marquees, hoardings' (2003). Critically, Vasudevan also prompts us to 'see this space in relation to a broader space, in the market, near factories, schools, offices blocks, in a mall, in residential areas' and to interrogate 'how it is located in the depth of this space or on its margins, near main arterial thoroughfares, linking one space to another' (2003). Needless to say, the spatial distribution of leisure facilities within the urban environment has a major impact upon how people move around their city, while the particularity of each location has an equally critical affect upon how (and by whom) this leisure infrastructure is accessed.

As such, the urban geography of the multiplex must be related to current patterns of development in India's metropolises. These are processes that are leading to increasing suburbanisation and evermore marked differentiation between urban districts and between segments of the population. Accordingly, we seek to demonstrate how these tendencies have impacted upon the deployment of the multiplex in the major metropolitan centres. To fully understand the spatial relationships between multiplex cinemas and urban redevelopment programmes, we must consider the inevitable collisions between the rationale of the multiplex format and the realities of existing social spaces, where significant local variations in economic conditions, traditions of public culture and political forces are all factors which influence how the geography of leisure is being defined and contested in different cities.

Catchments, enclaves and selective development

Many of the more hyperbolic statements about the transformation of India's cities in the popular press suggest that all parts of the urban economy are undergoing massive transformation, but in practice recent developments have targeted highly-specific locations. In turn, the multiplex and mall operators target the resulting clusters of New Economy activities (such as IT, BPO and call centres) in conjunction with established high-wealth areas (such as central business districts and 'old money' suburbs). Thus, while traditional theatres were built predominantly in areas of a city with the highest volumes of occupation, multiplex operators' analysis of the urban landscape at the metropolitan scale seeks to identify pockets of affluence with the highest average incomes. Tushar Dhingra at Adlabs suggests that this logic means a focus on very specific localities:

> I'm not talking a town. I'm not talking a city. We're looking for a catchment. A catchment is ten minute's driving distance. That defines the demographics, psychographics, the propensity to consume outdoor entertainment outlets. Disposable income etc . . . It is not about being in Bombay. I will not invest in Bombay. I am looking at a particular location in Bombay and what is around it. Or that defines what I am going to do in Ahmedabad or Baroda or somewhere else. It is very catchment specific.
>
> (interview 08/01/2007)

Catchment, then, is a fundamental conception that governs the modus operandi of the multiplex industry, representing the area from which a multiplex can expect to draw its patrons. In the first instance, this requires an assessment of the immediate environs in terms of economic activity. As Dhingra explains,

> There are key indicators . . . you want to define whether it is a good catchment to get into or not. So demographics: number of cars sold, number of credit cards, these things. What kind of monies people have in the banks? Very real indicators, or how consumer goods are performing in that area. What is the penetration of telecom? These are good indicators, and if we require it, we normally do market research of a catchment before we enter.
>
> (interview 08/01/2007)

Similarly, media releases from INOX emphasise the critical importance of location. INOX planning indicates a balanced approach between traditional concentrations of purchasing power and new areas of economic concentration within the shifting landscapes of India's cities. In either scenario,

> Location is just as important as content in the multiplex business. While the right content helps in reaching out to the right target audience, the right location attracts higher footfalls and purchasing power. This is why all INOX multiplexes are located in high-traffic, commercial areas, or in the midst of affluent residential areas.
>
> (INOX Leisure Ltd. 2006d)

Within these contours, however, the mobility of people within the city impacts on their lived experience and imaginaries of places (Graham and Marvin 2001). The integration of production and consumption experienced in the practice of everyday life, and its formal exploitation through corporate economic planning, therefore highlights the importance of not only commercial and residential districts, but also of the patterns of movement established between these districts. Accordingly, location choice for a multiplex goes beyond the marketisation of populations expressed by demographic indicators to consider the likely trajectories of consumption arising from the capacity of suitable customers to access particular urban spaces. Dhingra's temporal and spatial definition of a multiplex catchment provides ample evidence of this critical dimension of the geographies of urban transport. The catchment within a ten-minute drive clearly has to encompass a range of contingencies such as the quality of transport infrastructure and the growing importance attached to the ease of travel as a factor governing consumption choices. Concentrations of wealth and available lands may determine the site of a multiplex, but it is travel time that effectively delimits the catchment area.

Hubbard's (2002) identification of the relationship between car travel and the typical location of multiplexes on the periphery of British towns has encouraged Collins, Hand and Ryder (2005) to formulate a model for calculating the interplay of travel time and location on the consumption of cinema. These calculations, based upon the British context, may not be directly transferable since they assume a far greater access to private car ownership than is the case in India. Nonetheless, what this approach adds to the discussion of cinema catchments is a recognition of the importance of commuting consumers in augmenting local residents within the overall audience. Certainly, there is a close relationship between the massive growth in car ownership underway in urban India and the pursuit of profitable catchments for new multiplex developments. However, while undoubtedly making new locations for leisure viable by creating greater mobility for consumers, increases in car use also bring their own limitations. Anand Moorthy at FUN Cinemas in Mumbai is acutely aware that:

> Because now most Indian time is spent on the roads commuting, because they are selling so many cars and scooters with such kind of pace it has taken ahead of the infrastructure which is not ready. So convenience becomes again important.
>
> (interview 06/01/2007)

The congruence of affluence and convenience for the multiplex customer thus requires a considerable degree of infrastructure support, intimately aligning multiplexes with road and metro-rail developments. As Paul, Shetty and Krishnan (2005) note in Mumbai, the construction of new road links creates new hubs for redevelopment schemes, as well as faster travel between them. Whilst ostensibly separate private developments, the physical connection of upmarket residential developments, retail hubs, multiplexes and other leisure facilities creates a new leisure network in which the different components are closely oriented towards each other. However, this massive series of interventions in urban space remains an ongoing process at present, with the sheer density of the existing built environment and of the urban population continuing to be a major factor in inhibiting movement even for those with private transport. The limitations to catchment size imposed by transport infrastructure constraints is a reminder of the difficulty of constructing seamless networks of consuming mobility within crowded and contested urban domains. In cities like Mumbai, this makes catchment areas relatively small by international standards, as Shriram Krishnan from Shringar notes:

> I think that we have to understand that India has an infrastructure constraint. So travelling times is, the time it takes from your house to the multiplex, is what determines your radius. Because of infrastructure constraints, with the density of population being what it is in this country, I believe that a three to four kilometre radius is needed to take into account of travelling time.
>
> (interview 20/01/2007)

While earlier cinemas were built in response to growing urban populations during the twentieth century, the first wave of multiplexes in India were instead built in anticipation of future wealth. In recent years, multiplex developments have been targeting areas identified for growth in the urban redevelopment plans now being adopted across India, anticipating a larger consuming public spreading beyond existing pockets of affluence and occupying suburban and satellite townships in what were until recently brownfield and greenfield sites. As such, the materialisation of broader regulatory and political conditions at the scale of the metropolis, including land rezoning, infrastructure provision (especially roads) and complementary retail and residential infrastructure, has influenced the placement of multiplexes. The particularities of these conditions arise from the varying political, historical and social contexts found in different cities.

There are obvious limits to the extent that these stories can be told here in full. Our study of the multiplex to date has incorporated seven cities in India's eastern, northern and southern regions, ranging from the largest metros down to the so-called 'second-tier cities', including: Delhi NCR, Mumbai, Kolkata, Bangalore, Baroda, Durgapur and Panjim. Here, we discuss the distribution of multiplexes in the Delhi-NCR, Bangalore and Kolkata, which are three major cities situated in northern, southern and eastern India respectively. We present a spatial analysis of the distribution of multiplex sites and, at a finer scale, we also examine a number of specific catchments in terms of their immediate neighbourhoods and the areas from which they draw their audience. In doing so, we demonstrate that the manner in which each catchment is formulated follows a general logic as a whole, while remaining markedly variable in size and scope due to specific urban conditions.

Delhi and the National Capital Region

The area that makes up Delhi today encompasses a series of historic cities established during the centuries of Muslim domination in north India. As the capital of British India since 1911 and of the Republic of India since independence in 1947, Delhi has been massively enlarged through the past 100 years in a series of distinct stages. The construction of New Delhi, south of the historic walled city of Old Delhi between 1911 and 1931 was a large-scale development of a spacious capital designed to accommodate the machinery of colonial government. As such, the planned city of New Delhi was intended to be both a functional and a formal expression of British imperial power. After independence, Delhi was constituted as the capital of a federally-organised nation. Housing the central government, Delhi became a Union Territory independent of the newly organised regional state administrations in 1956. The Union Territory of Delhi included both Old Delhi and New Delhi, along with a substantial belt of rural land. As we noted previously, early attempts were made to plan the future development of the territory through the DDA, although these were only partially realised.

The steady growth of the public sector economy and the expansion of India's administration saw Delhi grow significantly throughout the first four decades of independence. The residential suburbs of South Delhi expanded to serve the administrative district of New Delhi proper. The long-term influx of labouring populations from neighbouring states, along with migrants from Punjab in the immediate post-independence period and again during the 1980s, greatly increased the areas of conurbation around the western and eastern districts (the latter being located across the Yamuna River that flows south along the eastern edges of Old and New Delhi). Although initially an administrative centre rather than an economic powerhouse like Bombay, the growing population and the location of central power in the city (aided by the increasing government role in the post-independence economy) saw Delhi steadily increasing in economic importance. The famous circular central business district of Connaught Place, lying between the walled city of Old Delhi and New Delhi functioned as the hub of commercial life in the city.

In 1991, the Union Territory of Delhi became the National Capital Territory of Delhi with nine administrative districts and its own legislative assembly and chief minister, effectively becoming a state in its own right. At present, Delhi is second only to Bombay (now Mumbai) in commercial importance, and it is attracting major investment inflows. At the same time, the public sector continues to employ three times as many people as the private sector, with the latter being overwhelmingly constituted by goods and services. The population of Delhi has now reached over 14 million, making it the largest city in India. The rapid growth Delhi has experienced throughout the liberalisation era has been facilitated by extensive rail and road infrastructure projects. The inner and outer ring roads around Delhi are eight-lane highways that now bypass congestion points via dozens of flyovers, facilitating large volumes of orbital traffic. Nonetheless, with 5.5 million vehicles now registered in Delhi, road transport infrastructure is struggling to keep pace with traffic growth. Pressure on the system also comes from high volumes of entering traffic from five of India's major national highways that intersect with these ring roads. Given that 60 per cent of commuters using public transport are still serviced by the Delhi Transport Corporation bus network, the ever-increasing rates of car ownership in Delhi suggest further strain on road networks.

The major response to rising congestion has been the construction of the Delhi Mass Transit System. This massive urban rail network, commonly known as the Delhi Metro, was originally envisaged in the DDA Master Plan of 1960, although construction was not actually undertaken until 1998. The completion of the extensive first phase of the network was achieved in 2005, three years ahead of schedule. The second phase is presently under construction, taking the network across the state boundaries. Two further phases are intended to extend the network throughout the National Capital Territory and adjoining states. The extent to which highway upgrades and the Delhi Metro are transforming the spatiality of Delhi, and its relationship to its hinterland, cannot be easily overestimated (Delhi Metro Rail Corporation 2007, Siemiatycki 2006).

It is easy, however, to understand why the multiplex boom began in Delhi. The opening of PVR's retrofitted sites in upmarket South Delhi from 1997 onwards occurred at the cusp of a major outward expansion of the city. Since then, the completion of the various stages of road and rail infrastructure projects and the rezoning of agricultural land on Delhi's periphery have driven a building boom that has inexorably drawn major new commercial and residential developments to the outlying areas. Massive growth in malls and multiplexes across Delhi have been seen as positive proof of India's growing economic importance, but it has also become contentious due to widespread violations of planning laws with scores of large-scale illegal developments. Although the removal of squatter structures has been part and parcel of various urban renewal programmes conducted in Delhi since independence, the demolition of illegally-built shopping malls in upmarket South Delhi suburbs during 2006 was highly controversial (*Hindustan Times*, 2006). With the Delhi government seeking to orchestrate its own renewal programme for the 2010 Commonwealth Games, these demolitions were a clear attempt to reassert control over the chaotic nature of development across the city.

One of the most visible outcomes of the new policies concerning resource allocations to the various Indian states and of the wealth being generated within the National Capital Territory has been the push by neighbouring states to substantially develop districts immediately adjoining the National Capital Territory. The re-zoning of land in these areas has paved the way from compulsory government purchase and its on-sale to private developers at favourable rates. Along with the upgrading of transport connections between these areas and Delhi proper, this has had the effect of drawing the expansion of the capital across the state borders. The success of these satellite conurbations has brought into existence the larger entity of the Delhi-NCR. The NCR is an area including the National Capital Territory of Delhi, along with rapidly-growing satellite developments in the states of Uttar Pradesh, Haryana and Rajasthan. The ready availability of land and the imminent arrival of major transport upgrades in these areas have been accompanied by favourable planning regimes and other incentives. In the case of the multiplex, this includes the introduction of Entertainment tax exemptions in Haryana and Uttar Pradesh. This has made the multiplex story symptomatic of the rise of the NCR, since if we take aside the retrofitted cinemas operated by PVR within Delhi itself, almost all of the 21 multiplexes in the NCR are located in the satellite towns of Gurgaon and Faridabad (in Haryana) and NOIDA and Ghaziabad (in Uttar Pradesh).

While the satellite townships of the Delhi-NCR are sometimes treated as a single group for analytical purposes, they have quite different characteristics. In the case

Table 5.1 Ownership and frequency of multiplexes in the NCR.

Sub-division of NCR	Companies represented	Number of multiplexes
Delhi	M2K (2) PVR (6)	8 (6 retrofits)
Gurgaon	DT (2) PVR (2)	4
Noida	PVR (1) Wave (1)	2
Ghaziabad	Adlabs (2) FUN (1) Gem Shipra (1)	
	M4U (1) MMX (1) Movie World (1)	
	Movie Palace (1) PVR (1)	
	SM World (1) Silver City (1) Wave (1)	12
Faridabad	PVR (2)	2
Total	**13**	**28**

of the NCR, we believe that it is useful to make a broad distinction between more closely planned New Economy developments (Gurgaon and NOIDA) and the more ad hoc residential and retail satellites of Ghaziabad and Faridabad. Accordingly, these locations represent markedly different catchments for multiplex operators. The indicator of the placement of IT and BPO industries favoured by the major national chains proves instructive in this regard, since the NCR's IT and ITES sector is second only to Bangalore in significance. However, there are clearly other factors at work since Ghaziabad has the greatest number of multiplexes – despite having a comparatively small IT and ITES sector compared to Gurgaon or NOIDA.

The rise of Gurgaon began in 1997, when the state government of Haryana acquired a large area of land adjacent to the National Capital Territory. This land was made available for private-sector development of technology parks and other New Economy infrastructure. A large portion of this area was acquired by DLF, the largest landowning company in India. Gurgaon saw rapid development as IT companies, BPO operations, call centres, management colleges and financial institutions began operations. This expansion of the informational economy saw Gurgaon (along with Koremangala in Bangalore) becoming synonymous with India's economic boom. The wealth being generated by the offshoring economy has attracted a large number of grandiose residential, hospitality and retail developments.

Gurgaon has become a major source of revenue for Haryana, contributing up to one-third of state revenues. The Haryana State Government co-operated with the Government of Delhi on the upgrading of the NH8 connecting Delhi, Indira Gandhi International Airport and Gurgaon. The further development of this route as part of the Golden Quadrilateral scheme implemented by the BJP-led central government of Atal Vajpayee has made it the most significant corridor of wealth in India today. The acquisition of land by state governments for IT campuses, call centres, BPOs and gated residential complexes has had major implications for the local leisure economy. In Gurgaon, the privileging of multiplex and mall developments as non-polluting industries has encouraged the growth of a sprawling commercial infrastructure serving those employed in the New Economy, transforming Gurgaon into the so-called 'City of Malls'. The aptly-named 'Mall Road' in

Gurgaon now houses one the largest stretches of retail space in Asia, making Gurgaon a major shopping draw for the residents of South Delhi and affluent visitors from other states and countries.

The DLF Group is a prime example of the kind of corporate interests involved in the transformation of peripheral farmlands into high-value commercial townships. Gurgaon remains one of the most significant areas of interest for DLF, who currently operates four major malls in the area, alongside a suite of other developments. Further, DLF is the parent of DT Cinemas, a wholly-owned subsidiary operating multiplexes in two of the huge DLF mall complexes in Gurgaon. One of these multiplexes is part of an integrated township called DLF City and a another is located in the heart of Gurgaon at DLF CityCentre mall. In 2007, DT Cinemas announced their intention to spend an additional 160 crore rupees to expand within the NCR by adding multiplexes in Shalimar Bagh, Saket, Vasant Kunj, Delhi and Gurgaon (*Business Standard* 2007). An additional 35–40 screens were to be built within a year to complement the new malls opening in those areas. DLF certainly has the capacity to become a much more significant player in the mall-multiplex market since its land reserves throughout India total 10,255 acres, including 5,269 acres in the Delhi-NCR (*Indian Express*, 2007). While Gurgaon is frequently associated with DLF, there are many other players investing in IT, ITES, residential and retail developments here. Both Ansal and Unitech, through companies incorporated offshore, have major office developments underway in collaboration with finance and construction companies like Infrastructure Leasing & Financial Services Ltd (IL&FS). Other major players that are active in Gurgaon include Tata, Parvsnath and Emaar-MGF (*Business World* 2007, *Financial Express*, 2007, The Press Trust of India 2007).

PVR, who has located their company headquarters at DLF Corporate Park in Gurgaon, operates two multiplexes here, at the Metropolitan Mall and at the Sahara Mall, with a third site due to open at Ambience Mall. The catchment for the four multiplexes operated jointly between PVR and DT in Gurgaon corresponds with the desired model in most respects with both a high-income population working and/or residing in the area (albeit alongside a large number of low-income labourers involved in the construction of the district) and upgraded transport links drawing patrons from outside the neighbourhood (albeit primarily by private vehicles, with only limited bus services and Metro connection still under construction). Gurgaon's status as an IT hub and as the City of Malls is a further indicator of its capacity to draw a high-value crowd with disposable income. Easy access to Delhi's airport is also a significant feature, suggesting a floating population of affluent long-distance visitors that augments the local population and visiting Delhi residents. Thus, there are three distinct groups of patrons served by this catchment. The division of the Gurgaon catchment between PVR and DT also suggests a relatively stable field of competition, with other multiplex operators unable to enter to date.

The New Okhla Industrial Development Area (NOIDA) has also become a significant area for IT and ITES, although on a lesser scale than Gurgaon. NOIDA is located to the east of the National Capital Territory, on the other side of the Yamuna, and lies within the state of Uttar Pradesh. The story of NOIDA is distinct from that of Gurgaon, with its development originating in the period of authoritarian socialism in the mid-1970s. The brainchild of Sanjay Gandhi, the area began to be transformed from peri-urban land to its current status in April 1976 as part of Emergency-era measures to reverse urbanisation in Delhi (Government of Uttar Pradesh 1976). NOIDA was conceived as an industrial development beyond the city limits with a resident labouring population, thus removing both polluting industries and a large volume of the labouring population from the capital (Potter and Sinha 1990). Following the end of the Emergency period, the development of NOIDA was stalled for several years as the master plan for the area was reformulated and delays were compounded by frequent shifts of the administrative responsibility for NOIDA at the district level within Uttar Pradesh. Perhaps reflecting the era of its origins, NOIDA has a markedly different layout from Gurgaon, with a regular grid structure and numerically-designated sectors. The population in NOIDA is now growing rapidly, although it has taken a long time to achieve momentum. This is partially because of a reluctance of industrial and commercial operations to relocate there during the 1980s and early 1990s and partially because of the success of Gurgaon from the mid-1990s onwards (Potter and Kumar 2004).

Despite competition from other areas in the NCR, NOIDA has prospered in the post-liberalisation era, particularly as the focus of development has shifted from industrialisation towards a New Economy agenda after the Gurgaon model. As such, the percentage of land use for manufacturing has decreased overall, whilst the presence of the services sector has increased (Ansari et al. 2000). NOIDA has attracted several hundred IT companies during the last decade, although they have tended to be smaller players than those found in Gurgaon. NOIDA has also benefited from the media boom brought on by the deregulation of broadcast television during the 1990s. NOIDA is now the site of Film City, which serves as the hub for many of the television stations serving the Delhi-NCR as well as all-India broadcasters and the Asian Academy of Film and Television. NOIDA has also attracted an array of tertiary- and secondary-level education institutions and numerous private hospitals. With the shift towards services activity and office work, NOIDA is now modelling itself as a best practice urban area, with a pro-active development agency that privileges high environmental standards and non-polluting commercial development. However, this transformation has not been without further controversies (particularly relating to land deals) (*The Times of India* 1998).

NOIDA is known for the Sector 18 market and its Centerstage Mall, where the Chadha Group operates the most significant of its three Wave Cinemas multiplexes. One of the most profitable multiplexes in the NCR, Wave Cinemas at Centrestage is often the location for Bollywood premieres and appearances by Bollywood stars, bringing glamour to the area. Parveen Kumar, Operations Manager at the site, emphasises the rapid transformation of NOIDA in recent years:

> The whole of NOIDA was just barren land . . . [now] the place is very big . . . We have residential areas here, plenty of them, because we don't have land space in Delhi, and the way that the NOIDA authority is helping the normal

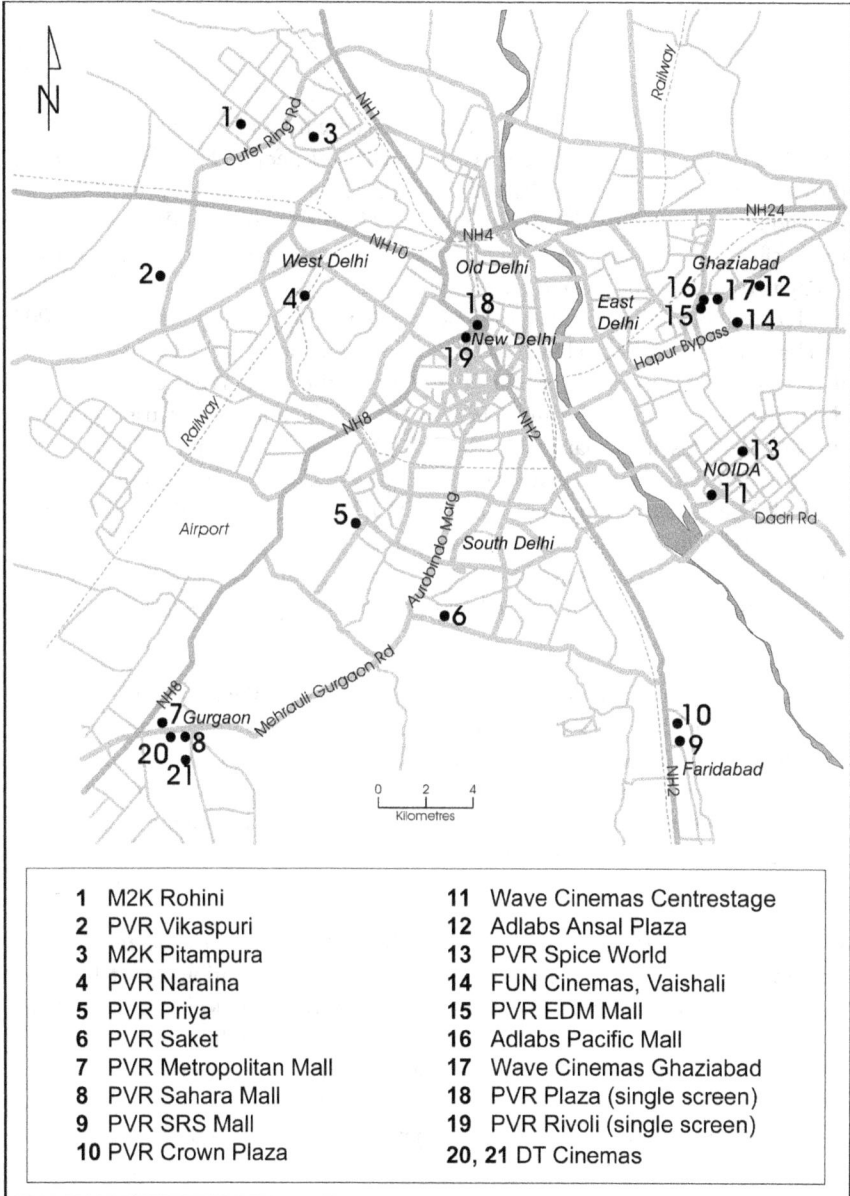

Map 5.1 Distribution of Multiplexes in Delhi-NCR, March 2007. (Tracy Connolly and Adrian Athique)

person to get a better class of services. Later it will be transport. We are getting Metro here, we are getting monorail here and buses services is increased now. Even electricity and liquid water, everything. Everything we are getting it world class.

(interview 09/03/2007)

Noida also contains India's second-largest capacity multiplex in the Spice Mall, a PVR site which boasts eight screens and seats 1,821 people. For Wave and PVR, the catchment in NOIDA is substantial, with the local population approaching half a million. However, NOIDA is certainly not all New Economy, and this makes it far less exclusive than Gurgaon. As a city that attracts a great many migrant workers from surrounding rural areas (as well as from Bihar and Bangladesh), much of NOIDA's population is far from the SEC A+ demographic (Potter and Sinha 2004: 2). High property prices in Delhi have also directed a large number of working families, as well a significant segment of retirees, to the area. What offsets the local demographic profile for the multiplex operators is the quality of transport connections to Delhi itself. In particular, the NOIDA Toll Bridge and the Ghaziabad-NOIDA-Faridabad Expressway provide easy access to South and East Delhi. In some respects, this is a mixed blessing for NOIDA. It alleviates the need for businesses to relocate to the area and as much as 50 per cent of NOIDA residents still commute to Delhi for work. For the consumption economy, however, the ease of access from Delhi guarantees a steady influx of visiting patrons from the city. As Parveen Kumar explains,

> Sixty percent of my clientele live in South Delhi . . . We have got a toll bridge and I think that gives a lot of boost to our place because they can move from their home and they can catch flyover and they can be here within twenty or twenty-five minutes. And if you say twenty-five minutes in contrast to Delhi time, travel time or commuting time is very less compared to the average commuting time of a person in Delhi. It's a happening place now.

(Interview 09/03/2007)

Given the population pressures in the NCR, NOIDA remains poised for future growth, and ironically the reduction of its original population target has been accompanied by rapid population growth. The development of a further satellite city, Greater NOIDA, to the southwest is further increasing the conurbation of this area. With the proposed second airport for the NCR (Taj International) and a substantial railway station planned for Greater NOIDA, the Delhi-NOIDA-Greater NOIDA trajectory is being remade as a significant transport hub, further increasing the desirability of residential developments along this route. Nonetheless, the wealth of the local population will take a long time to match that of South Delhi, which means that the visiting clientele will remain a mainstay of the local multiplexes for the foreseeable future:

> Bear in mind that Delhi people are more expending, [those] people are spending in nature. their culture is that if you have the money, then it is for

enjoyment. The same thing hasn't happened in UP. We are getting executives, we have got new companies, we have got the executives whose purchasing power is high, but still they are new and they don't want to expend it. Their primary concern is to build a house of their own, car of their own. Later on they will think about amusement and entertainments. It's a secondary thing. The type of population is different in Delhi . . . it's the new people [who] are coming in NOIDA, who will want to do something with their lives, who want to excel. They are hard working and they want to do well. This is a new place. So once they fill up the place with [people] who are established well in their own terms, they will be people like that.

(Parveen Kumar, interview 09/03/2007).

NOIDA's status as a planned township housing a more socio-economically diverse population gives rise to a qualitatively different catchment from that found in the more exclusive enclave of Gurgaon. However, attracting wealth from Delhi itself remains a primary concern for commercial concerns in both of these satellites. This is even more the case for the two other satellites in the NCR where the multiplexes have appeared: Ghaziabad and Faridabad.

Ghaziabad was a sub-district of Meerut in Uttar Pradesh until it became a district in its own right in 1976. Ghaziabad lies east of the Hindon River, which flows north to south about ten kilometres east of the Yamuna. It is a major rail junction for north India, with large railway workshops, other industries (e.g. steel and pharmaceuticals) and a major gateway from the capital into the large state of Uttar Pradesh. Despite its incongruity with the target demographic for multiplexes, Ghaziabad is home to more multiplexes than Gurgaon and NOIDA combined, hosting 12 sites in 2007. It is abundantly clear, however, that the catchment for these facilities is not Ghaziabad but rather the capital itself since they have been constructed in a concentrated area around Kaushambi and Vaishali, neighbourhoods that lie immediately east of the National Capital Territory and Uttar Pradesh border. This places them west of the Hindon and about eight kilometres from Ghaziabad proper, immediately adjacent to East Delhi. Lying immediately south of the Sahibabad Industrial Area, Kaushambi and Vaishali are both marked out for new residential developments.

Again, the rationale for building here appears to have arisen from favourable access to land and the upgrading of the NCR's transport infrastructure. Patrons from New Delhi and South Delhi can reach the multiplexes and malls here on one of two major roads (the NH24 bypass or Vikas Marg). In the near future, Ghaziabad will further benefit from the expanded Eastern and Western Peripheral Expressways and the Delhi–NOIDA link section of Delhi Metro. The concentration of multiplexes here began with the building of Wave Cinemas in 2003. Along with the opening of nearby Ansal Mall, this led to a transformation of the area, as Tapu Boram, a shift manager at Wave Cinemas, Ghaziabad explains:

Before it was like a dump. That was all you could see for a large distance. Even the mad dogs used to come to this place, because Ghaziabad was not a very safe kind of place because of criminals and activities that were going on. People over there were a bit sort of badly educated you could say, because they are not from the urban areas, instead from the rural areas of India. That's why the people didn't have the guts to open something like this here. Now it is completely changing, with the people and all the apartments coming up . . . and you can see Ansal here and after going into Vaishali all the modern apartments are coming up . . . Now the mindset of the people is changing. We are getting decent crowd here . . . People are now coming from Saket, from 28km south of here.

(interview 06/03/2007)

The capacity of Wave Cinemas and the Ansal Plaza Mall to attract large crowds from the capital led to a rush of developments in the area, culminating in the expansive Pacific Mall housing and Adlabs multiplex. Unlike Gurgaon and NOIDA, where just two operators in each case are running sites, the large number of facilities in Ghaziabad are operated by many different companies (with the exception of Adlabs, which runs two sites). Although both Adlabs and PVR are present, the majority of sites there are run by smaller operators. Given the initial impetus provided by Wave Cinemas, it is clear that more regionally-specific capital is a prominent feature of the multiplex landscape in Ghaziabad. However, having such a large number of players in a small area has inevitably created intense competition, which appears to have quickly saturated the market and driven down occupancies and ticket prices. Despite the numerous residential developments under construction in the area, and its contiguity with East Delhi and NOIDA, it seems highly unlikely that this catchment can support so many operations for long. Boram at Wave recognises this problem:

Now we are surrounded by mushrooming of multiplexes . . . 7200 people can sit together to watch a movie at a single time, so how many multiplex can we be surrounded with? . . . Before it was 2400 only. So it has been impacting on how we are getting the crowd.

(interview 06/03/2007)

Faridabad, the remaining satellite in the NCR, lies south of the capital territory in the state of Haryana. The conurbation of Old Faridabad was extended in the post-independence period to house refugees from Pakistan. It has since developed into Haryana's major industrial centre. Faridabad is spread out some considerable distance southwards, running between the parallel courses of the central railway, Mathura Road (NH2) and the Agra Canal. Faridabad now has a population of over one million, with a number of new residential districts under development. Despite its industrial focus, a large number of malls are now under construction in this area. PVR has two multiplexes operating in the Crown Plaza mall and at SRS Mall, which is part of SRS World, a combined leisure park development in Sector 12. Despite the current spate of redevelopments, Faridabad retains an industrial outlook and is a greater distance to travel from Delhi than NOIDA or Ghaziabad. This suggests that the local population represents much of the available catchment (at least until the Metro connection is completed).

If we assess the distribution of multiplexes across the NCR, it is apparent that the favourable conditions created by state policies in the satellite townships has given rise to a situation where Delhi's multiplexes have strong incentives to be located outside of the city limits, whilst at the same time taking advantage of upgraded transport infrastructure to draw customers from within the city. The major exceptions to this are the six retrofitted sites run by PVR, in Delhi itself, which draw audiences from their immediate vicinity. Given the difficulty competitors have in entering these established districts, the original PVR sites in affluent South Delhi (Saket and Priya) remain highly profitable, with their renovation of famous cinema halls in Connaught Place (Rivoli and Plaza) staking their claim to the city's old commercial heart. Other PVR sites in West Delhi (Vikaspuri and Naraina) appear to have fared less well, whilst nonetheless remaining viable propositions due to the greater distance of West Delhi from the various satellite developments. The dominance of PVR across the city, and its reputation as the first mover, has allowed them to establish a good spread of catchments that exploit the entire multiplex market. By comparison, other operators remain confined to the NCR satellites, where they compete with PVR for market share.

The present geography of the multiplex in the NCR clearly provides support for the close relationship between multiplex cinemas and suburbanisation experienced in other countries, and for the importance of transport infrastructure in determining the viability of multiplex catchments. With the largest number of multiplexes for any city in India, it is apparent that the market is now highly competitive, and there are questions about saturation in some areas due to the clustering of sites. Nonetheless, current rates of growth in the NCR remain high, which suggests that underutilised sites may improve their performance provided that further developments do not expand too rapidly and outstrip demand. Perhaps the most important observation to be made here overall is that the massive developments on the city periphery, of which the multiplexes are part, have turned Delhi's geography of leisure quite literally inside out over the past decade.

Bangalore

The city of Bangalore, in the southern state of Karnataka, has become synonymous not only with India's economic boom over the past decade, but also with the rise of the global network of IT hubs that underpin Castells's (1996) formulation of a global network society. In recent years Bangalore has also become closely associated with anxieties about losses in services jobs in the West, due to the impact of the widespread outsourcing of IT, BPO and call centre work to the city by multinational businesses. Originating in the sixteenth century, the city of Bangalore came under British control after the Mysore wars of the eighteenth century. For the remainder of the British period, it was divided between a native city administered by the Princely state of Mysore and a cantonment under British control, which saw a large influx of population from the neighbouring Madras Presidency (that today makes up the states of Tamil Nadu and Andhra Pradesh). After independence, Bangalore became the capital of the state of Karnataka. This encouraged an influx of population from across Karnataka, with the city reaching a population of 1.2 million by the early 1960s. Despite being a long way behind the metropolises of Calcutta, Bombay and Madras (as they were then known), this made Bangalore India's sixth largest city.

With a healthy industrial sector developing in the city, decisions were taken during the Nehruvian era by the central government to locate major public sector telecommunications and aeronautics research infrastructure in the city (Stremlau 1996: 50). This transformed Bangalore into South India's major technology hub, supported by a range of strong, English-medium technical institutions producing a large pool of skilled engineers. With the added incentive of cheap real estate and an agreeable climate, Bangalore underwent another major transition from the late 1980s onwards to become the centre of India's IT industry (Heitzman 1999: PE-7). Bangalore's contemporary status as the 'Silicon Valley' of India took its impetus not only from the presence of government and high-technology infrastructure and quality education institutions, but also from the entry of Texas Instruments in 1985. The close connection subsequently fostered between multinational technology companies and the Karnataka state government became the major driver of economic growth in the city, and indeed the entire state. The new era of the outsourcing economy that would transform the city landscape was heralded by the establishment of Software Technology Parks of India (STPI) in 1991, including the country's first satellite earth station (undeniably an important factor in enabling its transition to an offshore and call-centre powerhouse). The announcement of a new IT-focused economic policy in 1997 by the Karnataka government was aimed at further accelerating the growth of the industry. Bangalore is known internationally for being the headquarters of Wipro and Infosys, two of India's largest software companies and both major international players. Public sector involvement also remains significant with Karnataka State Electronics Development Corporation Limited (Keonics) playing a major role. In recent years, the arrival of biotechnology industries has further augmented the suite of hi-tech operations that now largely determine the economic life of the city.

The favouring of a campus model amongst the various technology developments over a long period has had the effect of separating the new Bangalore from the old to a significant extent. This is reflected spatially in the extensive redevelopment of the old cantonment and the southern suburbs of the city, seemingly at the expense of the old native town and the central district. Population growth has been as rapid as the advance of the technology industry. The population rose to three million by the 1980s and is now estimated at six million. However, it remains the case that the specialised skills sets required by these industries have restricted the capacity of the overall population to take part in the information economy. Therefore, the technology sector constitutes no more than eight per cent of Bangalore's total workforce, with some putting it as less than four per cent (Benjamin 2005: 9). Indeed, according to NSS statistics: 'In 1991 . . . the difference between the lowest 20 per cent and highest 20 per cent in Bangalore was 1:5. By 2001, this had increased to

1:50 . . . .[I]f we include a much wider definition of societal groups, such differentials may be significantly higher' (ibid.: 6). The disparity in incomes between those employed in new industries and those who are not, along with such rapid population growth, has put considerable strain upon communal and class relations in Bangalore, despite (or perhaps because of) its long-standing reputation as South India's most cosmopolitan city (Chakravartty 2008, Rao 2007, Srinivasaraju 2007). Thus, there is a strong counter-discourse in Bangalore that positions the city as one that has fallen into moral turpitude compared to the idealised past when it was a 'pensioners' paradise' (Suchitra and Nandakumar 2008).

Similarly, the rapid expansion of the technology sector has put considerable strain upon the infrastructure of the city in terms of power consumption, transport infrastructure and sewerage. Given their economic dominance, there can be little dispute that the needs of the technology companies have had a disproportionately large influence on the re-shaping of the built environment over the past two decades. With a great deal of resources being devoted to satisfying their needs, and their localisation in particular clusters within the city, Bangalore today appears to display all the characteristics of a two-speed city. This pattern of urban renewal was formalised with the introduction of a new governance model under Chief Minister S. M. Krishna, who set up the Bangalore Agenda Task Force in close collaboration with Infosys and Temasek Holdings (a Singapore government concern). The IT corridor and international airport redevelopment were facilitated via the single window clearance scheme of the Karnataka Industrial Area Development Board (KIADB). These programmes were made possible because after 1999 the state government acquired vast amounts of land at negligible prices and built complementary infrastructure (Benjamin 2005: 7).

Given its reputation over the past decade as a prime example of a modern hi-tech Indian city, and the conscious targeting of the IT/ITES workforce by multiplex operators, it is relatively surprising that Bangalore currently has just three multiplexes in operation. This places Bangalore well behind both Delhi and Mumbai. This is mitigated to a certain extent by the scale of Bangalore multiplexes, with PVR's 11-screen facility at Forum Mall in Koremangala being the largest multiplex presently in operation in India. INOX also operates a site within the Garuda Mall on McGrath Road and Innovative, a local player, operates a large complex on the city's outskirts. The locations of these three sites all have a distinctive character: Innovative is located beyond the city outskirts; PVR Forum Mall occupies prime real estate in the city's southern suburbs; and INOX at Garuda Mall is in the heart of the city's major commercial district. If we relate these locations to Rolee Aranya's (2003) mapping of the concentration of the information economy in Bangalore, we see that PVR Forum Mall is located in the heart of the most concentrated area of activity, whilst INOX's more central location at Garuda Mall is surrounded by the next highest level of concentration. The proximity of PVR to major institutions of tertiary education in southern Bangalore is also a major contributor to its catchment. In terms of transport infrastructure, the location of INOX on McGrath Road places it at the intersection of major roads from all directions. PVR is located on the NH7 that runs north-west to south-east and bifurcates the concentration of IT operations in Jayanagar (west) and Koremangala (east) respectively. Gagan Bindra, Corporate Relations Manager at PVR Forum Mall, describes the attractiveness of Koremangala as a high-value catchment:

> When this mall has started, the centre of Bangalore area was called Brigade Road, which mostly did not have the kind of place to provide for such a mall . . . Koremangala was then a developing and very upcoming colony, which probably brought about the development of land over here . . . Koremangala now is pretty much the central bank of the city as it has expanded. It's really spread out. So it is a very ideal location . . . it is a perfect blend of offices and residential areas. So you anyway have a good captive audience. Cinema is a locational business ultimately. For convenience, this mix is perfect . . . Normally, you're either in a commercial hub or you're in a residential hub. This is a perfect blend.
>
> (interview 14/02/2007)

The decision of INOX to choose the alternative location in the middle of the McGrath Road-Brigade Road-Residency Road area is a reflection of their overall strategy of developing a downtown presence (as they have also done in Mumbai and Kolkata) which sets them apart from the other brands. In this case, the decision of the Bangalore Metropolitan Corporation to lease land for a combined car park and mall on McGrath Road provided access to an area where real estate was costly and difficult to acquire. Leasing space in the Garuda Mall enabled INOX to make a conspicuous entry to the market in Bangalore. General Manager Mohit Bhargava explains the value of the INOX catchment:

> This is the heart of the business district. So there are a whole lot of people who come to work here. There are a whole lot of colleges. They form a very big audience. Offices form a very big audience. And even where residents are concerned, within a five kilometre radius . . . there are a whole lot of very upmarket residential areas. So we do look at a five kilometre radius as a catchment and fortunately for this particular location, it fulfils those needs whether it's for students, whether its for office-goers, whether it's for residents . . . We are part of the CBD of the city. See Bangalore doesn't offer much in terms of entertainment and sightseeing, so anybody who comes to Bangalore from anywhere has to come to this area. So that is also part of the importance of this area, because this is where the most glamorous shopping lies. This is also where most of the pubs are located. Most of the better-known pubs. Bangalore is very well-known for its pubs. It has the best pubs for any city in this country. So we are right in the heart of the happening area.
>
> (interview 06/02/2007)

With just two multiplexes operating within the city limits, competition within their respective catchments is non-existent. However, they are in competition with each other due to the comparative ease of movement within Bangalore. Despite the

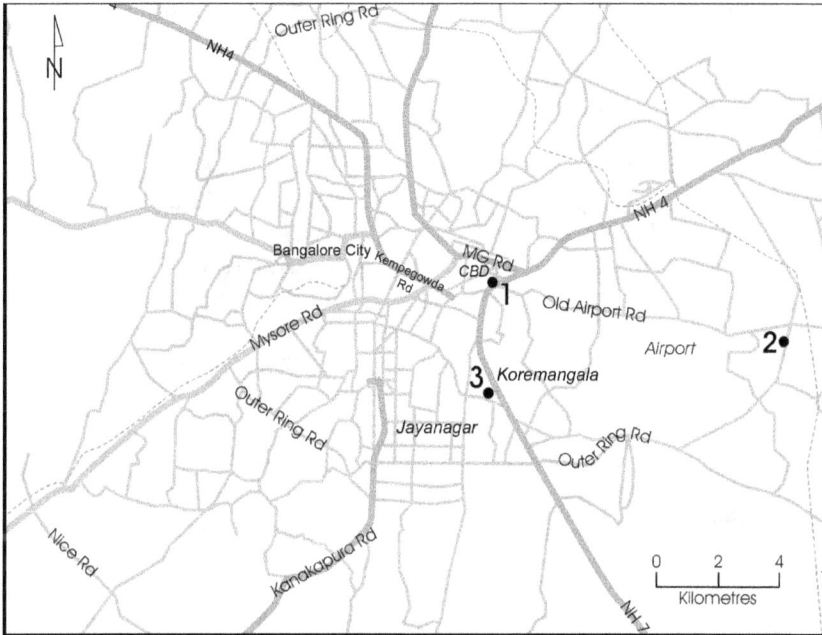

Map 5.2 Distribution of Multiplexes in Bangalore, February 2007 (1: INOX Garuda Mall; 2: PVR Forum Mall; 3: Innovative). (Tracy Connolly)

Figure 5.1 Satellite View of the Forum Mall, Bangalore. (Google Earth)

growing (and justified) complaints about serious traffic congestion in the city, Bangalore remains a much smaller city to traverse than the big metros. However, the extent of the future expansion of the city and current rates of growth in both population and car ownership suggest that this may change in coming years.

As noted previously, the recent developments in the southern districts and around Brigade Road have steadily shifted the focus of the city. Accordingly, the older neighbourhoods previously associated with cinemas (along Kempegowda Road and in the City Market Area) bear little resemblance to the locations occupied by the multiplex. Prior to the arrival of the multiplexes, Bangalore was a city served by a large number of cinemas, both in these two areas and spread around residential suburbs. A large number of these cinemas were constructed during the 1970s to serve the city's rapidly expanding population. Another reason for the profusion of cinemas in Bangalore was the diversity of the population, with significant Kannada-, Tamil- and Telugu-speaking populations all served by different film industries. However, this expansion of the theatrical market was followed in the 1980s by saturation in the most favoured areas, and a long-term stagnation in ticket prices has seen many single-screen theatres becoming derelict and closing down. Thus, Bangalore was seeing a reduction in overall screen capacity at the time the multiplex operators entered. By contrast, the growing wealth of the specific population segment targeted by the multiplexes has meant that their audience has increased rapidly, marking out a sharp difference in the fortunes of the two theatrical infrastructures. For Gagan Bindra, this is an underscreened market:

> In Bangalore, as of today, there is a lot of market. People come here and ask why we don't have 22 screens instead of 11. So given today's situation, I don't think distance is an issue even if you are going across the road a little bit. Three, five, ten years down the road, of course it will make a difference whether it is the same location or multiple locations. Because right now you have the entire Bangalore community, but other plexes will open. We are expanding and everybody else is expanding and obviously the catchment gets divided. As of today I don't think there is a limitation.
>
> (interview 14/02/2007)

The potential of a larger market for multiplexes is clear. It will doubtless be linked to the continuation of the campus redevelopments that have been the mainstay of urban transformation in Bangalore. For the multiplexes, the fact that the market remains open to new entrants is encouraging all the major chains to develop further sites here. The rocketing real estate market, and the requirement of mall and multiplex developers for sizeable lots, has seen both PVR and INOX recently acquiring some older cinemas in the southern suburbs for demolition and/or refurbishment. Two examples of this, the Nanda and Swagath halls, both in Jayanagar, are currently being redeveloped by INOX and PVR respectively into three- and four-screen sites. PVR is also planning another large 11-screen multiplex along the lines of their existing facility to be sited in a major township development scheduled for Mallesvaram, north-west of Bangalore, to be built by Brigade Group.

Compared to the Delhi-NCR, and in the absence of major satellite towns encouraged by competition between adjoining states, a different pattern has emerged in the development of multiplexes in Bangalore. However, despite being the Karnataka state capital, development in Bangalore has still remained subject to problems arising from competing jurisdictions between different state bodies (Aranya 2003: 11). Being a much smaller city, and notwithstanding the impact of the technology sector, there is also less wealth in Bangalore overall. This has encouraged a much more selective deployment of multiplexes sites focusing solely on the enclaves of New Economy activity fostered by the implementation of the Bangalore IT corridor. This trajectory between CBD, New Economy enclaves and airport links is a more limited range of catchments than is found in Delhi, and it is one that also has some resonance for the multiplexes in eastern India's major city, to which we now turn our attention.

Kolkata

The four multiplexes that were operating in Kolkata during 2007 were located in areas that closely correspond to the catchment model followed elsewhere in terms of their proximity to relatively high-income segments of the population and connectivity with major transport infrastructure. The pattern of multiplex developments in Kolkata are similar to the Delhi-NCR in the sense that they target what are known to be areas of established wealth that pre-date post-liberalisation redevelopment, as well as New Economy developments. The geography of these locations, however, is more resonant with Bangalore, with a strikingly similar trajectory of airport to CBD. INOX currently operates two sites in Kolkata and Shringar Cinemas is present with one of their Fame multiplexes. At the time of fieldwork, there was also a regional player, 89 Cinemas, that has subsequently been acquired by INOX, giving that company a dominant position in the market for multiplexes in eastern India. South Kolkata and Salt Lake are the locations that have attracted multiplex operators in Kolkata. To understand why, it is useful to trace the development of the city, whose spatial layout has been shaped by physical geography and planned interventions, as well as by broader historical contingencies.

The initial morphology of Kolkata (then Calcutta) was established by Job Charnock, developed in its first phase by the East India Company and later developed by the colonial administration. As such, the city was spatially divided so that the areas in what is now the CBD were the colonial district where administration, security and housing were located, while the areas to the north and east were where many of the low-wage workers lived (Banerjee 2007:148, Chakravorty 2000, Hornsby 1997). Since there was initially little industry, most of the new migrants who moved to what became capital of British India until 1911 worked for colonial concerns. The economic base of Calcutta changed over time as Fort William became an important military base and industries such as jute and manufacturing became progressively more significant. While Calcutta established itself as a significant entrepot, the so-called 'white town' of the European residents was prioritised in terms of facilities, with the 'native town' largely ignored by colonial authorities

(Chakravorty 2000). These divisions were not absolute, however, with considerable cultural overlap and people moving between the two areas (Chattopadhyay 2005). As in other colonial centres, the neglect of native areas was somewhat mitigated in later years as health and sanitation concerns forced the colonial administration to consider taking measures to improve those neighbourhoods (Beattie 2004). Concerted efforts to improve the living conditions for residents began with the establishment of the Calcutta Improvement Trust in 1912, an institution that was to remain significant even after other bodies such as Calcutta Municipal Corporation (CMC), the Calcutta Urban Agglomeration (CUA) and Calcutta Metropolitan District Authority (CMDA) became established (Dasgupta 2007).

The political economy of Calcutta changed radically after the capital of British India, along with much of the colonial administration, was transferred to Delhi in 1911. The city nevertheless remained vital to the economic base of the British Empire, particularly in terms of the maritime trade that made Calcutta first amongst equals when compared to the other important port cities of Bombay and Madras (Hornsby, 1997, Kosambi and Brush 1988). This significance was expressed spatially in the extensive port and dock area around Garden Reach and Kidderpore in central Calcutta and close to what was to become BBD Marg (De 2005). The significance of this maritime trade and associated manufacturing also led to the influx of many non-Bengalis into the city, these immigrants adding to the heterogeneous mix of people in central Calcutta that for many Bengalis is most exemplified by the Marwari moneylenders and traders who have occupied an important economic presence in the city since at least the nineteenth century.

The partition of India that came with independence in 1947 fundamentally changed the nature of the city in profound ways. Calcutta's most important trans-port links, markets and sources of raw materials were all lost as East Bengal became East Pakistan. Partition also meant the influx of at least one million refugees, com-pounding overcrowded conditions in North and South Kolkata. Many of the bet-ter-off refugees settled in new suburbs in southern Calcutta such as New Alipore, Ballygunge and Jodhpur Park, forming *paras* that were contiguous with those of more established areas such as Bhowanipur, where Bengalis of similar class back-ground traditionally resided. Further urbanisation occurred in a haphazard fashion in the southern suburbs of Dhakuria, Jadavpur, Baghajatin and substantial parts of Tollygunge, with the expansion mostly clustered around the route of the rail lines (Dasgupta 2007: 321). In contrast to the mixture of old and new affluence of South Calcutta, the northern suburbs and Howrah on the western bank of the Hooghly were the most crowded and remain comparatively impoverished today.

In the early 1960s, Dr B. C. Roy, then Chief Minister of West Bengal, rejected suggestions to simply replicate the Delhi master plan that had been developed in 1956. Instead, the Calcutta Metropolitan Planning Organisation (CMPO) was cre-ated with assistance from the Ford Foundation. The resulting Basic Development Plan (1966–1986) prescribed an ambitious set of measures to be implemented over the next 20 years. Banerjee argues that the BDP 'was unprecedented in scope, not just for a developing country but for developed countries as well' (Banerjee 2005:156) The implementation of these plans was facilitated by the setting up in

1970 of the Calcutta Municipal Development Authority (CMDA, later the KMDA). While many of the planned measures have not been achieved, it is notable how many of them have been attempted with some success in the face of political and economic turbulence in the post-independence period.

Despite the intentions of transforming the city laid down in the BDP, broader forces have problematised this process enormously, with Calcutta becoming synonymous with economic decline and poverty. Many of the causes of this downward turn lie in the complex historical circumstances of the post-colonial period. A great deal of industry, managerial expertise and capital relocated to Delhi and Bombay in the aftermath of partition. The potential advantage of having a mineral-rich hinterland disappeared after freight equalisation in 1956. The India-wide recession in the late 1960s, following the Indo-Pakistan War and severe droughts (1965–1966 and 1966–1967), was particularly disastrous for the economic base of Calcutta (Bagchi 1998: 2975). At that time, much of Calcutta's industry consisted of engineering firms reliant on government contracts, and during this recession many of these contracts were scaled back or cancelled and never reinstated (Bagchi 1998: 2976). A tumultuous political period followed in the late 1960s and early 1970s, spurred on by increasing industrial disorder and, in turn, further crippling an economy that was by now characterised by ageing manufacturing with low productivity.

International events were also to add to the pressures on the city. The independence of neighbouring Bangladesh following the war of 1971 saw further influxes of refugees into Calcutta. Domestically, the populous but increasingly poor hinterland of eastern India (including Bihar, Orissa and the north-east states) has contributed great numbers of migrant labourers to Calcutta each year. The rise of the Communist Party of India (Marxist)-led Left Front government in West Bengal from 1977 has achieved much in alleviating distress in the rural areas of West Bengal (Hill 2001). However, their tenure hurt the reputation of Calcutta in the early years, as *hartals* and *bandhs* became frequent and industry resorted to lockouts and widespread capital flight (Mayers, 2001, McLean 2001). Accordingly, many commentators suggest that Calcutta remains one of the most problematic mega-urban areas in South Asia, with poverty, overcrowding and sanitation problems evident in the city's many *bastis* and with many thousands living on the streets every night.

Despite these socio-economic upheavals, the morphology of the city has continued in a significant sense to be conditioned by the physical geography of its setting, so that most of Calcutta remains closely confined to the eastern bank of the Hooghly and extends in a north–south direction (Dasgupta 2007: 319). However, the spatial dynamics of this conurbation were changing during this period, as the outer metropolitan areas grew much faster than the inner city (Dasgupta 2007: 315). Indeed, the development of BidhanNagar (Salt Lake) in the area known as Salt Lake Waters was the beginning of a significant reorientation of the city, with the draining of wetlands providing land for the new area that by 1990 had grown to have 175,000 residents. Most of this population is middle and upper middle class, a pattern belying the original intentions to have a mix of low- and middle-income communities. This growth of the outer metropolitan areas, that also eventually extended to Patuli-

Bhaisnabghata township in the south-east, is despite the fact that the drained wetland areas are a RAMSAR-declared site of international importance. There is arguably an element of hypocrisy about the Left Front's continuation of these outer metropolitan developments because the need to limit eastern expansion and conserve the wetlands has, rhetorically at least, been a constantly reiterated feature of state government policies (Dasgupta 2007).

The 1990s saw the Left Front government attempt to attract more private sector investment into West Bengal, and Calcutta in particular, with the setting up of the West Bengal Industrial Development Corporation in 1994. Despite a slew of memorandums of understanding (MoUs) signed during the initial period of the Left Front government's investor friendly volte-face, the reality has been very slow progress in attracting foreign or domestic investment, with the opening of the petrochemicals complex at the new port in Haldia being the only significant achievement (Hill 2008). Leftist organisations and trade unions with strong links to the Communist Party of India (Marxist) (CPI(M)) remain somewhat suspicious of the implications of the New Economic Policy (NEP) initiated after 1994. The coercive actions of the Calcutta Municipal Corporation and CPI(M) cadres during Operation Sunshine (1996–1997), followed by further slum clearances – often without adequate compensation – have only exacerbated the political difficulties for the CPI(M) (Roy 2003: 173). Attempts by the Left Front to reassure its constituency that it was true to its ideological roots was occurring even while the Left Front canvassed advice from international consultancy companies such as McKinsey about how the state could restructure its economy by expanding ITES and food processing.

It was arguably not until the retirement of Jyoti Basu from his post as India's longest serving Chief Minister and the installation of Buddhadeb Bhattacharya in 2000 that investor confidence in Kolkata (as it was by then renamed) began to increase. Bhattacharya has pursued an economic path directed towards liberalising the economy rather than mollifying the traditional constituencies of the CPI(M) (Basu 2007). As such, areas such as Salt Lake have continued to expand in recent years, with Sector V, devoted to IT and ITES, becoming an important contributor to the New Economy in West Bengal. Outer metropolitan growth in Kolkata has gained added impetus with the development of Rajarhat, located in the north-eastern part of the city between Salt Lake and Subhas Chandra Bose international airport. Rajarhat has quickly became one of the most expensive areas in India – the Kolkata equivalent of Koremangala and Gurgaon – and the New Economy is continuing to expand rapidly on land acquired by the state-run Housing Infrastructure Development Corporation (HIDCO) at prices that some suggest are vastly below market rates (*Times of India*, 2007).

While Kolkata has received substantial private sector investment since 2000, the majority of this has been domestic investment (in stark contrast to metros such as Bangalore). Shaw and Satish (2007) argue that the reluctance of international investors is now diminishing as the establishment of an IT Ministry (2000), an ITES policy (2002) and surplus electricity generation have added to investor confidence (Shaw and Satish 2007). As with other major cities, Kolkata has seen substantial growth in its real estate sector. Rajarhat and Salt Lake have been the most visible indicators of this latter trend and the main growth areas for the future are projected to be Prince Anwar Shah Road, Rajarhat and along and beyond the Rashbehari Connector of the Eastern Metropolitan Bypass (Mukherjee 2008). The older south Kolkata neighbourhoods have also benefited, with Park Street, Alipore and Ballygunge all appreciating substantially, although the potential for new developments in the city proper has been constrained by the government's refusal to repeal the Urban Land Ceiling Regulation Act (ULCRA).

Arguably, it is for this reason that three of the four multiplexes in Kolkata (INOX Salt Lake, Fame Hiland Park and 89 Cinemas) are all located in the outer metropolitan areas associated with new development programmes. Thus, Fame Highland Park, a four-screen multiplex located within the Metropolis Mall, is adjacent to the Bengal Ambuja Metropolitan Development Authority's newly-established residential quarters of Hiland Park and Udoyan. These two complexes contain buildings between 18 and 28 storeys, which were considered somewhat trail-blazing at the time of construction in what is historically a fairly low-rise city. Fame Hiland Park's location on the EM Bypass also makes it easily accessible for those coming to the area by car, buses and auto-rickshaws. The INOX at City Centre, Salt Lake (discussed in greater detail in Chapter 6) is located right in the middle of the upmarket satellite township of Salt Lake. It is predominantly aimed at the resident population, but it also caters to those living and working in upcoming peripheral developments nearby, such as Rajarhat and Patuli-Bhaisnabghata, who can access the area easily following the construction of major bypasses. This INOX site is a central component of the extensive CityCentre Mall in Salt Lake, built by Bengal Ambuja Metropolitan Development Authority (a joint venture between the KMDA and Gujarat Ambuja Cements).

89 Cinemas, a four-screen multiplex with a total seating capacity of 1,024, is located on the Eastern Metropolitan bypass (opposite Salt Lake Stadium) and adjacent to Swabhumi, a renowned Heritage Plaza with which its operators hoped the cinema would form a complementary audience. Established in 2004, 89 Cinemas is somewhat less opulent than the INOX or Fame facilities and screens a greater number of popular Bengali films (perhaps indicating a different clientele). Prior to the recent takeover by INOX, this multiplex was owned by Calcutta Cine Pvt. Ltd, a joint venture between the Bengal Ambuja Group and Consolidated Entertainment Pvt. Ltd (CEPL). The building was planned by Delhi-based architects Morphogenesis and the interiors were completed by Era architects, a Mumbai-based firm. INOX Forum, the only multiplex in the centre of the city, is situated on the top floor of the Forum Mall on Elgin Road, located within Bhowanipore, which is the oldest locality in South Kolkata. Along with Ballygunge, Bhowanipore is arguably the most prestigious of Kolkata's older suburbs. As such, the intended catchment for INOX Forum is clearly the established elite of South Kolkata. This core constituency is augmented by commuting traffic from main arterial roads, such as A.J.C. Bose Road.

As with Bangalore and Delhi-NCR, the confluence of multiplex developments with the highly selective geography of contemporary urban renewal is highly apparent in the case of Kolkata. Furthermore, the significance of the state role in

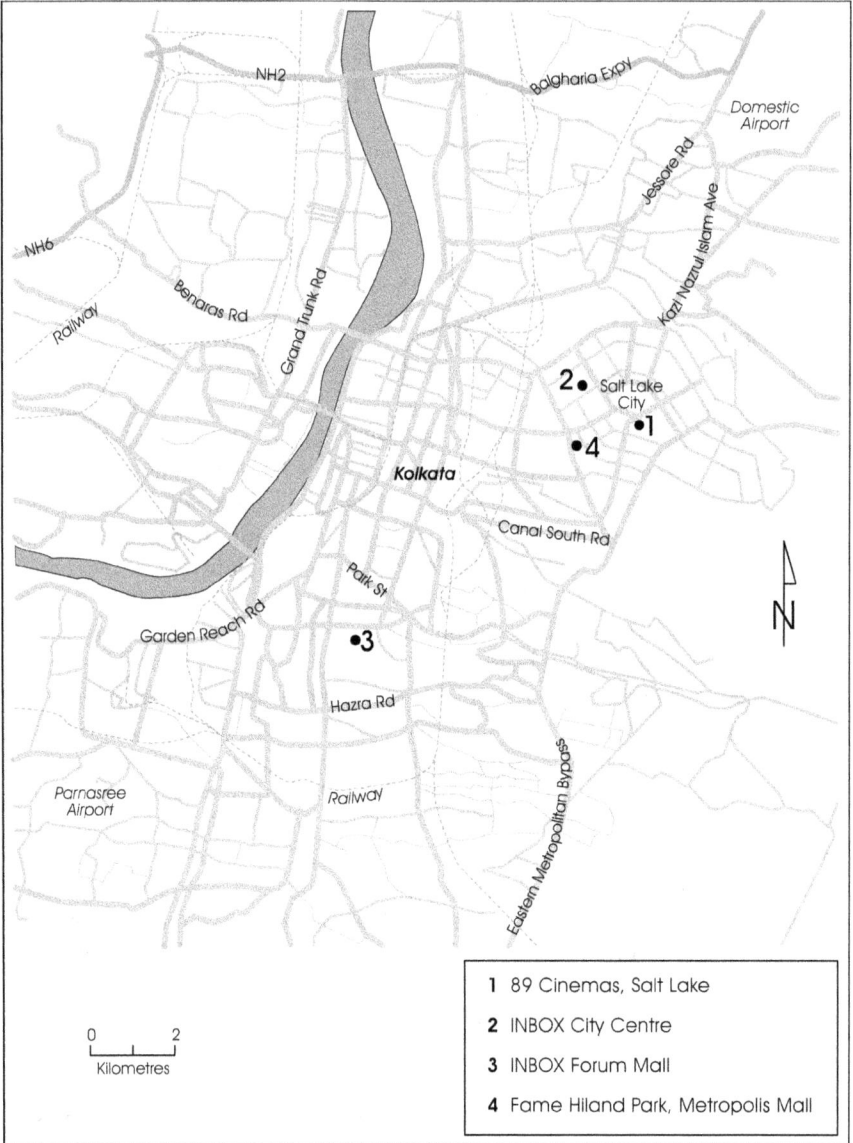

Map 5.3 Distribution of Multiplexes in Kolkata, January 2007. (Tracy Connolly)

facilitating the development of multiplexes can be noted in all of these cases, despite the markedly different political climate of these cities. In Kolkata, this is evident in the extent to which the majority of large-scale real estate developments were located under the auspices of the Calcutta Metropolitan Group Limited (a 50/50 joint venture between the United Credit Belani Group (UCBG) and the Kolkata Metropolitan Development Authority (KMDA)), along with a selection of private sector companies, including Hiland, Southside and Ambuja. Whatever the stated intentions of the West Bengal government, there is no doubt there has been a pronounced bias towards the wealthier districts in terms of infrastructure provision and towards the interests of the upper middle classes in terms of the kinds of leisure, retail and residential developments being pursued. This preference is expressed differently between Kolkata (under the aegis of the KMDA), Bangalore (Bangalore Task Force Agency (BTFA) prior to 2004) and the NCR (various agencies), so it is clear that state-level politics and local public culture mediate how this agenda is expressed in different places. Nonetheless, it is the same agenda.

Multiplexes in urban space

We began the chapter by noting that multiplex operators assert a strong relationship between multiplex patrons and consumers of other artefacts of the New Economy in the retail, residential and leisure sectors. We have subsequently illustrated where the infrastructures serving these activities are currently located, and the spatial relationship between these developments and the multiplexes in our three case studies of Delhi-NCR, Bangalore and Kolkata. Our analysis suggests a measure of consistency in the identification of suitable sites for multiplexes within significant and highly localised patterns of urban geography emerging from processes that we have situated in the contemporary era as well as within a longer historical trajectory. Further, in spatialising our interpretation of Dhingra's elaboration of the catchment of a multiplex, our discussion inevitably gravitates towards a wider assessment of the dispersal of old and New Economy wealth in urban India.

Within these contours, INOX has followed a distinct strategy by developing a small number of highly visible sites in central downtown districts (such as Nariman Point in Mumbai). The strategy of the industry overall, however, has been to develop sites either close to existing wealthy suburbs (such as Elgin Road in Kolkata), in up-and-coming areas associated with the New Economy (such as Koremangala in Bangalore), in areas where re-zoning has made land very cheap and is attracting residential developers (such as Ghaziabad near Delhi) or along the arterial routes and flyovers that now connect central commercial districts with these middle-class suburban enclaves (such as Andheri in Mumbai). As land becomes available at the urban fringes and a credit boom provides funds for property purchase and the growth of car ownership, the simultaneous improvement of roads is enabling the younger generation of the middle class to finally vacate the crowded conditions of the inner cities. As such, a multiplex invariably comes with a substantial provision of (fee-paying) parking.

While India's older cinema halls are typically located in places where large crowds are formed (such as city markets) and areas around public transport hubs (such as railway stations and bus depots), access to multiplexes is a matter of private transport. In a certain sense, the case of the multiplex is resonant with the paradox of private transport in that it is also a technology of personal consumption that requires support from large-scale public investment in infrastructure. The urban geography of the multiplex is also illustrative of the interests of the capital flowing into India's cities in the current era and how it is re-shaping the built environment and facilitating the emergence of new urban forms. These are not merely commercial interests at work, but also state interests. The doctrine of what Leela Fernandes calls 'urban developmentalism' as articulated by the relevant authorities in all the cases considered here inherently favours wealthier, more mobile sections of the population occupying new or gentrified suburbs (Fernandes 2006: 151). In this sense, the leisurely practice of visiting the multiplex cannot be easily separated from the priorities of state governments, municipal authorities, private sector developers and wealthier citizens. The multiplex is not the purpose of such programmes, but it is hard to see how these facilities could flourish without the wider agenda that is re-shaping urban India.

Invariably, then, the blossoming of multiplexes and other artefacts of the New Economy in particular parts of the city (and not others) serves the interests of particular groups of people. This raises a myriad of questions about India's urban future, but we will restrict our final comments here to one particular question, which is whether the doctrine of selective development, and the urban ecology of enclaves that it inevitably engenders, provides a sustainable basis for the new leisure infrastructure. The size of these enclaves, both in absolute terms and relative to the city overall, become important here. This is not least because it is notable how few suitable catchments have been located and exploited to date in the cites that we have examined. Half a dozen catchments in a city of, say, 12 million people is a very small number by any standard. Broadly, this indicates that the New Economy remains very small in proportional terms, but for the multiplex chains more specifically, it raises serious problems of overcompetition in desirable catchments. Thus, while the initial wave of multiplex construction in Kolkata and Bangalore is clearly viable, the example of Delhi-NCR suggests that the possibility of market saturation is ever present. As Shriram Krishnan at Shringar notes:

> I think if these pockets were spread right across the city, I think probably everybody is doing well, but if we are all within the same radius, with short travelling time, I think there are pockets, Gurgaon is one that is going to be an issue, Indore is already an issue, I think that Ghaziabad is another problem area. You see so much multiplex in that place . . . In Ahmedabad, there is three in a row.
> (interview 20/01/2007)

There is clearly a tension between the kind of clustering seen in Ghaziabad and the catchment model that multiplex operators work from. In part, these situations arise from the inadequate consideration of planning applications for copycat developments. However, they may perhaps also indicate a collision between the long-standing spatial practices of Asian cities, where activities and occupations are associated with particular districts, and the suburban monopolies for which many of the new architectures of consumption were designed. Mall Road in Gurgaon is a good example of this since the rationale of the suburban mall is to capture a local population, not to stand shoulder-to-shoulder with dozens of other malls. Exactly the same thing is true of the multiplex, and the major chains take some care not to co-locate sites. As Alok Tandon puts it:

> One has to be careful not to have all the multiplexes on one stretch . . . of road or one area, or one locality of a city. It should not happen that in a radius of five hundred metres, we have three multiplexes, because that will not serve the purpose. We will be eating into each others pie. The pie is big enough in India for everybody to survive, for all the multiplex operators to survive . . . One suburb, if you have three or four multiplexes, there's no point of having that, because the software is the same. Software is the same. The only different shaping factor over there is your service, how good is the mall where you are and, number three, the parking facility. That is the main thing.
>
> (04/01/2007)

In a time of exuberance, however, it is difficult for the multiplex chains to prevent other entrants to the market. As such, they are inclined to play a longer game by anticipating future growth in new areas rather than rushing into catchments that are already crowded. As competition increases, multiplex operators focus even more on the visual impact and aesthetic environment of their facilities, seeking to differentiate themselves from their competitors on this basis. In Chapter 6, therefore, we examine the built environment of multiplexes as a distinctive urban form, taking note of how these new chrome and glass architectures impact upon the urban skyline as well as the leisure experience of their patrons.

6 Spatial politics of the multiplex

An environmental model

Chapter 5 discussed environmental aspects of the multiplex in terms of the neighbourhoods where multiplexes are located. We demonstrated how these locations were conceived in relation to catchment and to the networks of infrastructure that linked together nodes of the New Economy. In this chapter we examine the architectural environment of the cinemas themselves. In so doing, our attention turns more explicitly to the deployment of space inside the multiplex. It is of primary concern of multiplex designers to anticipate the manner in which patrons will perceive and inhabit these buildings. As such, the functional form and visual aesthetics of the multiplex environment reveals much about the space that operators seek to create, and the kinds of urban sensibilities and taste cultures to which they cater. The careful design of all these aspects has numerous consequences for the patterns of leisure taking place within a multiplex. In this chapter we examine the iconic nature of multiplex architecture, both exterior and interior, before providing detailed accounts of specific examples of the Indian multiplex. Throughout our analysis, we remain interested in both the social production and social construction of the built environment, and in how these two aspects work together to generate spaces characteristic of urban leisure and consumption.

In order to understand what makes the experience of the multiplex distinctive for its patrons, it is useful to initially consider the typical organisation of older, single-screen Indian cinema halls since the contrast between these two spaces is always implicated in the popular assessment of the multiplex. The typical single-screen cinema tends to be found in a reasonably central part of the city where crowds gather. Its entrance adjoins the pavement, with a façade dominated by the largest possible hand-painted posters. Adjacent to, or just inside, this entrance is a ticket window providing a point of destination for a long snake-like queue (or, occasionally, a minor riot) in the public space outside in the period leading up to showings (established 12pm, 3pm, 6pm and 9pm show times). Also significant to the layout of the cinema is the area immediately around it, which, although not part of the cinema as such, constitutes an extension of its presence into public space, served by any number of food vendors, cigarette- and *paan*-wallahs and, inevitably, shady operators selling tickets 'on the black'.

Once inside the cinema entrance, patrons traverse into a short foyer, from where they separate into the two classes of 'stalls' and 'balcony'. This area would also include a less than salubrious toilet and a fitfully-manned refreshment counter which (sometimes) springs into operation to dole out popcorn during the intermission, when patrons pile outside to cool off or smoke during the break. Inside the cinema itself, the seating is divided into a split-level auditorium, where patrons typically sit in rows of fold-out metal or well-worn padded chairs with wall-mounted fans providing some relief from the often intense heat that comes from a thousand or more people crowded together in the Indian climate. The interior of these cinemas is characteristically rundown and there may or may not be carpet. If carpet exists, it (and the walls) will most likely be profusely stained with the distinctive red marks of *paan*-spitting. Showings are attended by local police officers there to ensure that public safety and morality is being maintained (Srinivas 2000b).

Architectural expressions of the new India

The multiplexes can be differentiated from the older style cinemas in almost all of the respects described above. The cinema halls of the past have developed an organic relationship with their environment over a period of time, and collectively they are also reflective of gradual changes in the built form over a period of a century. By contrast, the multiplexes that have appeared within the short space of a decade stand in stark contrast to the built environments that they have entered or replaced (variously shop fronts, suburban streetscapes, slum settlements or peri-urban farming villages). The conspicuous steel and glass architectures of the multiplexes, in keeping with the wider architectural characteristics of the new suburbs and the renovated areas in which they are located, articulate a symbolic break from the past. As such, multiplexes are not simply ultra-modern cinemas, but they are inextricably part of a broader post-liberalisation trend of re-branding urban space in India. Because these new buildings on such a grand scale so clearly diverge from older forms of the built environment, recent developments such as malls, residential complexes, IT buildings and multiplexes have to be understood as 'spectacularised urban spaces' that declare a remaking of the city (Debord 1999). For this reasons, India's multiplexes converge with Leslie Sklair's definition of 'iconic' architecture in as much as they are 'imbued with a special meaning that is symbolic for a culture and/or a time, and that this special meaning has an aesthetic component' (Sklair, 2006: 26).

The distinctive architectural styles associated with the contemporary period are closely linked to buildings with very specific purposes. It is the designers of habitats for the New Economy that have re-deployed the panoptic architectures of global commerce within the Indian context. By clearly demarcating the sites of the New Economy from those buildings that existed before as part of the old economy, these architectures are obvious examples of the way that spatial design is implicated in the ideological construction of urban spaces (Kearns and Philo 1993). One of the most consistently astute commentators on the contribution of architecture to India's public culture and politics is Anthony King, whose recent work (2004) demonstrates the significance of India's new built environment in creating 'spaces of global culture' which provide a physical reference point for the aspirational goals of the new consuming class. Thus, the new architectures of liberalisation are not simply reflective of the new values, but are themselves powerful interventions in public space that guide behaviours. As King observes, 'where such developments are built they have a significant impact as models of domestic consumption on the new upper middle class. It is here where financial, economic, cultural, discursive, as well as spatial and architectural manifestations of globalization overlap' (2004: 135).

India's new architectures must therefore be understood as part of a transnational project that gives physical form to the proscriptions of late capital, and which endows consuming society with a material reality in the same way that the concrete infrastructure of India's previous epoch gave socialism the semblance of productivity. The buildings of India's New Economy emulate the rejuvenated financial districts of Manhattan, London and Singapore. They have appeared as part of a three-decade long wave of commercial building that is also now breaking upon China's eastern seaboard. In the contemporary period, the global technical knowledge and globalised taste cultures reflected in the multiplexes are useful examples of what, following King, we might call 'transnational architectures' in that their design is the consequence not only of the immediate environment, but also of cultural and architectural shifts occurring elsewhere. This process mirrors a pattern found across the world where prestigious architectural commissions are given to global firms charged with re-branding existing cities as world-class, global cities (for Shanghai and Vancouver see Olds 2002, for Beijing see Ren 2008).

King singles out DLF City in Gurgaon for his discussion of India's aspirational architecture. However, similar developments are now highly evident in many of India's other cities, not least those in which we conducted our research. To assert that international architecture takes on special meanings in the new India is not to suggest that India has been closed to outside influences in the past. Le Corbusier's Chandigarh and Luyten's New Delhi are obvious prior examples of how architecture has previously been a significant part of India's engagement with a broader international trajectory that subsequently shaped India's perceptions of modernity. King, in his earlier work, demonstrates that the colonial bungalow was itself a form of global architectural bricolage whose design, construction and built form was the consequence of a network of internationalised actors, such as architects and planners, who collectively produced a hybridised taste culture that impacted upon the design of the bungalows (King 1975/2006). The same can be said of the colonial-era cinemas prior to the long process of their indigenisation that really began in the 1940s.

In the present moment of their celebratory newness, the multiplexes replicate this trend in ways that both enforce and elide the repetitive nature of appropriation and renewal in modernity. Nonetheless, it has been a point of pride for the operators that many of the multiplexes that we discuss in this chapter were designed by global firms who have built similar complexes in other parts of the world. According to Jamie Pickford of New Zealand-based architectural firm Walker and Associates, responsible for INOX sites in Bangalore, Panaji and Kolkata, the tendency for the ideas of global firms to dominate the design of a new multiplex is potentially exacerbated by the fact that local developers are generally uncritical of the designs that international architects present to them:

They see you as the consultant and if that's what you reckon it should be, then that's what it should be . . . That's sort of what happens at the start when they bring in someone from overseas. Cause they are after ideas, [from] people who have done it before. They're aspiring to things that they have seen in America or the UK . . . And the same thing will happen with the shopping centres that we do. But at the same time, we are trying to say, 'don't just do what they are doing in Dubai, which is kind of international kind of stuff, make it more local'. And they really respond . . . that makes a big difference if you go in with that attitude.

(interview 04/12/08)

Given the influence of international architects in the design of multiplexes, it is appropriate to question the extent to which multiplexes in India conform to a global template, compared to the extent to which the local conditions, tastes and materials are incorporated into each design. Despite their global convertibility, and the importance of this to their symbolic coherence, both architects and the operators who commission the buildings tend to emphasise the need to balance international style with the local environment. In a series of recent articles, David Mesbur, one of the principle partners of the Toronto-based firm Mesbur+Smith, who have designed over 400 multiplexes worldwide (including many commissioned for India by Shringar), argues that the design of multiplexes needs to be conscious of local tastes and preferences, whilst also stressing that there are certain design principles that are necessary to incorporate in any cinema (Mesbur, 2001: 10). From the industry perspective, however, the air of internationalism remains critically important for the associations that the industry is seeking to make on the minds of the public. Mohit Bhargava, General Manager of INOX Bangalore, is representative of a broader cross-section of opinion that equates multiplexes with the visual impression of an Indian city that is achieving a global standard:

For the last decade and a half . . . Bangalore has had the image as a hi-tech city . . . So definitely, with that image, malls and multiplexes have got to be there. You are looking at an international workforce, you are looking at an international clientele, you have to provide other facilities also at an international level . . . so in that way I think malls and multiplexes fit in beautifully.

(interview 06/02/2007)

Travellers arriving at Bangalore's airport in 2007 were greeted with a series of banners that proclaimed Bangalore as a 'city of malls', a 'city of multiplexes', a 'city of IT' and a 'city of the future'. The fact that multiplexes have become regonised in India as indicators of progress, development and modernity is highly significant in itself. Placed in the wider context of the New Economy experiment in Bangalore, it is clear that such facilities have had the effect of altering Bangaloreans' perception of their city, even though their benefits are highly localised within the city itself. The introduction of these new kinds of buildings during the 1990s, largely because of the rise of IT corporations and call centres, marked a distinctly new phase in the role of architecture in Bangalore in contributing to public culture (Stallmeyer 2006). As

Partha Chatterjee (2004: 144) notes, it was Bangalore and, to a lesser extent, Hyderabad that were singled out for transformation into New Economy cities during the early 1990s – an experiment that is now being repeated elsewhere.

The choice of Bangalore had much to do with the technical institutes founded there during the pre-liberalisation era, but this was also a location much more amenable to an architectural blank slate than cities like Mumbai or Kolkata. Prem Chandavarkar argues that most of the distinctive changes in Indian architectural approaches in the post-colonial period have occurred within the three cities of Delhi, Ahmedabad and Mumbai. Therefore, areas outside this north-western triangle have not undergone a visual transformation in their architectural environment to a similar extent (Chandavarkar 2007: 79). Chandavarkar (2007) argues that prior to the liberalisation era, Bangalore's architecture developed in such a way that new developments were not distinctively different from what was already there. This legacy of the architecture of the background has been powerfully reversed with the arrival of malls and multiplexes in Bangalore. These attempts to create landmark facilities, so conspicuously different from what existed before, are an indication of why Bangalore was selected as a city that the liberalisation era could remake in its own image.

If we describe that image in the form of the multiplex, what we see is a large-scale construction clad in expanses of plate glass and adorned with hoardings and moving screens advertising branded goods in the English language. Large blocks of contrasting colours are juxtaposed with bold lines marked out in chrome. In order to compete with their competition, multiplexes are increasingly augmented with architectural flourishes such as towers, balconies and irregular lines and curves. Even when nestled amongst buildings of a similar type, the multiplex consciously stands apart from its setting, cordoned off by traffic barriers and an expanse of parking spaces for private cars. In locations such as Bangalore's suburb of Koremangala and the satellite towns of the NCR, the concentrations of malls, multiplexes, residential apartments and office towers express themselves in conscious opposition to the environs and the historical architectures of the cities from which they sprang. The impression that these developments seek to create is one of an exclusive and futuristic space of high activity, new technologies and ostentatious wealth.

In places like Mumbai, where space is at a premium, the multiplexes are instead parachuted into the spaces created by the demolition of the city's industrial past (D'Monte 2005). Here, they jostle for attention amongst the architectural expressions of the commercial ambitions of the past. In the second-tier cities where they are now appearing, multiplexes built on a much smaller scale are generally sufficient to reshape the skyline of the city. In each and every case, the architectural exterior of the multiplex is primarily intended to shout for the attention of the affluent motorist passing by on arterial routes.

The leisure environment: Designing spaces of pleasure

Whilst the exterior of the multiplex is designed to grab the attention of an increasingly mobile public, it is the interior spaces of these buildings that customers pay to

Figure 6.1 Garuda Mall, Bangalore, home to INOX Bangalore. (Adrian Athique)

Figure 6.2 SRS Mall, Faridabad, NCR, home to PVR Cinemas. (Adrian Athique)

access. For this reason, the inside of the multiplex receives, if anything, a greater degree of design than the façade. The purpose of the design process is the creation of a stimulating and fantastical world for leisure and consumption, an arcadia beyond the humdrum experience of daily life and an environment to which patrons will seek to frequently return. The internal spaces of the multiplex are sites of visual performance in their own right. As such, the lobbies of Indian multiplexes are typically themed with a distinctive, eclectic, post-modern style rarely seen elsewhere and decorated throughout in vibrant, distinctive colours. India's multiplexes reflect a noticeably bolder and more colourful aesthetic than their Western counterparts, but they still correspond with what David Mesbur defines as the overarching purpose of interior design for a multiplex: to 'convey a sense of fun, drama, and fantasy through the creative use of colour, materials and architectural motifs, express a consistent theme from the entrance through to the auditorium details and reflect local taste, owners' preferences, the audience profile, and the type of films exhibited' (Mesbur 2001: 11).

As Phil Hubbard (2003) notes, a further function of the multiplex interior is to achieve a certain cognitive effect that puts customers at their ease. A relaxed and non-threatening space for leisure spending engenders a sense of ontological security amongst customers that encourages them to spend the time required to partake in commercial activities. For this reason, the interiors of multiplexes can also be viewed in a wider societal context as a form of architecture that is expressly designed to convey notions of mutually agreeable and well-regulated behaviour. Through its expansive glass walls, the orderly and hygienic interior with its omnipresent muzak and air conditioning is at once separated from, but also powerfully contrasted with, the hot and frenetic space of urban India outside. One way of reinforcing this impression of distance between the leisure environment and the outside world at the boundaries of the building is through the use of opulent interiors and spacious lobbies. As Shriam Krishnan at Shringar puts it:

> in a dark hall, everything is the same. But I think that when you step out into the lobby and you see a lot more food offerings, a lot more buzz happening, something or the other happening around you, I think people expect that from multiplex . . . You really feel that you are there.
>
> (interview 20/01/2007)

The design of the lobby is also significant for the practical functions it serves, as Mesbur points out:

> A well planned lobby contributes to the success of a multiplex . . . . [It can] enhance patron convenience and increase revenue by utilising innovative ticket booth layouts to accelerate ticket sales and minimise queuing time, maximising concession exposure, organising pedestrian traffic to avoid congestion and conflicts, arranging other entertainment uses for easy, direct access yet isolated from auditoriums to prevent noise intrusion and providing ample, convenient public washrooms using materials and finishes that minimise maintenance.
>
> (Mesbur 2001: 10)

In this sense, the spatial layout of the multiplex lobby is very different from the narrow thoroughfare found in the older-style cinemas and its attendant street gatherings. The multiplex lobby is explicitly designed to minimise time at the ticket office and to encourage a more evenly-dispersed flow of people through the facility. Furthermore, given the importance of food and beverage concessions to operator profits – profits generally lost to pavement vendors for the older cinemas – the multiplex lobby is designed as a space where patrons can linger comfortably and consume these products. A wide range of food and beverage products is available from concession counters modelled on fashionable US-style fast food outlets. The facilities are staffed by a relatively large number of young, well-groomed, English-speaking attendants dressed in smart jeans and t-shirts (which continues, due to its novelty and Western providence, to be much more upmarket attire in the Indian context than it is in Europe and America). To increase the impression of space, ease and safety within these spaces, tight and highly-visible security at entrances assures the clientele of the non-threatening nature of the multiplex experience, instantly negating any fear of unwanted mixing with undesirable elements of society. At the same time, highly-controlled access to leisure facilities also imparts a sense of value by reinforcing the perception that the experience on offer is a socially-exclusive and desirable privilege.

Upon exiting the lobby, multiplex patrons enter auditoriums that are far smaller than those found in traditional theatres, typically featuring around 300 seats. The screens themselves are also smaller and in keeping with the reduced width of the auditorium. By further contrast, multiplex auditoriums are configured for comfort, not capacity. They are always fully carpeted and air-conditioned, with back-up generators installed to counter the frequent power cuts that are a daily feature of life in metropolitan India. Sound and visual equipment is generally comparable, if not superior, to that found in multiplexes in Western countries and the distance between the front seats and the screen is also generous in relative terms. The seats themselves have high backs and are well padded with arm rests. Multiplex auditoriums are on a single level with raked seating and do not feature a balcony class, although some auditoriums will have more expensive seating located at the rear. Those paying the higher prices will not be spatially separated by any boundary, but they will enjoy wider and more luxurious seats. Deepak Srivastava describes the environmental conditions of the INOX brand in all its locations:

> All INOX complexes offer an option of 3–5 auditoriums, state-of-the-art facilities in terms of modern projection and acoustic systems, THX certified or compliant auditoriums, stadium style high back seating with cup-holder armrests, internationally designed interiors, high levels of hygiene, varied theatre food, selection of Hindi, English and regional movies, computerised ticketing and most importantly high service standards upheld by a young and vibrant team.
>
> (interview 28/12/2006)

Compared to other parts of the world, multiplex operators in India also place particular emphasis on the quality of toilets. This is an area in which the middle-class

Figure 6.3 Concession counter at INOX Bangalore. (Adrian Athique)

Figure 6.4 Arcade to auditoria, INOX Bangalore. (Walker and Associates)

audience has found the cinemas of the past highly unsatisfactory. As such, these are important parts of the facilities that represent a significant point of differentiation to local customers. While all multiplexes are outfitted conforming to these broad spec-ifications, increasing competition means that the multiplexes must now differenti-ate themselves not simply from the old single- screens, but also from each other. As Jamie Pickford from Walker and Associates notes:

> Everybody's got similar technology in terms of the projection . . . the size of the image, the comfort of the seat, just getting in and out, all those practical things that don't interfere with your enjoyment: so you can't hear the air-condition-ing, you can't hear the sound of the rain on the roof during the monsoon, so you can get totally lost into that . . . . If everybody is doing that, because they are all in competition with each other, the only thing is the foyer . . . People are not going to look at the air-conditioning. There is a certain ambience, a certain feel that has to come through.
>
> (Jamie Pickford, interview 18/11/2008)

While all multiplexes market themselves as a departure from older-style single-screen cinemas in terms of facilities, comfort and crowd, the scale and opulence of lobbies and the spending on decorative elements throughout the building can vary considerably between multiplexes. This is because the standardisation of all of the functional features of multiplexes means that there is a need to differentiate the facilities on the basis of these other elements. The attention paid to interior design is a device for assisting companies in gaining a competitive advantage. Spending on these elements is based on judgements made by operators about the perceived audi-ence for individual sites. Thus, a multiplex seeking to draw its primary audience from more upmarket areas will spend greater sums of money on the look of its inte-riors and amenities. The ability to judge the quality of fittings needed to impress a target audience in any specific location is obviously particularly important for those who are trying to overcome the first-mover advantage of their competitors who are already established in a good location. This was the situation faced by INOX in Bangalore when opening its site in competition with PVR's flagship 11-screen facil-ity. The INOX strategy was to try to distinguish its new, smaller multiplex on the basis of its more opulent furnishings:

> Bangalore already had two operating multiplexes, so the most important thing was to make something striking and spectacular in terms of the architecture, so that when people came and they said, 'wow we have come to a different kind of place'. So physically it had to be different and of course in terms of service we had to set a new standard. So everything that we did from an interior point of view, from a facilities point of view, had to be geared towards providing better service. And interiors had to have the 'wow' factor.
>
> (Mohit Bhargava, interview 06/02/2007)

While this need to distinguish sites from competitors on the basis of the outfitting of facilities is something which was also true of the more upmarket single-screens in their heyday, the scale of such spending in the multiplexes is striking, particularly in the metropolitan centres. Pickford notes that his firm's experience with building multiplexes in India to date suggests that this degree of expenditure may not continue to be adopted so readily in the future. Thus future multiplexes will likely see smaller foyers relative to the size of auditoria, as well as reduced expenditure on interior detailing. While developers were previously enthusiastic about having facilities like monitors on the walls of urinals, for example, the high cost of land and the growing competitiveness of the market mean that while initially there were many added extras, over time these are likely to be toned down:

> It always comes back to the money, it always comes back to the accounting but within that we have to be creative . . . [Multiplex companies] have set formulas which will only work if they lease from a developer and that's all they are willing to pay for, and that has to stack up and so as that is becoming more evident with the land going up of some of those things that you love to throw in they're less inclined to do. The capital cost is too high relative to the value of the land.
>
> (Jamie Pickford, interview 18/11/2008)

The shift seen in recent years away from purpose-built multiplexes to leasing space within mall developments has had obvious repercussions in the design of the multiplex environment. Most obviously, the mall itself provides the façade and the grand lobby for the multiplex located on the upper floors. As such, the importance, and scale, of the lobby within the multiplex itself is reduced. The multiplex operators believe, however, that the wide expanse of leisure space and entertainment facilities provided by this format support and supplement the footfalls of the multiplex (and vice versa). The tenant mix of a mall, especially the quality of the food court, is highly significant in attracting footfalls to the in-mall-multiplex. As a result, these multiplexes become dependent upon the location of the mall and the other tenants. They are necessarily integrated into the environs of a larger commercial retail neighbourhood and the purposeful design of its public space. It is worth noting that, unlike the interface of traditional cinema halls with city pavements, the mall-multiplex combine is an interior neighbourhood operating as a privatised public space. This has a determining effect upon the ways in which patrons experience these environments – a point that we return to in the conclusion of this chapter.

Inside India's multiplexes: Case studies

We can distinguish three different kinds of multiplexes in the Indian market: retrofits, purpose-built multiplexes and in-mall-multiplexes. The latter two categories both appear in urban space as distinctive examples of the fashionable status of large-scale post-modern architecture with the extensive use of glass frontage and large areas of bold, primary colours on both interior and exterior surfaces. The retrofit multiplexes, which appeared first on the Indian scene, are the least architecturally distinctive of the three models, being a modification of an older cinema hall. Whilst they share the livery of the newer sites, they lack the distinctive architectural features of contemporary structures. Where the three models primarily differ from each other in design terms is in the balance of cinematic, retail and eating activities that they accommodate.

In the case of the purpose-built multiplex it is a grand entrance, an opulent lobby and the layout of the auditoriums which take precedence for both the interior and exterior design. Retail outlets for rent are typically included, but they are generally located in areas of the complex that are marginal to its overall visual effect. By contrast, in the case of the in-mall-multiplex, the entrance to the multiplex will typically be located on an upper floor and will be relatively modest with only a small foyer found inside. The ticket counter will often be incorporated into the space of the mall rather than being located in the small lobby of the cinema proper. The brand colours of the multiplex operator and their logo occupy a large volume of the exterior space of the mall in which it is located. However, the signage of the multiplex operator has to share visual space on the exterior of the mall with other retailers and advertisers to a far greater extent in this model. The sites chosen for retrofitting are generally located on a small shopping plaza in a well-to-do area. Access to this plaza is usually manned by private security or a functioning police *chowki*. Aside from the control of the spaces they occupy, what the retrofits share with the new multiplexes is the use of high-impact interior designs and the high visibility of the livery and logo of the operator on the exterior facades. All of these models, for which we detail specific examples, reflect the received logic of the industry: the ambience of the multiplex experience rather than simply content is what draws patrons.

PVR retrofits in the NCR

PVR is credited with starting the multiplex boom in India, but their first four sites were all refurbishments of existing theatres rather than new purpose-built multiplexes. As such, the sites run by PVR in the Delhi-NCR are undoubtedly the best-known examples of the retrofitted multiplex cinema. Although the emphasis has definitely moved away since 2001 from refurbishing older cinemas to building new multiplexes or operating within malls, the retrofit model remains attractive in some downtown locations, where space is at a premium and planning regulations make demolition of existing structures extremely difficult. As such, Shringar refurbishes and operates traditional cinemas outside of their Fame multiplex brand and, despite owning more purpose-built multiplexes than its competitors, INOX is now opening two retrofitted cinemas in Jaipur. More commonly, however, it is the owners of existing cinema halls who have been refurbishing their buildings as multiplexes (such as the Roxy and the Apsara in downtown Mumbai), where their location is profitable enough to justify the expense.

Of the six PVR retrofits operating within Delhi proper, it is important to note that only three (Anupam, Naraina and Vikaspuri) have actually been split into the multiplex format. The remaining three (Priya, Plaza, Rivoli) are premier single-screen facilities that have undergone exterior and interior refurbishment (and re-branding within the PVR chain) without actually being transformed into multiplexes. However, location is just as important for selecting sites for retrofits as it is when building new sites. In South (Anupam at Saket, Priya at Basant Lok) and West Delhi (Payal at Naraina, Sonia at Vikaspuri) the cinemas chosen by PVR are all large halls located in purpose-built community centres in suburban districts that provide pedestrianised open space to the front of the hall. Along with regulated car parking, the mix of local retail franchises in the immediate vicinity is also an important component of all the retrofit sites. A suitable blend of international brands and boutique stores provides the environmental context seen as suitable for attracting the multiplex crowd. In this sense, despite their status as dedicated cinema halls, the PVR sites in suburban Delhi all function in practice as components of open (or 'flat') shopping malls. (PVR Vikaspuri also incorporates shopping space along the building exteriors.) Similarly, the two heritage cinemas in central Delhi are both located in the colonial-era circular commercial centre of Connaught Place, arguably India's first modern shopping mall.

In carrying out the refurbishment of their sites in New Delhi, PVR worked closely with Delhi-based 'intelligent' architects Morphogenesis Pvt., who had previously designed corporate buildings in Gurgaon. Sonali Rastogi of Morphogenesis, in an interview with Anand Vivek Tanaja at SARAI, claims that prior to refurbishment, the Priya cinema was an 'alienating space' and hence one of the major moves was to open out the front of the cinema, to have the space of the cinema extend 'from the popcorn stand in the lobby to the *paanwallah* outside'. Morphogenesis thought of literally extending the cinema into the space of the city, to link the renovation of the cinema with 'urban renewal' (Tanaja 2008). This attempt to rejuvenate cinemas by alleviating architectural alienation also has a wider social dimension. Whilst PVR Anupam was a successful cinema with an affluent catchment even prior to refurbishment, some of the other PVR retrofits have sought to transform the catchment for the site along with its architecture. In sites such as PVR Naraina in West Delhi, retrofitting represented a conscious attempt create a new upscale audience in place of the audience which frequented the cinema previously. For this reason, we have to understand the process of retrofitting as one of social, as well as architectural, engineering:

> PVR Narayana, formerly Payal . . . was a highly disreputable and unsafe location, according to Sonali. The ill-lit front of the cinema hall, [was] next to a fire station, and *dhabas* selling butter chicken and hooch . . . One of the first things they did in Narayana was to again open up the front of the cinema, so that the audience gathered/gathering in the foyer can see the approach to the hall. This approach, the exteriors/parking lot of the hall were also well lit up in their plan, despite not being part of the cinema building, so that the whole area was well lit and visible from the hall, hence immediately making it 'safer'. The coming of the PVR brand, and the perceived/expected change in clientele changed the nature of the space around the hall, a perhaps 'exemplary' example of Morphogenesis's contribution to urban renewal . . . The restaurant where they often ate 'on site' hiked up the prices of its basic dish from rupees 12 to rupees 26. Pepsi and Coke provided the restaurants with attractive signage, to attract the more upmarket clients soon expected. the butter chicken and

hooch selling restaurant turned respectable (damn!), and even the decrepit Fire Station got a new coat of paint.

(Tanaja 2008)

For the PVR retrofits, the refurbishment process includes an extensive visual redesign of the exterior faces of the building. This involves the application of the bold blue and yellow PVR colour scheme and prominent brand signage along with chrome fittings. For the interior spaces of the building the refurbishment involves the use of bold pop art motifs, with blocks of primary colours again providing a high degree of visual impact. (In the case of Priya, it is red that predominates and at Anupam it is yellow that predominates.) Backlit display signage and lettering are used extensively, along with dispersed overhead lighting designs. Hard modern edges and chrome fittings delineate the functional architecture of the lobbies and the McDonalds-style food and beverage counters further implicate the Western modern. Orderly behaviour at these food concessions is subtly encouraged through the use of small, standing barriers. This interior domain, both heavily stylised and markedly functional, creates a purposeful environment between the open space of the plaza frontage and the more muted space of the auditoriums. Rastogi describes this combination as a 'time slice' of cinematic design, combining 1980s style retro, American diner and Elvis imagery, neon, backlit glass displays, movie information system with plasma screens (MIS) and modern steel and glass minimalism (ibid.). For the patron, the overall visual impression is post-war Americana with the colours turned up to the maximum, contrasting with the cooler corporatism of the exterior facades.

The refurbishment process within the buildings naturally entails extensive modifications. In the case of the three multiplex retrofits, this involved the transformation of large-capacity halls (approximately 1,000 seats) into either three or four smaller auditoriums apiece. Where possible, the lobby inside the building is extended to provide more space for patrons to relax inside the building itself. As such, in the case of the two single-screens in Connaught Place, refurbishment has seen the overall capacity of the cinemas greatly reduced in order to make space for food courts within the building. The auditoriums themselves are re-equipped with THX audio systems, re-carpeted and re-seated with wider, high-backed padded chairs with cup holders. There are 15 seats to a row at PVR Anupam in Saket, marking an increase of space per patron as opposed to the decrease which characterised the early multiplexes in the US In the sense of the visual environment presented to patrons, the commonalities between the PVR retrofits and the deployment of the multiplex aesthetic in other forms of architecture is striking, despite the obvious limitations of space available for re-positioning auditoria. For this reason, it is defensible to make the case that the multiplex phenomenon is defined as much by environmental ambience as it is by multi-screening per se.

INOX Goa, Panaji, Goa

Perhaps the most iconic purpose-built multiplex in India is the INOX at Panaji, Goa. It was built in co-operation with the Goa state government to re-house India's

Figure 6.5 PVR Naraina (formerly the Payal) in West Delhi. (Adrian Athique)

Figure 6.6 PVR Vikaspuri (formerly the Sonia) in West Delhi. (Adrian Athique)

International Film Festival, which was seeking to re-locate from its traditional home in Delhi. A tender was put out to the private sector by the state government; INOX was the successful bidder to clear, build and operate the site for a five-year period. INOX Goa is located behind the former Goa Medical College building on DB Road as it runs along the Mandovi Riverfront. Between the INOX frontage and the well-maintained colonial-era GMC building is an open plaza with several encased trees providing shade, along with the canopy that projects from the front of the building. General Manager Deepak Srivastava explains the challenges of fulfilling the tender for the site:

> There was an old building which had to be demolished and then the founda-tion laid again, and then the construction. So the land was provided by the gov-ernment. The funds were provided by the government. The know-how and the manpower was ours. That's how we took it up. We actually designed it. The government approved it. This is how it worked. We had an idea person. We had an architect. Then we had a landscape person. Then we had several builders, as such, and then we had engineers, basically . . . all these agencies were working 24 hours because time was not there, and we had to go through monsoons. So that was a big challenge . . . This was the only site with a lot of expanse around it. Mandovi river at front. Heritage building on site. A nice courtyard here in the centre. Market behind. It is a really central location. So, the accessibility of people from all areas to Panaji is very easy at this site.
>
> (interview 28/12/2006)

To the immediate east of the INOX site are the Panaji markets, the city's main com-mercial district. To the west is a medium-sized ground-level car park that belongs to the complex is staffed by security guards at its entrance points. Security guards are also positioned at the rear of the building at the goods access point and at the entrances to the plaza. The entrance to the cinema itself is staffed by a number uni-formed security guards. Patrons enter through a detection booth and are then searched with body scanners. Cameras and digital recorders must be placed into a cloakroom facility. The secured plaza at the front of the building gives not only a sense of security, but it also provides a sense of space that extends the scope of the building itself both visually and in a practical sense. As with the retrofitted sites dis-cussed previously, a large, secured expanse at the front of INOX Goa is important in terms of everyday operation since the ticket office is on the outside of the build-ing. It is also required for accommodating the large crowds that attend the International Film Festival:

> Since it was going to host the International Film Festival. The brief was that it must have the best equipment. Whether it is the projection equipment, whether it is the sound, whether it is the screen, whether it is the seats or whether it is the materials that are used: It has to be world class and it has to be number one. And that's what we have chosen. That's what we have developed and that's what we have been complimented on. It has to be hygienic and it has

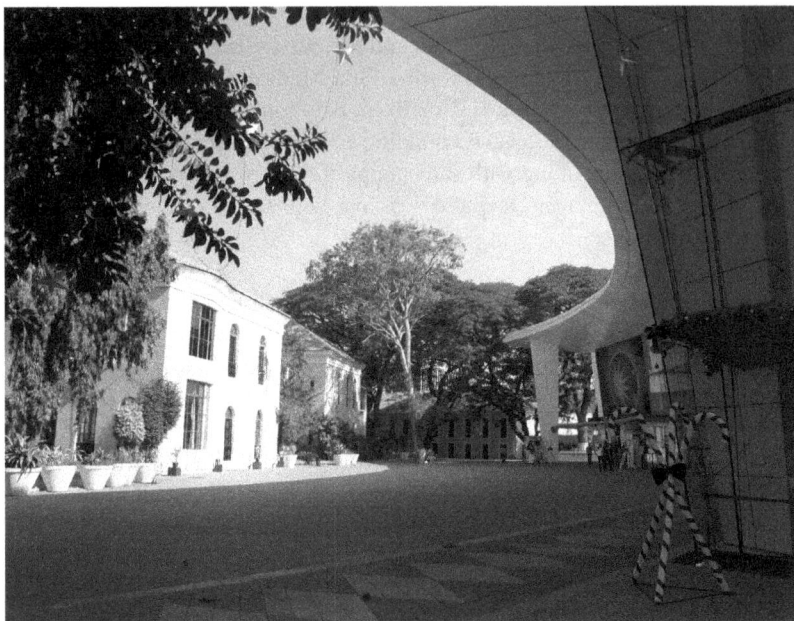

Figure 6.7 Plaza between the former GMC building and INOX Goa, Panaji. (Adrian Athique)

Figure 6.8 Lobby at INOX Goa, Panaji. (Adrian Athique)

to look good, with all the elements of nature coming in too. Because we have space, and it should have four screens with 1272 seating . . . This is the number which was given to us . . . We have disabled access and that's why all of our screens on the ground floor with ramps and so for wheelchairs the reach is available here . . . because of the International Film Festival people might come with that kind of requirement and so we have got that.

(interview 28/12/2006)

The firm responsible for designing the INOX facility at Panaji, Walker and Associates, intended its glass exterior to function in juxtaposition with the historic Portuguese-era GMC building which sits adjacent to it:

At night there is a floodlights and its all lit up on the side, but in the day you get a reflection of the old building in the new, that was the concept, that was part of it. See they also have ambitions towards the future, so you have a juxtaposition between something that was really modern and simple, relatively simple, against something which is old and ornate and historic, rather than trying to imitate it or anything like that – this was then and this is now, this is the future and this is where we are heading, so that was important- rightly or wrongly that was our concept and they loved it and that's what they wanted to do . . . We wanted to make use of the courtyard between this and the GMC as one large space, that the forecourt flowed right into the foyer so it feels like one even though you go from air-conditioned to non-airconditioned, so you could be either inside or outside depending on how big the movies are and how many people come. they set up tents in the courtyard and make it quite theatrical, so its one of those 'do's', they can have cocktails and wine . . . We saw it like a stage, the whole building is a backdrop to a stage and the culture is the people who go in there.

(Jamie Pickford, interview 18/11/08)

As with all of the multiplex formats, advertising and signage play an important role in the operating environment. The building makes good use of its glass frontage with window advertising along with hanging banners on the solid walls. In December 2006, the placard and banner advertisers were HSBC, Airtel Mobiles, Senior Shoe Shop Goa (display booth), Bombay Bazaar Mall & Baron Clothes (display booth) and Dimples Cine Advertising. Airtel provided a free phone re-charge stand within the foyer. Given the importance of Christmas to Goa's largely Christian population and to the state's tourism industry, there were also Christmas decorations, foam candy sticks, a nativity diorama and a Christmas tree. Aside from INOX's 'Refuel' food and beverage concession, there are also a small number of retail facilities inside the foyer: Baskin Robbins Ice Cream, Crazy Cupcorn and a bookshop stocking English-language books and periodicals. There was also a portrait sketch artist and a stand selling scented soaps and candles. The INOX complex also houses a function room with a bar facility that is not open to the general public. This is where stars reside during premieres, and it is also rented out for private children's parties. Although this is a small multiplex by international standards, and even those found in metropolitan India, the bespoke design of the building and its particularly favourable location allow for the provision of a full multiplex environment at this smaller scale.

PVR Forum Mall, Bangalore

As an example of the in-mall-multiplex as an operating environment, the 11-screen PVR Cinemas at Forum Mall in Bangalore is perhaps the most obvious example, being India's largest multiplex at the time of writing. Opened in November 2004, this site is housed in the Forum Mall, a large-scale shopping mall development standing on Hosur road in Bangalore's suburb of Koremangala. The Forum Mall has four floors with balconies encircling a large central space at the midway point of each floor. Elevators located along the longitudinal axis of the building on both sides of the central circle regulate the flow of customers between floors. The mall is large enough that it fills the space at the apex of Hosur and Marigowda Roads, with entrances in operation at either side of the building. Access from both roads greatly assists the accommodation of a large circulation of visitors. Aside from the internal rotunda, two other circular elements, breaking up the rectangular shape of the building from the exterior, are the car park access towers located at two corners on the north-western face of the building, serving 800 parking spaces. The Forum Mall was developed by the Prestige Group, who invites their customers to:

> Close your eyes for a moment and imagine a shopaholic's paradise – a shopper's dream – 650,000 sq.ft. of futuristically designed shopping space, offering a multi-brand bonanza with top global levels, wooing and attracting the shopper . . . open your eyes and you have The Forum . . . a place one can go to for almost anything one wants to buy.
>
> (Forum Mall 2008)

Along with a long roll call of international brand franchises and newly-established national brands offering 'everything from shoes to exercise equipment, from home furnishings to electronic goods, from books to video games', the Forum mall hosts a wide-range of food retailers, including South India's first McDonalds. The operators describe this highly successful mall as:

> an accomplishment the Prestige team is truly proud of. The building management systems, close circuit security, computerised parking management systems, ATM machines, 100 per cent generator backup, centralised air conditioning and line-in-music completes the loop, to offer a world-class 'view of the future' ambience. The popularity of this mall is such that almost all the celebrities who visit the city of Bangalore make it a point to drop in here.
>
> (The Forum 2007)

The PVR multiplex occupies the entire third and fourth floors (over 100,000 square feet) at Forum Mall, with the auditoriums arranged along both sides of the mall.

The open floor area of the two levels thus functions as a gigantic foyer for the cinemas, with the placement of the escalators feeding patrons onto the cinema levels at two different points. The multiplex crowd is further dispersed by the arrangement of four different ticket counters at various points around the third floor. All of this works to make optimum use of the available space and avoid congestion, whilst maximising exposure to the retail levels below. As Gagan Bindra, Public Relation Manager, explains:

> The layout was planned so that for the first time in India we offered three distinct different categories. The Classic, Europa and the Gold. The gold is the first of its kind in India. Three options in the same place and the convenience of getting your tickets. Independent ticket counters for each class and two counters for the classic. With eleven screens and two thousand you have to ensure that. The exists and entrances, I mean, its very customer friendly. Its just a natural flow that happens over there.
>
> (interview 14/02/2007)

The large number of screens at Forum allows PVR to cater to Bangalore's diverse population with regular screenings in six languages. It also allows for a greater accommodation of India's status- and luxury-conscious society through three self-contained classes of seating. Thus in addition to the regular standard of multiplex auditoriums on seven screens, there are two 'Europa' class auditoriums with better seats and an enclosed lounge area for patrons, offering a more extensive refreshments menu. At the top of this hierarchy is the 'Gold Class', consisting of two small auditoriums with a dedicated drinks bar, 32 overstuffed and fully-reclining chairs and a full in-seat waitress service. According to Bindra, the importance of the Gold Class extends beyond its actual takings to setting the reputation of the site:

> The brand pull is the Gold Class. There is no doubt about that. Not everybody goes into the Gold Class to watch a movie but the Gold Class is by itself important. People talk about it. Plus, I would definitely say, the convenience of getting tickets. The convenience of the cinema also. The seating of the cinema also. It is far more comfortable I would say than any other plex. Not only in Bangalore you can go national. With the Gold you can go global. It's a different category altogether . . . It is a landmark in the South of India. It's not just me saying it as an employee but that is what we hear from people. From well-placed people. Senior people of the city. PVR Bangalore is the best cinema . . . When you talk cinema in Bangalore, PVR comes first. In Karnataka, PVR comes first. So it has definitely changed the image [of Bangalore] . . . People come here just to see PVR. It is a landmark.
>
> (interview 14/02/2007)

The manner in which PVR Cinemas is integrated with the architectural space constructed by the Forum Mall itself is a good example of mall-multiplex combine on a large-scale. In other locations, multiplex operators may operate on just part of a

Figure 6.9 PVR multiplex, third and fourth floors, Forum Mall, Koremangala, Bangalore. (Adrian Athique)

Figure 6.10 Central rotunda, Forum Mall, Koremangala, Bangalore. (Adrian Athique)

floor. Nonetheless, the mall plays the same role in replacing the space not only of the outside pavement, but also the foyer of a traditional cinema. In many cases, the ticket counters are also located outside the cinema itself and integrated with the larger building. These might be situated on the exterior the building or in a kiosk on the ground floor. Again, this has the effect of dispersing the cinema crowd and creating an interior space that is more easily managed. As such, there are architectural and commercial synergies in this model. Naturally, the fact that in-mall-multiplexes must be incorporated into pre-existing spaces owned and designed by others places limits on the capacity of operators to control their own architectural space to the same extent as they can in a purpose-built multiplex. However, for Bindra, these disadvantages are offset by the advantages of occupying an environment built around combined leisure activities, thus in a purpose-built site:

> You have more independence. It's your property. But I would say again, today time has come in retail boom. It's absolute, at least in India . . . For the people living around here, this has become an outing. Because they come here, they have a place to eat, they can go down to the pub, there's an entertainment centre for the kids and cinema also, but if you're a standalone cinema, you're a standalone cinema. You're ultimately not a multi-utility mall, so people only come to watch a movie. Here people come to shop to watch a movie to spend time or it could be reverse.
>
> (Gagan Bindra, interview 14/02/2007)

INOX Salt Lake, Kolkata

Opened in 2004, INOX Salt Lake, Kolkata, is part of a unique facility intended to cater to the sensibilities of Bengal's cultural elite. This multiplex, comprising four screens and able to seat 1,200 people, is one of two operations that INOX has in greater Kolkata (the other being located in the central thoroughfare of Elgin Road). This INOX screens a combination of mostly Hindi blockbusters, along with alternative fare and English language movies. INOX Salt Lake is discreetly embedded in one corner of the bottom storey of the CityCentre Mall complex, which was designed, with the cooperation of the communist-led Left Front State government, as an iconic statement for the new suburbs of Kolkata's eastern fringe. Salt Lake and nearby New Town (Rajarhat) are the most significant areas of growth for the New Economy in West Bengal. As such, in terms of catchment, the CityCentre Mall is targeted towards a particularly well-heeled audience since this multiplex is situated in the middle of what is arguably the most affluent part of the city. The INOX website recognises that the positioning of CityCentre mall accommodates the established upper middle classes of Salt Lake, as well as anticipating the future shape of Kolkata, when 'this location will emerge as the nucleus of tomorrow's metropolis' (INOX 2007).

As a symbolical marker of place in the middle of Salt Lake, the CityCentre complex is imbued with a profusion of cultural markers that make reference to both pan-Indian and locally-specific cultural idioms. These are intended to mark it out as something that is new, but which remains in keeping with (and respectful of) the culture of Kolkata and, indeed, broader Indian motifs. The complex was designed by Charles Correa, perhaps India's most famous architect and a figure known for his commitment to all sectors of society. His involvement is indicative of the extent to which the complex has been developed by the West Bengal government (via the KMDA, a major joint-venture partner in its development) as a statement of their response to liberalisation project. This integrated housing, retail and leisure development aims to provide a place where the effects of economic and cultural globalisation can be mediated in ways which are meaningful to Bengalis in particular.

Architecturally, the combination of covered and open-to-the-sky spaces is a radical departure from the glass boxes that constitute most malls in India and is in keeping with Correa's long-standing assertion that access to the sky is an Indian architectural tradition that contemporary architects should aim to utilise by incorporating terraces, verandas and courtyards into their designs (Correa 1989: 95). The website of the CityCentre argues that the 'architecture of the complex embodies the spirit of Kolkata' (CityCentre 2007). This concern with localism is clearly evident in numerous symbolic features of the design. Showcasing the significance of art to Kolkata's identity, the complex features *Kalighat* paintings and an art wall, the latter showcasing recent additions from artists from around the city. Of course, the self-conscious syncreticism of Bengali identity, which clearly informs the symbols of CityCentre, also demands a reference to the colonial era, as the legacy of Calcutta's former place as the second city of the British Empire has been a common theme in the way that Calcutta has represented itself in the post-colonial era (Chattopadhyay 2005). Accordingly, CityCentre mall has a restored horse-drawn tramcar located next to the open *kund* and intended as an acknowledgement of the history of the Raj period.

Along with nods to the colonial era, the CityCentre complex attempts to be something more than just an expression of globalised culture, primarily in order to appease the locally-specific ambivalence to the liberalisation agenda (see Scrase and Ganguly-Scrase 2001). This is a retail environment where 'heritage, culture and indomitable Kolkata spirit are not trampled over by rampant commercialism' (CityCentre 2007). As such, CityCentre caters to the self-perception that Bengali identities and imaginaries are politically progressive. In keeping with this sentiment, alongside the ubiquitous chain outlets found in other malls (such as Pizza Hut, Planet M, Moustache), there are spaces in CityCentre where the underprivileged elements of society are referenced. Akriti, which showcases products from NGOs working with the poor, is an example of this. The ethos of an inclusive and locally-distinctive society is reinforced by the mixture of food outlets. While the brands typically associated with liberalisation-style culinary and retail shopping remain prominent in the complex (such as Pizza Hut), the Bengali staple of *muri* is also available, while the vernacular-inspired Tea Junction (*chayer dokan*), where patrons perch on low chairs, is self-consciously different from the globally-styled Cafe Coffee Day outlet upstairs. The CityCentre website (2007) therefore argues that in addition to promoting local culinary traditions, the cultural innovations of art, heritage and social compassion counterbalance the commercialism and generic global modernity associated with the mall environment.

The design of the complex around public and community-conscious spaces supposedly facilitates the perpetuation of public conversation, or *adda* (Dipesh Chakravarty 2000, Swati Chattopadhyay 2005: 182–187). This public space includes a central *kund*, drawing from traditions of the ancient bathing area, as the centrepiece around which all the other features of the complex are constructed. The INOX multiplex is no exception in this regard: it is both spatially and visually subordinate to the overall design in an almost total inversion of the prominent and celebratory presence of multiplexes in other malls across the country. This had unique implications for the development of the INOX facility at the site. While Correa's designs for CityCentre have attracted a great deal of interest both in India and abroad, winning many national and international awards, the highly structured nature of the complex meant that Walker and Associates, the architects working on the INOX multiplex, had very little latitude in what kinds of design features they could include since the area was very tight and their own ideas had to sublimated to the overarching vision of CityCentre's chief architect:

> The Salt Lake INOX was probably the most blinkered that we have ever had to do because . . . Charles [Correa] had an idea about the way it was going to be, and he is the main architect . . . It was quite rigid what we could and couldn't do, the whole entrance was dictated to us . . . . There was so much dictated by the shell, there wasn't much room for us to move. It was different from what we normally do. We normally work the whole thing out, We sort out the auditoriums and make it all functional, worked around on the inside, working on the levels and ramps.
>
> (Peter Prosser and Jamie Pickford, interview 18/11/08)

This more limited brief made the interior decoration of the multiplex the main focus for developing the site, with the challenge of distinguishing the INOX interior from the mall exterior without creating too great a dislocation between the two for patrons entering the multiplex. Thus, while the great aesthetic similarities normally found in the mall-multiplex support their architectural synergy, this site is an example of a more uneasy correlation. In direct contrast to the norm for India's malls, at the heart of Correa's design lies the ambition to create a built environment that does not tightly control the flow of people or create socially exclusionary space. Therefore, CityCentre is not bounded by solid walls and entrance doors like most malls. Instead there is a deliberate integration of the mall with the broader immediate environs of Salt Lake. This is not merely an architectural conceit, but also a political one, in a site:

> Combining shops, a wedding hall, a multiplex, offices and apartments, CityCentre is the heart of Salt Lake City in Kolkata, provides community and public spaces, both covered and open-to-sky, that are at the scale of the city, and open to all citizens.
>
> (CityCentre 2007)

Figure 6.11 Shopping thoroughfare, City Centre Salt Lake, Kolkata. (Palash Ghosh)

Figure 6.12 Social space at City Centre, Salt Lake, Kolkata. (Palash Ghosh)

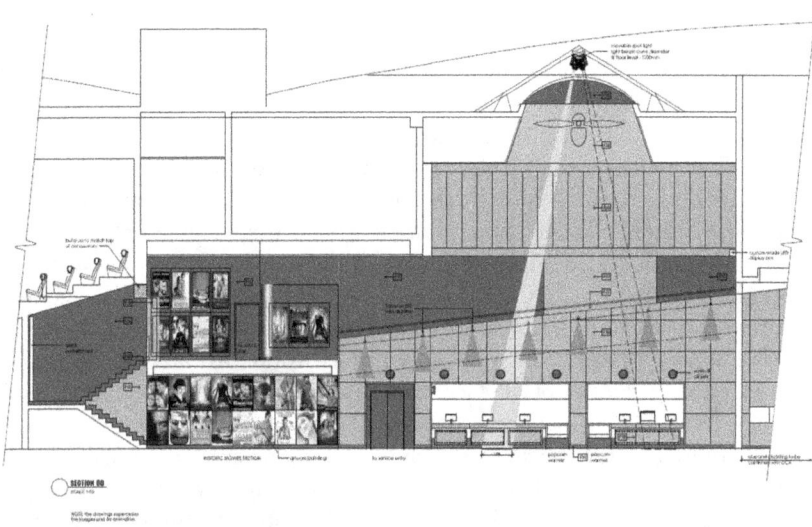

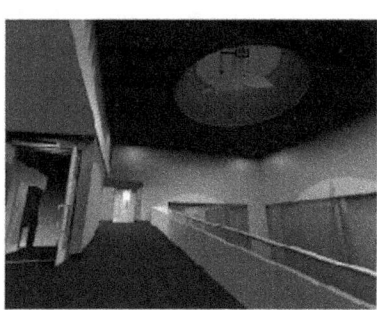

Figure 6.13 Architectural elevation plan and interior modelling for **INOX** Salt Lake, Kolkata. (Walker and Associates)

However, the extent to which it is successful in its stated objective of trying to cater to every segment of society and be open to everyone of all income and age groups is questionable.

Given the satellite suburban enclave in which it is located, not to mention the prices, it is immediately obvious that the intended patrons of CityCentre are in reality a reasonably narrow demographic. As with most of the other multiplexes we have profiled in this chapter, INOX Salt Lake caters to a social elite, regardless of their political persuasion. In this sense, it is of little surprise that CityCentre carries endorsements from all of the important players associated with the liberalisation project in West Bengal, such as captain of industry Ratan Tata, who calls it 'a very impressive enterprise' (CityCentre 2007). The complex also enjoys heavyweight political endorsement from Union State Minister of Housing and Urban Poverty Alleviation Kumari Selja, who sees CityCentre as 'world class' and 'something to be proud of'. The promotion of CityCentre as a place of significance to Kolkata is reinforced by other endorsements from famous Bengalis, such as cultural ambassadors Bikram Ghosh and Jaya Seal Ghosh, who (are husband and wife and) also feature on billboards throughout Kolkata endorsing GenX luxury residential housing. Usha Ray's comments that Salt Lake offers 'spacious and glamorous one-stop shopping' make the underlying ethos of post-liberalisation consumption equally apparent. Despite being so self-consciously antithetical to malls like Forum in Bangalore, CityCentre and its multiplex share the same objective of providing tightly-designed and well-ordered spaces for bourgeois activity.

The leisure experience: Cleanliness, convenience and security

The visual aesthetics and the functional design of multiplex architectures upon which we have concentrated thus far provide an insight into the spatial politics of the new leisure infrastructure. However, it is also important to pay attention to the ways in which these environments exert a controlling influence over the ways in which these environments are experienced by their clientele. These are, after all, purposeful designs, not least because the new correlation of movies and shopping is contingent upon the successful conversion of catchment to footfalls to purchases. How do multiplex operators understand the motivations for people coming to their facilities? Anand Moorthy at FUN Cinemas argues that the drivers of customer aspiration can be understood through the sub-categories of entertainment, leisure and convenience:

> These three things all had different definitions before. Today, these three things all have a very specific set of meanings to a separate group of customers. Entertainment is anywhere you can get entertainment, and it could happen at home or out-of-home. So, out-of-home, if you want to eat food, you want to watch a movie, a lot of things. Leisure is something that normally happens in a particular group of your kind of people, and at a place where you have time to spend. The third one is convenience, which again, by the growing density of population and less access to other things because of people getting busier . . .

Convenience is the most important thing. Otherwise, the customer has other avenues. So these are the three parameters on which it rests.

(Anand Moorthy, interview 06/01/2007)

The multiplexes are obviously designed to maximise all these elements in a way that is most appealing to the customers they seek to attract. Moorthy also emphasises that customers are active agents who will compare the merits of two cinemas before deciding which one to visit. This decision may change depending on whether a multiplex is offering not only an attractive level of service, but also a dynamic atmosphere. As Moorthy puts it, 'The customer is not loyal to one person, one place. He checks out both of the places and then he decides if he is coming with the family. He knows what is happening because he checks the buzz' (ibid.).

As a consequence of the need to attract customers on the basis of 'buzz', operators will try many kinds of marketing techniques. These may include conventional promotions within the lobby, such as competition stands for consumer desirables such as plasma televisions, mobile phones, two-wheelers and foreign holidays. They may also include augmenting the exterior of the buildings with themed installations. An example cited by Moorthy was when FUN Cinemas added a large Spiderman figure and web to the facade of their Andheri site to promote *Spiderman 2*. According to Moorthy, this high-visibility installation was so successful that FUN had the best revenue collections in the entire country for this film. While customers may be drawn to the multiplex by inventive promotions of this kind and the requisite mix of entertainment, leisure and convenience, it is also the case that cleanliness and security are vital components of a successful multiplex operation. As Deepak Srivastava in Goa points out:

Our typical customer is mostly the upper-middle class who do not mind spending a little extra for quality and service. Most of our clients are families. Because families look for two, three things. One is it should be safe. It should be hygienic. It should be congenial atmosphere. That means they don't want to see riff-raffs inside the multiplex. They want well-behaved people. With the ambience that we have created and the pricing, we have cut out that part – so we only attract the upper middle class. That is what the family wants.

(interview 28/12/2006)

Thus part of the environmental ambience rests upon conveying an expectation that once inside, patrons will only mix with 'respectable' people. For this reason, all of the multiplexes we visited were characterised by a high degree of security. All multiplex patrons must pass through detection booths and be frisked with electronic body-scanners. Bags must be searched and items such as cameras, audio players/recorders, motorcycle helmets and foodstuffs are prohibited. These measures are designed to combat film piracy, theft and the threat of attacks on the cinema. Although no multiplex has suffered a bomb attack to date, there have been numerous instances of traditional cinemas being attacked in this way. Unlike the regular theatres, however, there is no police presence in the multiplex auditoriums.

Instead, all the entrances and access points are guarded by uniformed private security guards (referred to, in an echo of the colonial past, as 'Ghurkhas'). For the in-mall-multiplexes, the presence of the operators' own security is further augmented by similar provisions at the mall entrances, as well as guards patrolling every level of the mall along and more guards hired to search bags in every store. As such, it is not uncommon when visiting a mall in Delhi during the afternoon for customers to be outnumbered by security staff.

> We [carry out] a frisk and we don't allow anyone with a slippers, don't allow anybody with slippers and anyone who is a little too shabby, don't allow that person in a mall. So once you'll get a very creamy crowd in the mall; only those can go to cinema. So why we are putting cinema in a mall, that gives dual benefit to us. First of all we are getting more of security sense because they are scrutinised twice, once in the mall entry and second at our entry.
>
> (Parveen Kumar, interview 09/03/2007)

To the multiplex operators, this high level of security, applied through dress-based judgements about the social class of potential patrons, is essential to ensure that upper middle-class families remain assured that no unruly behaviour will take place. This is because a select audience for the multiplexes is not only a pricing point, but also an environmental factor that is a crucial component of their appeal. In an older-style cinema hall, the practices of viewing continue to include raucous acts of mass participation, such as screaming, applauding, whistling and singing. Older-style cinema halls also provide space for inappropriate acts such as spitting, jostling, groping and making lewd remarks. In the balcony of cinemas, which still attract a family crowd, the experience of the film is often accompanied by the aroma of curry and the clunking of tiffin-tins from those accustomed to bringing their own food. By contrast the film-viewing experience in the multiplex is odour-free and marked by a relative silence. The sporadic ring tones of mobile phones and the subsequent mumbled one-sided conversations provide the only major distractions from the screen, with laughter at appropriate points in the film narrative (and only those points) being the only audible sign of shared participation. In this respect, the behavioural influence of multiplexes and their careful management is indicative of an era where

> the 'thrills' of the bazaar are traded in for the 'conveniences' of the sterile supermarket. Old pleasures are now exchanged with new pleasures of capitalism: creature comforts, an insatiable obsession with the body and the self (the pleasures of privacy), and the mythical freedoms of citizenship.
>
> (Chakravarty 1991: 29)

Multiplexes commodify these new social aspirations, prioritising cleanliness, safety and congeniality and providing a sensory environment that distances the well-off consumer from the immediate past of fear, discomfort and scarcity in public space. Thus, they appear to have much in common with similar privatised leisure spaces

Figure 6.14 PVR ticket booth inside Metropolitan Mall, Gurgaon, NCR. (Adrian Athique)

Figure 6.15 Looking out from Pacific Mall, Ghaziabad, home to Adlabs Films. (Adrian Athique)

in other parts of the developing world, where malls act as 'fortresses' of affluence, shielding their customers from deprivation and menace in the wider social environment (Bottomley and Moore 2007, Dodson 2000, Kuppinger 2005). As well as appealing to its core audience in terms of the safety derived from exclusivity, the multiplex interior is also significant because of its capacity to deliver an experience of personal space to a clientele living in some of the world's most crowded urban centres. The multiplex architects and operators work hard to disperse the customer flow and reduce the impression of being in the threatening, overcrowded space that is commonly associated with cinemas in India. This contributes to the third of Srivastava's criteria of 'what the family wants': congeniality. In a spatial sense, what is crucial for both purpose-built and in-mall-multiplexes is that the crowd formed by the audience is absorbed into the building itself and is no longer publicly visible as a crowd, either to onlookers or amongst its members. Since the multiplex is divided amongst a number of auditoriums with staggered show times, the multiplex audience is temporally dispersed, creating a cinema crowd that is no longer a potential mob occupying public space, but instead comprises a steady flow of consumers moving effortlessly and individually in private, commercial space. Indian multiplexes also feature a very wide egress compared with their counterparts elsewhere, which although ostensibly instituted as a requirement of fire regulations, has the benefit of further increasing separation between patrons.

One of the most significant ways that the multiplex is able to negate unwanted proximity amongst its customers is by making ticket purchases a quick and easy proposition compared to older-style cinemas. Thus, in the case of PVR Bangalore, there are multiple ticket counters. In other sites, ticket booths are commonly found in the wider space of the mall. Tickets can also be booked online or by SMS, helping patrons to avoid the queuing that is such a feature of Indian life. The convenience, and the privilege, of not having to queue is another luxury of the multiplex, the significance of which is much greater for women. Indeed, a critical aspect of these new interiors is that they are less discriminatory towards women than the older cinemas and the streets outside. Recent works on the gendered flows of moving through India's cities suggest that the urban experience is very different for men and women (Phadke 2007, Ranade 2007). While men are able to loiter in the public space without fear of harassment, women must always be purposeful in movement and frequently change their trajectory as they navigate past cinemas, *paanwallahs* and whisky shops. By contrast, the multiplex-mall complex, as a safe space, significantly reduces the necessity for women to remain attentive and mobile and, as such, provides an important opportunity for them to socialise and pass time freely, whether that means eating, watching a movie or window shopping. For female patrons, one of the major differences between going to a traditional cinema and the multiplex is the reduction in the need to queue in cramped lines with many unknown men. The fact that tickets can be acquired quickly and with limited interaction with others reduces the likelihood that they will encounter sexual harassment from dangerous others, which has been a longstanding concern for middle-class women at the cinema.

Another major contributor to the ambience of a safe leisure environment is derived from the marked emphasis on cleanliness at the multiplexes, which are kept spotless to an extent that is uncommon elsewhere in the world by a constantly mobile (and utterly anonymous) army of cleaners. As we indicated earlier, one of the major concerns of middle-class patrons with regular cinemas was the deplorable state of their toilets. The fastidious attention to toilet cleanliness by Indian multiplex operators is an acknowledgement of the significance of this. As Mohit Bhargava at INOX Bangalore observes,

> Earlier cinemas in India were not known for cleanliness. You would not want to use a toilet in a cinema hall. The seats would not be clean. The bowl would not be clean . . . So we want to create a notion that cinemas *could* be a clean place.
>
> (interview 06/02/2007)

The experience of leisure inside the multiplex is clearly conceived in relation to an exterior world seen as unruly, crowded and dirty. Thus Correa's ambition to integrate leisure facilities with their wider environs is incongruous when compared to the overall trend towards emphasising, rather than diminishing, the disjuncture felt by customers transiting between the overcrowded chaos of city streets and the spacious, safe and secure interiors of the multiplex. This intention to demarcate the environment of the multiplex from the world outside is reflected in the materials and colours that are used for the interiors of multiplexes. In the case of INOX Bangalore, it is the use of red leather cladding on the walls that accentuates the feeling of opulence, while the extensive use of marble and lighting systems adds a sleek, clean sensibility. Jamie Pickford confirms that these are elements that are consistently incorporated into Indian multiplex design in order to emphasise the contrast with the outside world:

> Outside its sandy, dusty and dirty and here its cool and slick and clean, without being sterile and that's where the colour comes in and there is different textures as well. But it has a cleanliness. Outside there is lots of rubbish piled up and its dusty and everything looks the same colour. So its a bit like a *sari*, the multiplex is like a *sari*, bright purple and yellow and that sort of stuff.
>
> (Jamie Pickford, interview 18/11/2008)

The powerful contrast between contemporary multiplex architectures in India and their immediate surroundings thus operates on many levels: juxtaposing saturated colours with dusty pavements, orderly pleasures with threatening chaos, spacious interiors with overcrowded cities, luxurious style with everyday discomfort, new-found affluence with ongoing deprivation, the cinemas of the past with the cinemas of the future. It is this symbolic function that underlies the significance afforded to these new buildings as part of a suite of new iconic architecture that has emerged in India in the post-liberalisation period. The multiplex forcefully interjects itself into the urban skyline and is imbued with meanings that have strong connections to transnational trends in urban design. At the same time, India's multiplexes are contextualised by local desires and sensibilities. They are particularly indicative of the imaginary arcadias of certain social groups currently laying claim to the cultural capital of the global modern. For all these reasons, it is reasonable to assume that the nature of the multiplex environment not only caters to the prior concerns of its patrons, but also determines their subsequent occupation of these spaces at a number of levels. In order to understand the ways in which these buildings are inhabited and experienced, we look in more detail in Chapter 7 at what these spaces mean to those who use them.

7 A 'decent crowd'

The social imagination of the multiplex public

In the preceding chapters, we discussed the spatial politics of the multiplex at a series of scales reaching from the national geography of opportunity down to the interior arrangement of specific sites. In each case, our discussion of the physical geography of the multiplex phenomenon sought correspondence with its human geography. As such, we drew attention to various aspects of this human presence. First, we recognized the role played by the formation of crowds around leisure activities in the contest over public space in India's urban history. Second, we noted the explicit focus on the high end of the cinema market in the business model of the multiplex chains, and specifically upon the so-called 'consuming classes'. For this reason, we have attempted to elaborate upon how the multiplex chains have sought to locate and serve this new public at the national and metropolitan levels. Whilst much of the discussion of this putative social formation has been necessarily quantitative in focus, we have taken care to emphasise that this is an *imagined* community that has been absolutely central to the ideological construction of India as an emerging economic power. Finally, in Chapter 6, we began to explore how the multiplex functions as an explicit device for the architectural disciplining of the body. From this perspective, the multiplex is constituted by a series of strategic spatial deployments designed not only to maximise profit, but also to instil a certain social order amongst its clientele.

In terms of the human experience of leisure, it is the articulation of a social imagination that provides the broadest expression of our relation with the consumption of media. Benedict Anderson famously postulated that it was the fundamental nature of the print media that produced the social imagination of modern nationalism by fostering a deep sense of fraternity amongst its readership (1991, 1998). Elsewhere, other scholars have also taken up this idea of media, encouraging larger and more abstracted social formations and applying them to television and the Internet (Appadurai 1996, Castells 1996). Given the undeniable complexities of quantifying such imaginative relations between media forms, their communicative content, their creative professionals and their consumers, it is not surprising that the advent of the mass media has instigated a rich debate across the humanities for almost a century. Almost every aspect of this debate remains unresolved to date. What is beyond doubt is that our engagement with the modern media is inherently a social practice, one that links us practically and symbolically, if not always physically, with others. Following this lead, this chapter begins to explore the social imagination that is being constructed around the multiplex, ultimately providing a rich speculative, descriptive and analytical account of the multiplex crowd.

We begin with the observation that any mediated social imagination necessarily extends beyond media consumers themselves. Crucially, those who speculate in the cultural industries (for themselves or on behalf of others) do so on the basis of their own interpretation of a potential market that is conceptualised in the form of an audience. This notion of an audience as an inhabited market is conceived of in terms of an interdependency between media providers and consumers which attributes agency, albeit unequally, to both. Naturally, the limitations of a market-based definition of 'community' arise from the restriction of social agency to choices based upon consumption. As such, the terms of the enquiry will always attribute more weight to the decisive act of consumption than to the production of meanings or pleasures. Nonetheless, this is undeniably imaginative work that is social in nature. This is also important work, whether it is undertaken by children's entertainers, classical musicians or by film professionals focusing on the successful exploitation of public taste. It is the capacity for imagining large numbers of plausible (but fictitious and essentially unknowable) consumers upon which commercial success often depends. For this reason, the multiplex operators are very conscious of their desired audience:

> I can definitely speak about our audiences, and they would be 18–34 age group, basically the college kids, and what we call the younger, the newly-married people. I think that the younger crowd, basically, they want to go out and have a nice time on evenings and enjoy themselves. In India we call them 'dinks', double-income no kids. It is that category that really is pushing it. Disposable income is going up. People are making more money so people want to spend that money and enjoy themselves.
>
> (Shriram Krishnan, interview 20/01/2007)

> Primarily we do fifteen to thirty five. Somebody who earns around more than one hundred and twenty thousand rupees. Typically someone who is at least a graduate, and who has money to spend but doesn't have time. So it is more of disposable time as a business person I am after, than disposable money. Today if you build something which deserves somebody's attention, people are ready to pay.
>
> (Tashur Dhingra, interview 08/01/2007)

The logic of the imaginative associations made here is readily apparent. The first component is the identification of a demographic with the requisite spending capacity and few financial commitments. This can hypothetically be translated into the desired spending behaviours, and thus company profits. Needless to say, the nature of this projection is somewhat arbitrary, but this capacity to rhetorically assume the role of an ideal consumer is a common feature of the way that media professionals describe their audiences. What it also represents in this particular case is an attempt to bridge the perceived disconnect between the wealth of India's middle classes and their desire to spend that wealth. Whilst the blue-sky projections of the purchasing power of India's middle classes provoked a frenzy of interest in the Indian market during the 1990s, the growth in consumption has lagged markedly behind its perceived potential (Fernandes 2006: 78). According to Mazzarella (2003), the major problem faced by India's advertising industry – itself perhaps the major beneficiary of the New Economy – has been that household incomes have been a relatively poor indicator of propensity to spend. However, according to the multiplex chains, their clientele represents a much more select segment of the middle classes – a segment that can afford to spend above the odds on non-essentials and, more importantly, is willing to do so. As we noted previously, advertising incomes for the multiplex chains are significant for this reason, constituting five per cent of overall incomes and growing steadily, according to Snehal Chitneni, Corporate Communications Manager at INOX:

> Corporates look at multiplexes as a very attractive venue for advertising, simply because of the kind of audience we attract. Most multiplexes are located in premium locations. The audiences that they attract are similarly SEC A+, SEC B. So basically, the upper to the middle classes are the ones who frequent multiplexes. Plus, we have a captive audience. When you run your ads in the interval or before a film, the audience are just sitting there because they have nowhere else to go. Plus a lot of corporates also do a lot of their product launches, setting up of kiosks. For example, if they are launching a skincare range they will have a counter where patrons can go and test it. So we have a lot of huge brands like Mercedes, Philips, Sony. The Levers of the world use INOX.
>
> (Snehal Chitneni 09/01/2007)

The multiplex crowd is thus not only selected for its own spending capacity within the confines of the mall-multiplex combine, but also for its on-sale value to advertisers. The multiplex crowd is thus both imagined and traded as a commodity. For the purposes of advertisers, the multiplex crowd is posited as an entirely different proposition from the regular cinema crowd. As Parveen Kumar at Wave Cinemas in NOIDA puts it:

> You know we advertise a normal good car in normal cinemas. OK, there clientele are like that, so they can put a more impact on local clientele. But if you are advertising for Nokia N Series, you have to play this thing in multiplexes because these people can afford Nokia N Series. Or let it be Windows Vista, in normal halls it doesn't matter any difference if we are advertising Windows Vista or Nokia because both things are out of their reach. So multiplex clientele matters, because Pepsi, Nokia, LG, Samsung, big business houses, we are investing more on their promotion or sales part, and we are their biggest consumers in that way.
>
> (Parveen Kumar, 09/03/2007)

The explicit construction of the multiplex crowd as a consuming commodity is a useful example of instrumental rationality at work in the social imagination. However, if we take into account the environmental conditions created by the visual impact of advertising at the multiplex and the bridging effect of the older tradition of the star-hoarding meeting the newer one of the film star as a clothes horse for innumerable consumer brands, we cannot help but be aware of how the multiplex patron is interpellated by a particular set of ideological conditions that equate leisure with consumption.

Iconicity aside, the physicality of the multiplex remains important here. The historical trajectory that is commonly marked out in metanarratives of the public sphere inspired by Anderson, Habermas and others, beginning with small-scale physical assembly and culminating in the virtual mass publics of television and the internet, tends to sideline the particular operating conditions of cinema. Cinema, despite being a mass medium, continues to require public assembly within specifically-constructed physical environments. Cinema is therefore implicated not only in the discursive functions of a symbolic virtual gathering, but also in the continuing material productions of public space and of public assembly. As such, the cinema continues to represent a unique interface between the mythic-symbolic and the architectural and biological dimensions of public culture. This is why the designers and operators of the multiplex are not only interested in what Indian English would designate as the 'creamy layer', but also in attracting the 'decent crowd'. This is because ambience is an important component of the environmental conditions seen as conducive to consuming behaviours. Ambience, of course, has a human element in which social mores and manners are emphasised. Thus, for some operators the high prices charged at the multiplexes are not only about maximising revenue streams, and certainly not about maximising occupancy. Rather, they are designed to ensure that particular kinds of people (and not others) go to the multiplex:

> This is why they don't want to reduce the prices, because we also have the fear that once I reduce the prices, you know – I can understand that even if I reduce the prices I can not get that much of impact on my general business – but I don't want to reduce my prices because then there's a chance that I'll get people which I don't want to be in the cinema . . . [In this multiplex] You will not find anyone hooting and shouting. It's very important. So being a manager it is my responsibility to give a sense of security to my customers. I don't want a couple of guys who can spoil the whole experience of the cinema for the rest of fifty or sixty people.
>
> (Parveen Kumar, 09/03/2007)

The inculcation and preservation of a sense of ontological security amongst patrons is an important behavioural aspect to the management of the multiplex chains that goes beyond prioritising the successful application of modern advertising techniques. In both respects, however, we might argue that the goal of the multiplex in India is to fashion a very particular kind of public through dynamic pricing, physical location and the architectural and paramilitary management of the built environment. When we pay attention to the degree of intent displayed in the conceptualisation of the multiplex crowd within the industry, there is a persuasive argument to be made that the multiplex has not simply arisen in response to an untapped demand for quality facilities amongst a more affluent public (as has often been claimed by the industry itself). Rather, the multiplex is more indicative of an agenda to re-create the Indian cinema audience in the mould of the elusive consuming class that the world's commercial entrepreneurs have been pursuing for more than a decade. It is equally clear that the multiplex is conceived as an environment capable of serving the hitherto elusive rational, modern and detached spectator (Rajadhyaksha 2000, Vasudevan 2000). For these reasons, the multiplex can be accused of 'audiencing', that is, of consciously seeking to shape its own clientele.

In the various aspects that we have encountered through this book so far, this is a programme of social engineering with fairly concrete material methods (e.g. placement, catchment, architecture, management). It is obvious, at one level, that the socio-economic filtering, architectural dispersal and ideological diffusion that are employed in creating the ambience of the multiplex necessarily imply a profound psychological effect upon patrons. At another level, what is less obvious is the extent to which these artificial conditions of existence actually reflect the social reality of the multiplex crowd. Thus, we need to gauge the extent to which members of this new public are aware of or identify with the ideal type of the multiplex spectator – the mould into which they are being placed. In order to understand the lived experience of the multiplex somewhat better, this chapter provides a qualitative account of the multiplex crowd found in a number of locations. The major focus throughout is upon the social imagination of multiplex patrons as manifested through their descriptions of the multiplex and who, and what, goes there.

Assessing the multiplex crowd: Findings from attitudinal surveys

In order to make a preliminary assessment of the claims being made about the composition of the multiplex crowd, we conducted several small-scale survey studies in Bangalore, Baroda and Kolkata during the early part of 2007. It was also our intention to provide adequate space within this book for multiplex patrons to vocalise their own motivations, desires and gratifications, as well as their concerns, surrounding their participation in this form of public leisure. For this reason, the survey was designed to encourage qualitative responses as well as basic demographic data. The questions were designed to address three primary lines of enquiry: 1) What was the primary motivation for visiting a multiplex? 2) How accurate were claims made by the industry that the multiplex crowd was socially (and socioeconomically) distinct from the regular cinema audience? 3) To what extent does the social imagination of multiplex patrons reflect the ethos of the multiplex and of the new regimes of consumption in general? The survey itself was conducted in English, in a paper form with three sections ('Basic Demographic Information', 'Viewing Habits' and 'Social Situation') over five pages. Of these three sections, the middle section ('Viewing Habits') focused on qualitative responses and comprised the largest part of the survey (four pages). As with the conduct of the study more broadly, the survey was conducted in a range of cities in recognition of the disparity between social attitudes and circumstances in different parts of the country. We subsequently staged a series of three focus-group discussions, where the issues emerging in the surveys were explored in more depth, during field visits.

It is obviously important to note at this point that a survey of a few hundred patrons accompanied by a small number of focus groups provides no empirical guarantee of the multiplex public, and equally the combination of quantitative and qualitative methods of audience research employed here makes no significant attempt to resolve the conflict between those two schools (see Alasuutari 1999, Gunter 1999, Brooker and Jermyn 2002). At the same time, however, drawing on the accounts provided by the industry itself, which correlate sales data and customer feedback with demographic and psychographic projections, it seemed reasonable to make our own assessment of those accounts, using similar methods drawn from the standard armoury of market researchers. In doing so, we uncovered a number of important factors contributing to the social context of the Indian multiplex that may otherwise have been omitted from our study. As an indicative account, our study of the multiplex audiences also raises a number of questions about the ideal types currently being employed by the industry itself.

Bangalore

In Bangalore, a city described in some detail in Chapters 5 and 6, 40 survey returns provided a useful indicative account of the multiplex crowd in India's Silicon Valley. The sample group was dominated by the youth demographic commonly associated with cinema audiences, with 14 respondents in the 16–21 age range and 17 respondents aged 22–25 years. This was overwhelmingly a male-dominated group with 29 male respondents and eight female respondents (three gender withheld). A large contingent of the sample were students from Christ Church College, with the rest being employed at various IT, BPO and call centre operations in Bangalore's southern suburbs. This geographical bias may have been a factor in the largest part of this crowd identifying PVR at Forum Mall as their preferred multiplex, with a far smaller number choosing INOX at Garuda Mall. No respondents indicated a preference for the peri-urban Innovative Multiplex.

In describing their motivations for their last visit to a multiplex, respondents identified a range of factors that would correspond with the logic of the multiplex format, such as distance, timings of shows and choice of films. However, the greater attention to patron comfort in Indian multiplexes, and the greater contrast of these conditions with the existing theatrical infrastructure, made environmental conditions of much greater importance to patrons when choosing the to visit the multiplex. The following are some indicative samples of survey responses [respondent identifier key: age (numeral) gender (capital letter) marital status (lower case letter)]:

20Mu: The sound quality was better compared to other theatres. I like the environment and basically the crowd is good.

21Mu: I couldn't watch films in other theatres 'cos the environment of the other theatres wouldn't be as good as that of the multiplex and also the comfort of watching movies in the multiplex is very good. Environment consists of people, the cleanliness of the place, etc.

21Fu: The good and decent crowd.

22Fu: Because of the picture quality, sound effects and especially the comfort. I prefer English movie in the multiplex. Indian movies have too many songs which are not suited to be played in multiplex.

18Fu: Because the crowd isn't very cheap. It is more comfortable. What I see as comfort is my basic priority for entertainment.

18Mu: There are a lot of choices offered. I could make last minute decisions. Also, there's the cool factor involved. People like to be seen in multiplexes. I would be too.

What becomes immediately apparent from these responses is that the environmental conditions that make the multiplex attractive to this audience have a human dimension. In this respect, the responses of the survey group echoed Parveen Kumar's concern with maintaining the selectivity of the multiplex audience, with six respondents identifying the make-up of the multiplex audience as a motivational factor for their own attendance.

From the responses collected, it was immediately apparent that film choice was a relatively weak factor in making a decision to visit a multiplex, which underscored

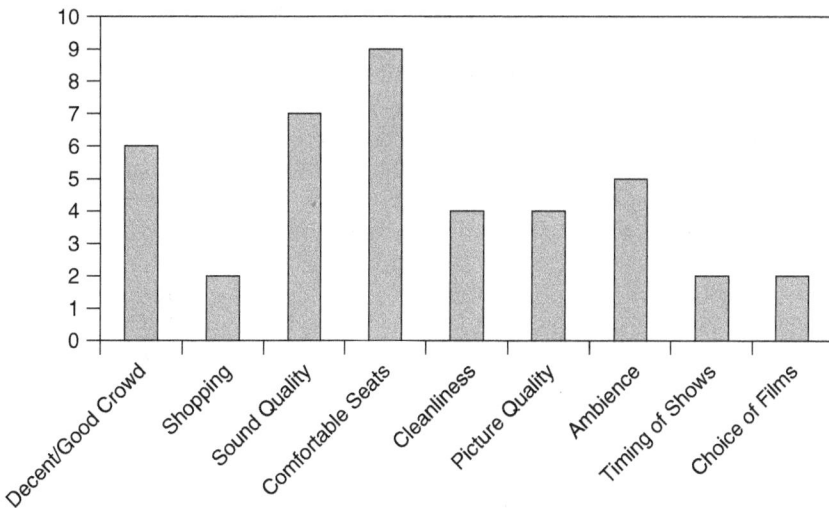

Figure 7.1 Factors influencing decision to visit multiplex in Bangalore.

the importance of 'ambience' as a major draw. The fact that the word was used specifically by five respondents serves to demonstrate the extent to which the commercial language of the marketing industry has entered the consciousness of this sample group. At another level, however, the following response is also strongly evocative of the 1950s commentators on cinema audiences discussed in Chapter 2:

> 17Mu: As multiplexes are more comfortable than a normal theatre. It is very much organised. Especially, 90 per cent of the crowd will be decent. Multiplexes are a huge advantage for ladies as ladies won't prefer to get squashed between a group of gents which usually occurs in a normal theatre. So to avoid the chaos, it's better everyone choose multiplex. Even the sound quality is better. Ambience is more and it is very, very clean.

Of the sample group, 32 respondents (80 per cent) stated that they were regular visitors to the multiplex, with 14 respondents visiting every month and eight respondents visiting three to four times or even more per month. However, only one-quarter of respondents (ten) identified themselves as 'multiplex-only' patrons. It may be due to the relatively small number of multiplexes in Bangalore in relation to the overall population that 32 respondents (80 per cent) also claimed to be visiting 'normal' cinemas. This indicated a significant degree of overlap between the multiplex crowd and the regular cinema audience. The 'multiplex-only' crowd was evenly split between males and females. The 'visiting normal cinemas' segment was far more reflective of the masculine bias of the overall sample (19 males to three females). This made 'multiplex-only' patrons a majority (62.5 per cent) amongst the smaller number of female respondents, but a clear minority (20.8 per cent) amongst male respondents. Obviously, it would be untenable to make large-scale projections from a sample of this size, but in light of the comment above, the greater frequency of females claiming to visit multiplexes exclusively appeared to be significant (as was their greater tendency to mention the nature of the 'crowd' as a motivating factor for doing so).

Despite the large proportion of the sample group who identified themselves as visiting normal cinema halls in addition to multiplexes, the image of Bangalore's regular theatres that emerged from their description of them was overwhelmingly negative, as the following examples demonstrate:

> 17Mu: There is too much of crowd left at a time. It is too dirty. No ambience. No proper parking. Dirty toilets.

> 21Mu: The sound, the crowd (generally cheap) the ambience.

> 21Fu: Cleanliness. All local people will come. Too much crowded.

> 21Mu: The seating quality is not good. The place is generally not clean and the washrooms and restrooms need more maintenance.

> 23Fu: Rats, cost, cheeking, etc.

27Fu: The choice of food/snacks at canteen – not like multiplex and – sometimes – bugs on seats.

21Mu: The picture quality, sound etc. (dislike). I do like the down-to-earth kind of movies.

21Mu: Likes: more economical. Number of cinemas are greater thus providing a larger variety of movies to choose from. Dislike: Not clean and hygienic. Too crowded. Crowd not good.

When we compare the following two tables that depict the most frequent terms of description used by respondents in relation to Bangalore's normal cinemas and the most frequent terms of description used by respondents in relation to Bangalore's multiplexes, we begin to see how the normal cinema hall was articulated as a negative inverse for the pleasures of the multiplex.

This almost dialectical representation bears a very strong resemblance to the claims of the multiplex industry, suggesting that they have successfully identified the major concerns of their target audience. From this perspective, it is hard to see why a greater supply of multiplex screens in the city would not instantly translate into a much greater 'multiplex-only' crowd. There were, however, some detractors from the overall polarity of this description. Two (older, male) viewers explicitly stated that they disliked the multiplex crowd, and while film choice was given as a positive factor by a respondent who liked watching 'English' movies, it was given as a negative feature of the multiplex by two others who preferred regional movies. Similarly, for one respondent the major drawback of the normal cinema was 'bad food', while for another the multiplex experience was diminished by the fact 'They won't let us take the snacks we wanna take'. The major inversion, however, of the 'bad' normal

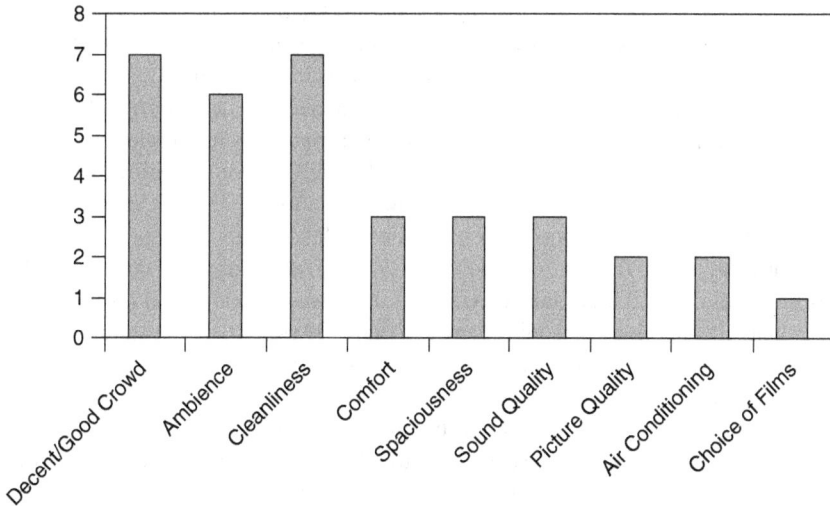

Figure 7.2 Positive aspects of multiplexes in Bangalore.

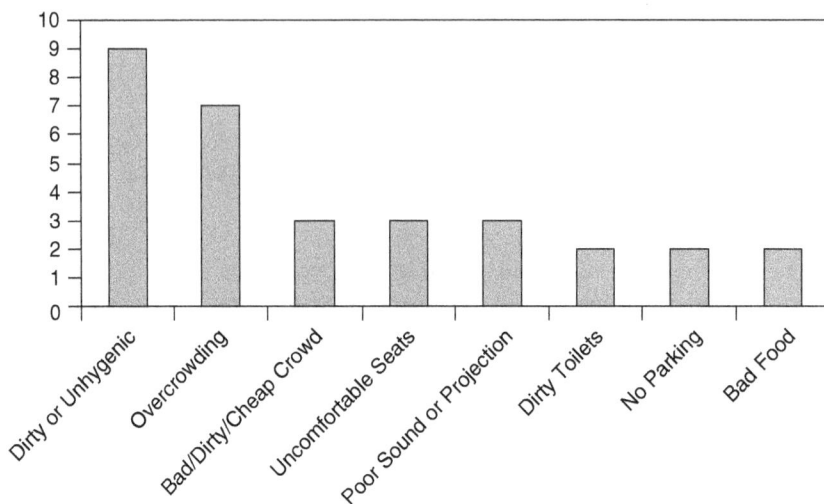

Figure 7.3 Negative aspects of normal cinema halls in Bangalore.

cinema versus the 'good' multiplex took place around the issue of cost. One-third of respondents to this question (11 of 32) thought that multiplexes were far too costly, variously stating that multiplexes were 'Too heavy on the pockets' and that the ticket prices were 'a little too high for the Indian economy' and therefore 'the price becomes a matter of concern'.

This reticence surrounding the cost of visiting the multiplex was reflected in the spending patterns that this group attributed to their multiplex visits. The vast majority of the group who specified their spending (27 of 38, or 71 per cent) claimed to spend less than 300 rupees on a visit to the multiplex, including ticket and refreshments, with 42 per cent (16 of 38) spending less than 200 rupees. These are of course, significant sums when compared with the average ticket cost of 40 rupees for a regular theatre in Bangalore, but they represent a fairly modest level of expenditure for the creamy layer. Indeed, despite the high degree of consideration that has been placed upon their consumer aspirations and Bangalore's reputation for shopping, only half this group (21 respondents) indicated that they spent money on anything other than their movie ticket and basic refreshments when visiting PVR at Forum Mall or INOX at Garuda Mall. Of those who would spend more money, over half (12 respondents) would spend less than 500 rupees, with just nine respondents (one-quarter of the survey group overall) indicating that they spent 500 rupees or more on other activities during a cinema visit. Again, the small sample size does not allow concrete projections about the spending habits of Bangalore's multiplex crowd. It is worth noting, however, that the large proportion of this sample that spent modestly on their cinema visits was not necessarily reflected in the consuming power of the group as measured by the traditional indicators of consuming power commonly used by the NCAER and others. For example, almost two-thirds of the sample owned a two-wheeler (26 of 40, or 65 per cent). More than one-third claimed to own a car (15 of 40, or 37.5 per cent) and just over one-quarter (11 of 40, or 27.5 per cent) held a credit card. Three-quarters of the sample had completed a tertiary qualification, and the remaining 25 per cent had completed 12th Standard and were attending college. In all these respects, the sample group appeared commensurate with the profiles prepared by the industry for its advertising clients. Despite this, however, this indicative study appears to suggest that only a relatively small proportion of the multiplex crowd, even in a major metro like Bangalore, were likely to be regular customers for Mercedes or Sony, at least in the immediate future.

Baroda

The next group of multiplex patrons that is considered here were located in the city of Baroda (now officially known as Vadodora) in the western state of Gujarat. The survey was conducted in January 2007. The city was selected as a useful example of how the multiplex phenomenon was developing in the so-called 'second-tier' cities. Baroda is also the headquarters of Gujarat Fluorochemicals Ltd., the parent company of INOX Leisure Ltd., which might explain why it was amongst the first of the second-tier cities to get a multiplex. Despite lacking the international profile of a larger city like Bangalore, Baroda has always been an important city in western India. In modern times, the city of Baroda was the capital of a Princely state founded by the Maratha General Pilaji Gaekwad in 1734 and lasting until independence, formerly becoming part of the Union of India in 1948. Industrialisation got underway in Baroda early in the twentieth century and the city has become a significant industrial centre in Gujarat, which is in turn one of the more heavily industrialised states in India. At the time of the 2001 census, Baroda had a population of around 1.5 million, making it the third-largest city in the state (Census of India, 2001). Baroda has a great concentration of the chemical industries, employing around ten per cent of the population. It is also a university town with 100,000 students attending the famous Maharaja Sayajirao University, the only English-language institution in Gujarat. Baroda was designated by the Confederation of Indian Industries in 2007 for further development as a 'knowledge city' with an IT focus (CII 2007). Both the NH8 and the Western Railway linking Delhi and Mumbai run through Baroda, placing the city firmly within the geography of opportunity.

At present, Baroda has three multiplexes which are found in a remarkably similar distribution pattern to that found in the much larger Bangalore: one in a central location, one in the suburban fringe and one outside the city proper. The first multiplex in Baroda, the Chandan, was opened in December 2001. It has a seating capacity of 1,500 over three screens, with two auditoria seating 600 patrons and third seating 300. Chandan was built on a greenfields site that is a ten-minute drive from Baroda proper. By contrast, INOX Baroda, opened in October 2002, is located within the city on Racecourse Circuit Road. It is fast becoming a focus for new commercial developments. INOX Baroda is a purpose-built multiplex with four screens that also houses a McDonalds franchise, a Pantaloons department store, Cafe Coffee Day and other retailers. The most recent multiplex opened in Baroda is the Deep Multiplex, which was opened in January 2005 at Ramvadi on the northern fringe of the city in an area currently not served by any of Baroda's existing cinemas. Developed by a local family operating a number of cinemas else-where in Gujarat, the site was originally purchased in 1996 for a single-screen cinema, but the development was altered to a multiplex due to the tax concessions implemented by the state government. Following the completion of fieldwork, the Deep has been leased by PVR and is now operated by that company. Aside from the three multiplexes, Baroda has eight independently-operating single-screen cinemas, all working in partnership with a local distributor. All of these theatres were established in the town by the 1970s.

The survey group in Baroda was comprised of 21 respondents, the majority of whom were recruited from the Maharaja Sayajirao University. This was again a group in which the multiplex's target demographic of 18–35 years predominated, with nine members of the group being in the 16–21 years range and a further eight aged between 22 and 25 years. Unlike the Bangalore survey group, this was a sample in which females predominated. Of the 21 respondents to the Baroda survey, 13 were female. The vast majority of this group was students, with relatively few of them having an income independent of their families. Of the three multiplexes operating in Baroda in January 2007, the survey respondents showed an over-whelming preference for the INOX site, as opposed to the Deep Multiplex. None of the survey cohort expressed a preference for the peripheral Chandan cinema.

Patrons in Baroda were much more concerned overall by the quality of the cine-matic facilities (e.g. sound and projection) and the co-location of retail and restau-rant facilities than the Bangalore sample when they were making their choice to visit the multiplex. This might in part reflect the far greater presence of mall devel-opments in Bangalore, where they are becoming more or less ubiquitous, as opposed to Baroda, where the presence of Central Mall's Baroda site is compara-tively recent and thus much more novel. Where the responses of the two groups reinforced each other most strongly was the emphasis on environmental conditions and the far lesser importance of the theatrical offerings in motivating patrons. In terms of the multiplex ambience as a draw for this group, the human aspect (i.e. the crowd) appeared to be an even more important factor for the Baroda sample. It was a consistently important factor for female respondents, as can be seen from a selec-tion of sample responses:

> F16u: I choose the multiplex because of its ambience. The comfortable seating arrangements, good sound system and also good quality foodstuffs. And even to some extent in a multiplex there are good crowd too. I choose any multiplex which is closer to my home, like INOX.

> F18u: I chose multiplex because multiplexes are comfortable. The crowd there is good. Security system is well-organised, no nuisance is involved over there. We can do window shopping or regular shopping along with watching the movie.

F20u: I choose INOX multiplex because INOX being a multiplex that offers a lot of facilities. I.e., one can visit Pantaloons, have food at McDonalds and of course watch a movie. So it's like having everything under one roof. Moreover, the gentry at multiplexes is better'.

F20u: Initially, I was enamoured by the luxury and ostentatiousness of a multiplex. As a school kid, when the multiplex euphoria began to catch up, it suddenly became uncool to watch movies in a normal cinema hall. One can also enjoy watching a movie in a multiplex without all the hooting and disturbance, that was the main attraction for me.

The importance of the multiplex to the group's cinema habits was clearly substantial, with three-quarters (15) of respondents describing themselves as regular visitors. Of these, three patrons did not specify the regularity of their visits in monthly terms. For those who did, roughly one-third attended monthly (four), one-third fortnightly (five) and the remainde, three (one) or four (two) times per month. It is worth noting that these are relatively low cinema attendance figures for India, where frequent and repeat viewings have been considered the norm (Derne 1999, Srinivas 2002). However, as a cautionary note, these figures are for multiplex visits only. In this survey group, we found once more that a significant number of patrons at the multiplex were also attending normal cinemas in Baroda (in most cases, the Aradhana, which was considered the most 'respectable' of the single-screen cinemas). However, compared to the Bangalore sample, there was a more substantial proportion of 'multiplex-only' patrons in Baroda, constituting around half (11 of 21) of the sample. In order to contextualise this, it is worth noting that Baroda had three operational multiplexes at the time of the survey – the same number as Bangalore (albeit with only half the screen capacity). If we consider that the population of Baroda is less than one-third of the population of Bangalore, it becomes clear that the former is far better serviced by multiplexes than the latter. Despite being a far smaller city, there are in fact already more multiplex screens in Baroda than single-screen cinemas, even though the latter still offer the greater overall seating capacity. This may well serve to explain why the proportion of 'multiplex-only' patrons was twice as high in Baroda.

Where we approach the multiplex crowd in gendered terms, male respondents displayed a 50/50 split (four each) between 'multiplex-only' patrons and those who also visited 'normal cinemas'. Female respondents showed a nominal bias towards exclusive use of the multiplex (seven to six). However, when these preferences were arranged by age, there was a marked bias (seven of nine) amongst the youngest cohort (16–21 years) towards exclusive multiplex use. This suggests that the recent advent of the multiplex craze may have successfully captured the younger cohort, while older multiplex patrons were more likely to also continue visiting the cinemas that they had been using before the multiplexes arrived. This disjuncture between generational perspectives can be most bluntly illustrated by comparing the two responses below, one from a younger, female patron and one from a male patron who was the oldest survey respondent:

F18u: Multiplexes are having wide space to move around. It's ambience is good, the whole premises are bright. Good crowd, i.e., people are sober, sophisticated, the premises are clean. There are many theatres, shopping malls are there. Eatables are good. Good facility of entertainment and good security arrangements and no havoc created.

M44u: I don't like multiplexes. They are too artificial. Eatables (junk food) are priced unreasonably. The aura around the multiplexes puts a strain to conform.

This male respondent claimed that, despite being a regular visitor to multiplexes, he visited the multiplex primarily due to 'peer pressure'. It would be erroneous, however, to imply that all the older respondents who also visited single-screen cinemas actually preferred them to the multiplex. One of the older female respondents (F35u) identified that she visited normal cinemas primarily for reasons of cost, and that she greatly preferred the multiplex due to 'Cordial surroundings, and to a certain extent, the viewers. As far as India is concerned there are categories of viewers. At multiplex, yes, the difference can be noted'.

As with the previous survey group, when we compare the overall description of the multiplex with the descriptions offered of the single-screen cinemas in Baroda, we can clearly see how one functions as the negative inverse of the other. The crowd at the multiplex is 'decent' or 'good', while the crowd at the normal cinema is 'dirty', 'cheap' or 'bad'. The seats at the multiplex are a draw, while at the normal cinema they are a drawback. There were some differences between the two surveys, however. Although cleanliness was still a selling point for the multiplex in Baroda, there were no specific complaints about the dirtiness of the single-screen cinemas, which

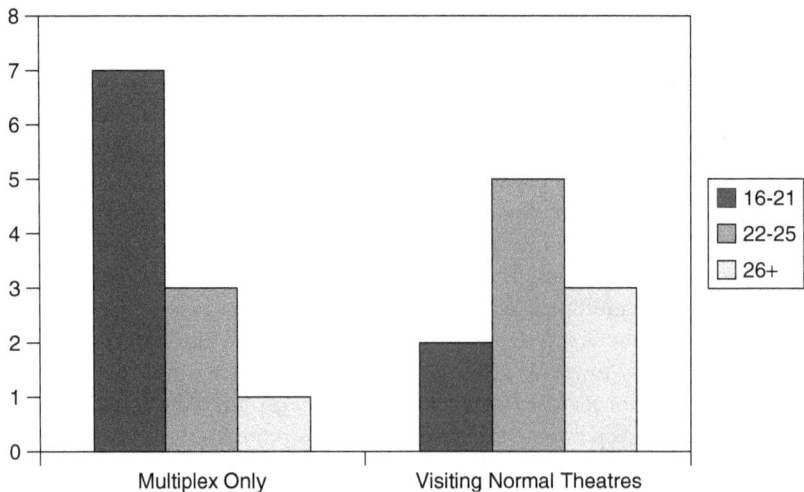

Figure 7.4 Multiplex only crowd vs. those visiting multiplexes and normal cinemas in Baroda, by age.

was the most common complaint of the Bangalore group. Another difference was that in Baroda, 'security' (and its negative inverse of anti-social behaviour at the normal cinemas) was a major factor.

For one young female respondent, the traditional cinema hall was described as a dark and sexually-threatening space. For a male respondent, the regular cinema crowd demonstrated a lack of appreciation for the cinema as an art form. Another female respondent specified that the noisy behaviour of regular cinema patrons was off-putting.

> F18u: Normal cinemas are not having wide space. Crowd is not good, has cosy premises, very crowded. Indecency is seen, the whole premises are not bright. Nuisances and havocs are created.

> M22u: What I like is the prices for the tickets is damn low here. What I don't like is the crowd it attracts. Not that I am against the lower classes but they don't appreciate good work.

> F20u: The hooting and screaming is one of the main reasons why I don't like normal cinema halls.

Some other respondents were more equivocal in their comparison of the multiplex with its architectural predecessor. For one male respondent, it was less a case of normal cinemas being dreadful per se, but multiplexes simply being better. The older male in the group claimed to prefer the 'atmosphere' of the regular cinema, even though he disliked the behaviour of patrons there as much as he did the behaviour of those at the multiplex.

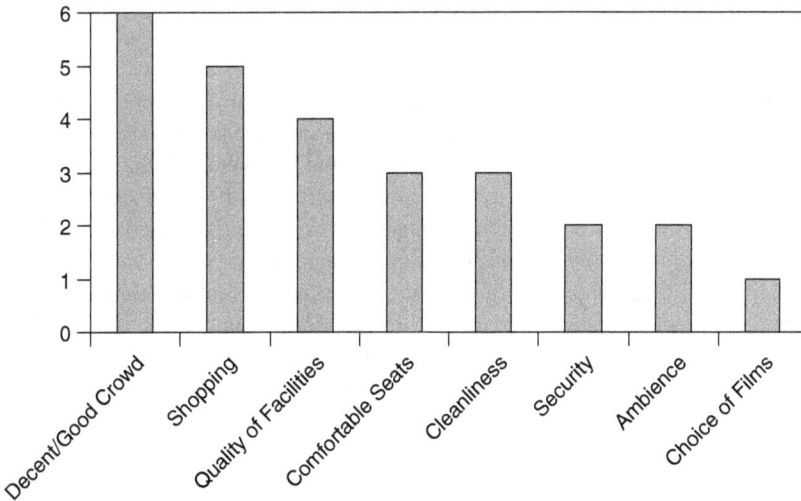

Figure 7.5 Attractive features of multiplexes in Baroda.

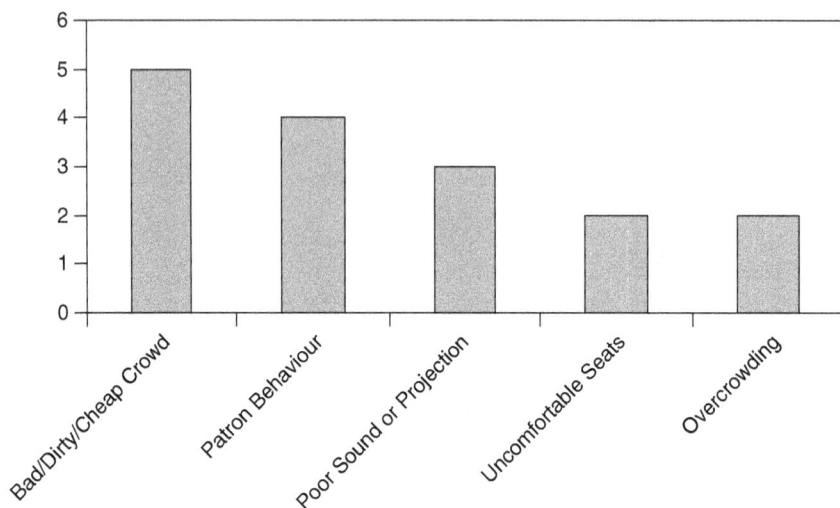

Figure 7.6 Negative aspects of normal cinemas in Baroda.

> M23u: Normal cinemas can also provide quite good facilities, but they are not in match with those of multiplex, and their quality is of no match to the multiplex.

> M44u: I like the relaxed atmosphere of normal cinemas, though the rats, spitting, smoking and lovers may be sometimes irritating. The crass crowd of the multiplex also uses their mobiles with a kind of unconcern for the other.

Even for those who found the presence of the 'cheap/dirty crowd' less of a problem, it was clear that visiting a normal cinema was seen as an uncomfortable and inconvenient experience. While Baroda's single-screen cinemas were not described as unhygienic, they were still considered as venues that were far from satisfactory for enjoying movies. When we take note of the fact that the average Indian multiplex is a good deal more comfortable than its counterpart in many developed countries, the enormous disparity between this exaggerated luxury and the hard and cramped seating found at the older cinemas is of major significance to the viewing experience. Even for those who enjoy taking part in, or simply observing, the raucous collective rituals of audience in regular theatres, complaints about the quality of seating have to be taken seriously when the average running length of an Indian film is over three hours. As one respondent (F37m) put it: 'In normal cinema, watching movie is like doing a work of watching. It's not leisure'. A younger respondent agreed:

> F18u: I chose INOX to watch the movie because it is the most happening place. Movie at a regular theatre is a chore but at a multiplex it is an experience.

The lightings, ambience, the smell of popcorn, the acoustics, add and enhance the whole experience of watching a movie. You feel sort of pampered and special. At other theatres, there are dirty chairs, tobacco-stained walls, scruffy employees and horrible visuals. Who in their right minds would go elsewhere?

While enjoying the relatively greater comforts of the multiplex, the 13 respondents who were prepared to detail their spending appeared to spend fairly modestly. Only one respondent spent more than 500 rupees on a trip to the cinema, and half of the group spent less than 200 rupees. However, this group seemed inclined to spend on ancillary activities while visiting the multiplex, with just one respondent spending nothing and two spending less than 100 rupees. The remainder of the group (nine of 12) claimed to spend between 200 and 500 rupees outside of the cinema during visits to the multiplex. With even smaller numbers in this sample, it is difficult to generalise about the value of the multiplex crowd in Baroda, but the consumer profile of the Baroda group was remarkably similar to the survey group in Bangalore. One-third (seven) had their own credit card. Over one-half (11) had a two-wheeler and almost one-third (six) had a private car at their disposal. Three-quarters (15) had completed some tertiary education and the reminder were engaged in tertiary studies. (Although, of course, unlike the Bangalore survey this was a sample entirely dominated by students.) Needless to say, this profile is far above the national average in every respect.

Kolkata

The Kolkata surveys conducted in December 2006 and January 2007 drew on larger samples than those undertaken in the other sites, with 238 respondents spread across the three sites of INOX Salt Lake (103 respondents), Fame Hiland Park (70 respondents) and INOX Forum Mall (65 respondents). A particularly useful aspect of carrying out a multi-site study within a large city like Kolkata is that it allowed us to look for the distinct make-up of the multiplex crowd in each site, and thus begin to assess the variations in audience across the different catchments. The industry model of the multiplex consumer strongly suggests that the multiplex audience as a whole is to be differentiated from audiences for normal theatres in terms of spending capacity and socio-economic status. The multiplex is intended to cater to the highest social classes in each location. The planning of sites in relation to catchments within each city, however, indicates a tacit recognition that there are different levels of wealth to be served by multiplexes in different parts of a city. The demographic data we collected on the sample audiences at the Kolkata multiplexes (presented below) provides some evidence of this variation. Fox example, compared to the other multiplexes, the crowd at INOX Salt Lake has higher levels of education, including a particularly large percentage of post-graduate education, and has much higher rates of ownership of consumer durables such as cars, scooters and credit cards. Fame Hiland Park and INOX Forum Mall by contrast had more mixed audiences in terms of these indicators. A further indicator of the differences between these catchments is the far greater number of respondents in the Salt

Table 7.1 Education attainment levels of respondents in Kolkata.

	10th Standard	10–12th Standard	Graduate	Postgraduate
Hiland Park	7.0	12.0	65.0	16.0
City Centre (Salt Lake)	0	10.6	59.4	30.0
Forum Elgin Road	0	15.7	67.0	17.3
Total	**2.6**	**12.17**	**62.17**	**23.06**

Table 7.2 Percentage of Kolkata respondents owning various consumer durables.

	Car	Scooter	Credit card
Hiland Park	24.6	15.4	32.0
City Centre (Salt Lake)	28.1	37.5	59.0
Forum Elgin Road	11.4	31.0	48.6

Lake surveys having been educated in English-medium institutions compared to Hiland Park.

These variations are important, and they reinforce our earlier comments about the unevenness of development in Kolkata. Equally, however, even though respondents at Hiland Park and Forum Mall were less affluent overall than the Salt Lake crowd, the majority of multiplex patrons in Kolkata were much better off than the general urban population. The high purchasing power of the multiplex crowd is a significant demographic variable consistently highlighted by multiplex operators and audiences, and one that we can broadly relate to class differentiation. In analysing the incomes claimed by multiplex patrons in these three sites in Kolkata, we found suggestive evidence that there is far from a single socio-economic class represented in the multiplex audience. In terms of income, while the majority of respondents earned more than 10,000 rupees per month and many earned substantially more, there was also a significant proportion who earned less than this. This was most obviously the case for the 81 respondents who were students receiving allowances from their parents (and are not represented in Figure 7.9). However, income differentiation also applied to multiplex patrons with an earned income. A significant proportion of respondents earned 10,000 rupees per month or less and, as such, were clearly not the wealthy SEC A+ consumers projected by the multiplex operators.

Differences also appeared between the multiplex catchments in Kolkata in terms of the relative balance of 'multiplex-only' patrons and those also visiting traditional cinema halls. A significant proportion of the Fame Hiland Park audience were not exclusively multiplex patrons. This was somewhat different from the audience at INOX Salt Lake, who in general were much less inclined to visit normal cinemas. INOX Forum Mall was situated between these two in terms of the split between 'multiplex-only' patrons and those who occasionally visit traditional cinemas. In all three cases, however, even those who did visit the older-style cinemas claimed they did so less often than they visited a multiplex.

As in our other surveys, it was clear from the Kolkata surveys that there is a wide variation in the frequency of visits made by patrons to the multiplex. However, the

**Income per month (Rps)
All Kolkata Multiplexes**

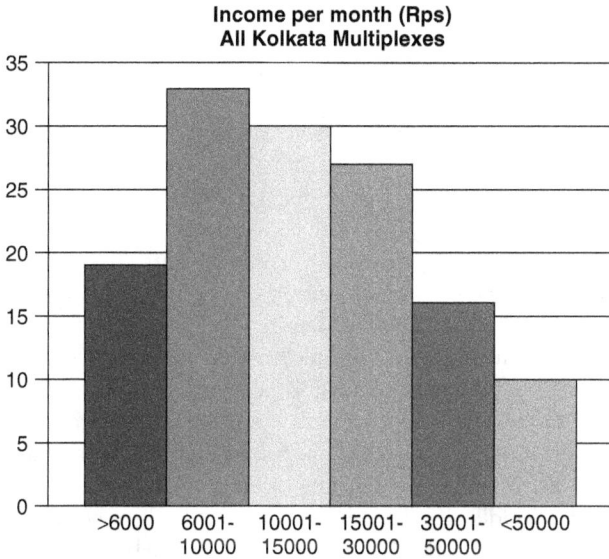

Figure 7.7 Income per month for employed multiplex patrons in Kolkata.

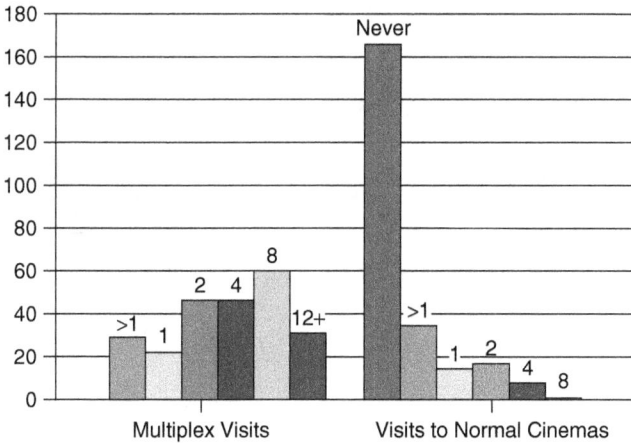

Figure 7.8 Frequency of visits to multiplexes and normal cinemas per month, Kolkata.

Kolkata audiences were much more frequent visitors to the multiplex overall than respondents in other cities. More than one-third (37.8 per cent) claimed that they visited the multiplex eight times or more per month, with 30 respondents (12.6 per cent) suggesting they visit multiplexes as much as three times per week. With 164 of the 238 respondents indicating that they never visited single-screen theatres, there was strong evidence to suggest that a large, exclusively multiplex-going public is emerging in Kolkata. For those who did visit single-screen theatres, the motivation was most commonly a desire to see regional films (as we found in Bangalore) and the difference in ticket prices between multiplexes and normal theatres was also a substantial issue for a significant number of patrons (as we found in Baroda).

As with our other sites, the gendering of the multiplex crowd became a major focus of our analysis here. The surveys from Kolkata demonstrated that there are significant numbers of women attending multiplexes in the city. In our surveys, female patrons comprised closer to one-third of the audience as opposed to the 50 per cent typically suggested by multiplex operators. Whether this indicates a lesser participation of women at the multiplex in Kolkata compared to elsewhere cannot be assessed on the basis of our samples, but our figures do suggest a much more substantial proportion of female viewers at the multiplex than can be found attending normal cinemas. However, while a much larger majority of women than men indicated that they never attended normal theatres, it was not the case that all women avoided them. This is at least partly because not all normal cinemas are as disreputable as the multiplex operators suggest they are. Many of our respondents were keen to differentiate between facilities such as Nandan or Priya in Kolkata, where upper- and middle-class women feel comparatively at home, and the more stereotypical single-screen cinema that is only frequented by lower-class men. Just like the overall pattern of cinema attendance, the percentage of women also attending normal theatres was highest amongst the Hiland Park survey respondents. In contrast, the numbers of women who did so amongst the Salt Lake respondents was very low. Overall, we concluded that Kolkata's multiplexes are important in terms of women re-emerging as a cinema audience. This reinforces the argument of the multiplex chains that this is an important audience demographic who enthusiastically responds to a safer and less male-dominated leisure environment.

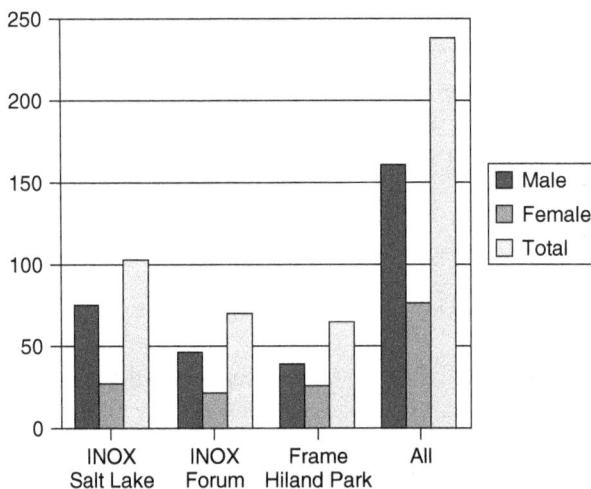

Figure 7.9 Gender composition of audience samples at Kolkata multiplexes.

The tenor of the qualitative responses comparing the multiplexes to normal theatres in Kolkata was very similar to the attitudes found in Bangalore and Baroda. The quality of facilities and the 'ambience' created by a 'well-heeled' crowd were most frequently cited as the draws to multiplexes. The benefits of multiplexes were again juxtaposed by many disparaging comments about the 'cheap crowd' and the poor facilities at normal theatres. The following short examples of positive comments on the multiplex are indicative of the overall responses:

> M25: You don't get the run-of-the-mill crowd, so you can enjoy the movie.

> M25: Shopping; a package of spending a day out, everything under one roof.

> M26: ambiance, seating arrangements, choice of movies.

> M36: We can meet people like us.

Not all of the comments on normal theatres from the Kolkata respondents were negative, but those that were negative referenced similar themes to the examples from our other surveys, including:

> M19: The environment is not good – people are talking and the seats are bad.

> M26: Crowd is not good, there is no options for different movies.

> F18: I dislike the ambience and crowd. They are chewing-paan speaking-Hindi Biharis from the lower class.

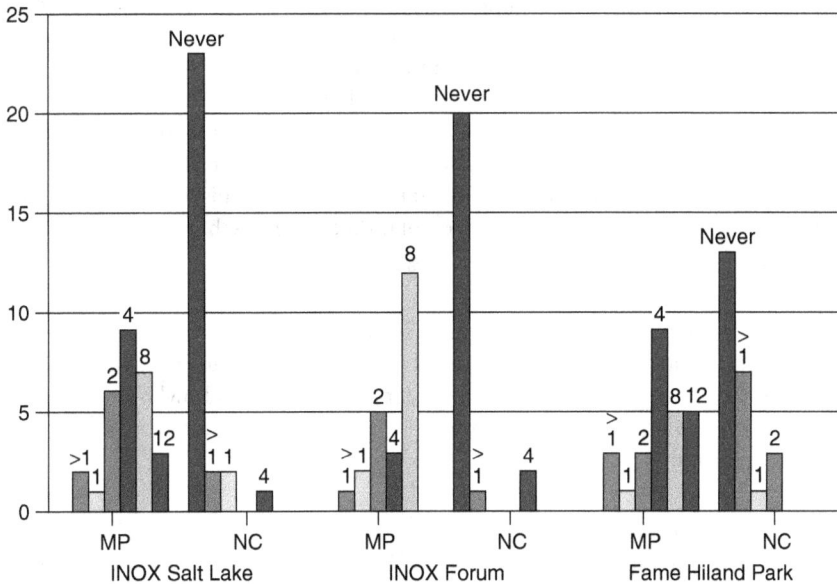

Figure 7.10 Trips per month by female patrons to multiplexes versus normal cinemas in the three Kolkata survey sites.

In making a general assessment of this multi-sited straw poll (which, in empirical terms, is perhaps the best way to frame this exercise), there appears to be sufficient cause for making the case that the multiplex crowd in Kolkata (and indeed in our surveys overall) is a far more diverse social body in socio-economic terms than is claimed by the industry literature. At the same time, the self-image of the multiplex crowd is remarkably conversant with the social values and 'psycho-profiles' deployed in industry marketing. Needless to say, the ensuing gap between the multiplex crowd as an imagined community and the multiplex crowd as a demographic reality becomes a crucial site for further enquiry, particularly in the context of such a large-scale ideological re-ordering of society as that which is being undertaken in India.

The multiplex crowd in discussion

In order to further explore the attitudes of the multiplex crowd reflected in the survey studies, a single round of focus groups was also held with multiplex patrons in Bangalore, Baroda and Kolkata in January and February 2007. These discussions were organised around an elaboration of the survey questions that queried the attractiveness of the multiplex in the first part of the discussion and invited opinions on the wider social significance of the multiplex in the second part of the discussion. The size of these groups varied, with five respondents in Kolkata, seven in Bangalore and 15 in Baroda. A range of venues was used for the three groups including a classroom in Baroda, a corporate meeting room in Bangalore and the confines of INOX Salt Lake in Kolkata. All of these group exercises proved to be lively affairs that canvassed a wide range of opinions and demonstrated the capacity of multiplex patrons to provide commentary on the sociology of cinema, the psychology of consumption and the ethos of the liberalisation era in India. In doing so, the opinions and explanations offered by the focus groups underscored the importance of understanding the multiplex cinema in India in relation to the local experience of theatrical exhibition. The statement made by this male respondent in Baroda was indicative of the general view of normal cinemas that emerged from the surveys:

> M: If you compare it to any normal cinema, you go there you have bad seats, you have bad lighting, you have a bad crowd, you have bad everything . . . You basically have people who basically start to hooting and howling at anything and everything that just comes up on screen. They can't sit quietly and appreciate the movie that's going on.

The following accounts provided by the focus group at CityCenter INOX at Salt Lake, an elite outer metropolitan suburb of Kolkata, are indicative of how members of the multiplex rhetorically differentiate themselves from the general cinema audience, even after conceding that they also visit normal cinema halls due to the very high costs of tickets at the multiplex:

F1: I am not trying to generalise but going to Jaya [a single-screen cinema in Kolkata], every damn person can afford. The crowd is not good.

M: We have different strata within our society. In this multiplex only the higher strata people come here, so there is a big deal of difference; in those other cinemas you have daily labourers, not only that, but lower middle class people also come there. So, their view of things and our view of things are very different.

F2: If you go to the other cinemas you can't enjoy the movie peacefully. They will shout and whistle and all and stamp their feet.

M: They will enjoy themselves. But here we can enjoy in our own way. They enjoy in a group. There is a psychological difference.

F1: I personally feel that there is no need to shout. Since this is a public place, people should be better behaved.

A large component of the eagerness of multiplex viewers to not mix with the 'cheap crowd', appears to stem from a rejection of the latter's emotionally demonstrative and 'undisciplined' watching of films. Lakshmi Srinivas (2002) describes Indian audiences viewing *masala* movies as actively participatory in nature, a tendency she attributes to overwhelmingly group-oriented social relations that she juxtaposes with the atomised, disciplined spectators of American cinemas. Similarly, in our focus groups, the older-style cinema halls were associated with raucous acts of mass participation, such as screaming, applauding, whistling and singing. However, for many of our multiplex patrons, this 'active' mode of spectatorship – where audiences boo the arrival on screen of the villain, sing and dance during songs and throw coins at the screen – was seen to devalue their own experiences of going to the cinema. As such, in the above comments, these members of the multiplex are stating a conception of appropriate behaviour in an auditorium that shows greater correspondence with Lakshmi Srinivas's dialectically-constructed American audiences. Having said that, we should resist the temptation to see the multiplex crowd as positive proof of Westernisation since their indignant dismay at the vulgar enthusiasm of the popular audience again reflects the attitudes of middle-class Indians of previous generations to the cinema (Srinivas 2000a).

However, for some of the male patrons taking part in the Bangalore focus group, the carnival atmosphere of the traditional cinema halls continued to be an attractive addition (rather than alternative) to their experiences at the multiplex. As such, it was less the case that they were disgusted by the exuberance of regular cinema audiences, but more that they considered different modes of spectatorship suitable to the occupation of different spaces and to different kinds of films:

M1: If I have to watch a regional movie or something, I'd rather prefer to go to a normal theatre. I can have fun there. Because usually in the multiplex, the crowd is very decent. So if I want to have some fun, for a regional movie, whistling and all, there's no-one throwing popcorn in a multiplex. Especially when there's your favourite actor and no-ones whistling, you know? So it is a different kind of thing, different kind of movie.

M2: If a regional star comes on screen, then people start whistling and howling. If Rajkumar is on screen there's whistling but if there's Brad Pitt, they'll just sit like that. That's the whole point. In a multiplex you're forced to be someone else. I mean, you're not yourself. If you want to shout at the screen. It's a sort of different experience. I mean you cant compare, it is just a different experience.

M3: Because the multiplex surroundings are made, are basically more posh but normal cinemas are more localised, they've been around for some time. There's not much renovation going on there, but the multiplexes are all new. They are all set on international standards.

M2: It doesn't bother us though. If it is a Telugu movie and it is really good, then I would prefer to watch it in normal theatres. We don't find it boring to put on someone else's shoes and go over there.

On the one hand, this notion of 'putting on someone else's shoes', or displaying the capacity to adopt behaviours appropriate to the viewing conditions they encountered, suggested that this group was more than capable of strategically applying themselves to join in with different classes and conditions of public participation. On the other hand, the coercive nature of the multiplex environment itself is clearly referred to in the phrase 'forced to be someone else'. There is a sense in these responses that despite their professed distaste for the boisterous behaviour of the lower classes of audience, these young men still felt that the orderly viewing conditions of the multiplex were somewhat arbitrary and artificial in nature. There was a general agreement that different viewing environments had a powerful affect upon their personal behaviour. The composition of the multiplex crowd – perceived as 'decent' or 'posh' – was as important as the architecture in achieving this effect.

However, the female members of this group were not able to move so easily between the two crowds. All three of them said that their parents would not allow them to attend normal cinemas in Bangalore, which were considered unsafe. The cause of this danger was the disruptive presence of 'locals'. The male members of the group also recognised that there was a gendered dimension that marked out the difference between the multiplex and the normal theatre environment for female viewers:

M: I was watching a movie in a normal theatre recently and all drunkards came and it wouldn't be safe for a girl. They were smelling of booze and all that. You know we guys are used to, we are more used to that crowd.

F1: It is not just a theatre. Even if it is a restaurant or anywhere, it always depends. If there is more of a local crowd there, we don't hang out there.

F2: That influences us a lot. It influences our thinking. If there are a lot of people, local people in any place, then we wouldn't go there. As simple as that.

Steve Derne (1999), in his writings on Indian cinema halls in the 1990s, emphasises the highly sexualised and threatening atmosphere of the cinema. For Derne, both the thematic content of the Hindi film and the traditions of spectatorship that surround it have encouraged the objectification of women. The practice of watching films thus engenders a state of aggressive collective sexual excitement amongst mostly male audiences that spills over into lewd advances towards female viewers and threatening sexual behaviour outside of the cinema hall. Derne observed that women were confined to more expensive balcony seats and, without the presence of male chaperones, were unsafe even there from harassment. This account provides a marked contrast to Lakshmi Srinivas's (2002) assertion that trips to the cinema in India are highly social in nature, broadly representative of the entire social spectrum and essentially represent an outing for the entire family. Without wishing to endorse either position, it is abundantly clear within the material collected here that safety is a major issue for female patrons, particularly the younger ones, and that the multiplex was widely perceived of as 'safer' than a regular cinema hall. At the same time, discussion of the relative safety of cinema halls did include a range of dissenting views, as the following examples from Baroda illustrate:

> F1: It happens even at INOX, hooting and howling thing, especially when Aishwarya comes on screen, I mean that does happen! . . . I think that about the crowd, the gentry, especially for women, they would definitely not want any teasers at their places, they would want safety out there.

> F2: Is a more upper class space more safer for you as a woman? I don't think so. I mean I walk around in our bazaar all the time. I do not get leched at, I do not get, you know, eve-teased and I think that that space is as sensitive of me as a woman as any other space would be. I, to say that a lower class, that the lower classes are always going to paw you, it's, I don't think it's a great notion at all.

> F3: The case of Gujarat or outside? Baroda is different but if you move to north India, it's very difficult. If I want to see a movie all alone, I can visit Baroda whether it is *Aradhana* Cinema or it is a multiplex. When INOX was not there I have seen quite a few movies *Hyderabad Blues* and all. We have all gone all alone, but that way Baroda is safe, but it depends on a region also. So see, every situation is specific.

One male focus group member was also highly critical of what Hubbard (2003) calls the 'ontological security' of the multiplex in more general terms. There appeared to be no doubt in this respondent's mind that multiplexes engendered a sense of security amongst their audiences. For him, however, the safety offered by new leisure architectures is as ephemeral as the sense of prosperity that it is also intended to articulate:

> M: Maybe the multiplexes make us think that India is shining when actually it is still not. Right, and I think that's very, very important because there are people who are much below the poverty line now, so-called poverty like, you

know what the poverty line is, right, and what's happening to them? And they are just being forgotten. All the safety, our notions of safety which didn't exist are equal, it's probably equally unsafe even now but people feel safe because they feel they belong to a higher income bracket and they can afford to see movies in safety and I think this is an illusion that we have and people live with this kind of illusion that there is something called safety here but in the old theatres there was none, 'OK so I am safer here', but I think it is just an illusion.

The impression of the multiplex as a safe environment was also reinforced by its association with modernity and progress. For many respondents, multiplexes were statements of the new India and a sign that India was now living up to international standards. They also saw the presence of multiplexes in their particular city as important markers of being on the right side of economic change. For the Bangaloreans, multiplexes were seen as a statement of Bangalore's prosperity and its status as a high-technology city:

> M: It increases our own value I think, that we have five multiplexes in our city.
> F: It's made it modern and more attractive.
>
> M: I mean if you're an outsider and you come down to Bangalore and you see all the multiplexes and everything, it sort of gives an impression of the city, I mean, that is, I think the word is hi-fi, or whatever, with technology . . .
>
> F: It's development.
>
> M: It's development, yeah.
>
> F: I think it makes the infrastructure more modern. So other states and other countries perceive Bangalore to be more modern.

And, similarly, for the group in Baroda, there was a belief that:

> F: Multiplexes have put Baroda on par with other big cities. People have their, aside, they'll ask you: 'you don't even have a multiplex in your city, what kind of a city, what kind of a village do you live in!' So it kind of puts you in the picture.
>
> F: The trend of the multiplex is here to stay because people once they've got accustomed to multiplexes, we cannot go back in time since we've been introduced. We can just say that maybe the single screen theatres, they would lose out, you know. Everything will be the multiplex concept, would, I mean it will continue because people cannot go back we cannot go back to single screen theatres now, we'll just advance now.

For one of the respondents in Kolkata, it was not simply the association with metropolitan improvement or regional pride that made the multiplexes important, but also their capacity to endow members of their audience with enhanced social status due to their association with luxury and upper-class affluence:

M: This multiplex is a status project. Status is a very big deal in multiplex. You can say that. At the top floor is a function room and we can book it like that for children parties and like that. I personally feel that if someone books it in the top floor of [INOX] CityCenter, then he or she is a status person. That's a very big thing. Obviously status is a hugely important thing for every person. I personally think that a person works hard day and night to earn money finally to improve our status. That's the main thing, I think, the motto of life.

At the same time, this respondent also felt that the importance of opportunities to enhance social status should neither reflect a callousness towards those less fortunate, nor underwrite an agenda of separate development. Other members of the group, who had previously challenged his material definition of status with one more oriented towards cultural capital, held different views on whether the exclusive nature of the multiplex was problematic:

M: When we are growing as a nation we should take each one with us as a group. Otherwise only a certain segment of India will grow and the others will be downtrodden. And that's not done. That's not acceptable.

F1: But that is very difficult. Even it is culturally impossible. So I think to start with we have to start with a particular section.

F2: Even in this case, I think most of the middle sections are being avoided. This influences society.

F1: Yes, but multiplexes are private investments, not public investments.

In charting the overall course of our focus groups, it was evident that the multiplex was inextricably associated with a certain socio-economic class of patrons that was assumed to have a commensurate behavioural profile that was well-mannered, disciplined and non-threatening. This crowd – the 'decent crowd' – was seen as being produced by the high ticket prices, the on-site security and the overall ambience of the multiplex environment. Multiplexes were seen as positive developments that increased access to leisure and produced a new form of public space that was resonant with the expression of modernity and the pursuit of affluence. They were also considered safer and more suitable than traditional cinema halls for middle-class women. Ultimately, the creation of this highly desirable environment was seen as a poor reflection of the conditions in which the majority of Indians obtained leisure. The question of the relationship between these new leisure spaces and the wider society remained unresolved.

Within these broad contours, there were inflections to the debate that were particular to the different locations in which the focus groups took place. The Baroda group was the most impressed by the novelty of the multiplex, which had clearly made a major difference to the overall availability of leisure facilities in the city for this group. It also contributed to their perceptions of Baroda as a 'small town' that was in the process of becoming a metro. However, there was also a sense amongst this group that economic development alone was not going to address the pressing social issues in their state. By contrast, the discourse of the Kolkata group was infused with a socialist vocabulary on the public sphere. This did not extend, however, to any desire to forego the attractions of being part of a more exclusive audience, and the status that this engendered, even if this meant having to save up for the necessary capital and going to the cinema less often that they would like. In Bangalore the gap between the focus group and the general population seemed very wide indeed, and there was very little in way of a critical response to the multiplex. For this group, the mall was 'like a second college', a natural environment for those most like themselves. They expected that the future would provide them with further malls in which to 'hang out' once they became bored with the sites that they currently frequented.

A 'decent crowd'

As this chapter has demonstrated, the audience research conducted at several sites indicated the pre-occupation of patrons with hygiene, security and shopping. However, it was the presence of an appropriate (or 'decent') crowd which was typically seen as the definitive factor in choosing to attend the multiplex. It was also the most critical factor in constructing the ambience of the multiplex and the most valued aspect of the multiplex experience. The 'decent crowd' of the multiplex was articulated throughout these audience studies as an imagined community strongly differentiated from the general cinema audience. As such, the modes of viewing at the multiplex were constructed in an inverse manner to the perceived norms of cinema spectatorship in India, and this difference was overwhelmingly attributed to the audience demographic. The multiplex crowd was defined by its exclusive nature, which was widely considered as the price that had to be paid for enjoying cinema in a manner that was not simply luxurious but, most importantly, disciplined and non-threatening. To be part of the decent crowd was seen as a marker of both affluence and good manners, and it allowed multiplex patrons to put themselves at a distance from the general movie-going public.

At the same time, despite seeing themselves as moving amongst an affluent crowd, most multiplex patrons also demonstrated personal consternation with the high costs of visiting the multiplex. In this sense, the decent crowd proved to be much more variegated in its spending capacity, habits and attitudes towards consumption than the description offered by the industry itself. It was evident in every case that the remarkably consistent description of the multiplex audience (amongst both executives and patrons) as the most wealthy, high-status and free-spending members of Indian society was not reflected by the demographics of the actual audience that we encountered. Rather, it appears that the multiplex functions as a major site for middle-class aspiration, and that multiplex operators were capable of marketing its socially-exclusive nature to a markedly wide cross-section of the middle classes.

It was also clear that there was more than simply a lack of available means behind the considerable overlaps with the normal cinema audience. For example, some members of the decent crowd showed continued taste for the indecent pleasures of the downmarket cinema hall and for their place in the 'cheap crowd' (or at least in the balcony seats). By contrast, however, there was also evidence that there is a significant cohort of young Indians for whom the only experience of cinema is the exclusively middle-class environment of the multiplex. This does appear to indicate that the multiplex crowd may well become more distinct from the general audience in the future. Finally, what is at once obvious, but nonetheless needs to be restated here, is that the content of multiplex programming was far less important to the multiplex crowd than the quality of seats and the people with whom they were sitting. This is not to say, however, that our investigation of the multiplex can be complete without turning our attention to what is on the screen.

8   Screening the multiplex

India is a country in which the institution of cinema has dominated popular culture for 80 years. The products of the film industry – both the films themselves and the star system they have created – have constituted an important component of national debates on major social and political issues since colonial times. Filmmakers have always needed to address the preoccupations circulating in Indian public culture. As a result, few topics of conversation produce as much commentary on contemporary society from Indian citizens as do debates on popular films. Arguably, this is why India is one of the very few countries in the world where audiences have demonstrated a clear preference for both locally- and nationally-produced films, and where the issue of foreign film imports as a form of cultural colonisation has been a relatively minor issue. It is equally important to note that Indian film culture is constituted as a multi-media industry. Popular music in India has long been an intrinsic component of the film industry, and other forms of popular culture, such as magazines, fashion and, more recently, television, are also closely referential to film culture. By Western definitions, film in India is neither a singular industry, nor simply one format of popular culture – it is popular culture. It occupies a prime location at the centre of a multidimensional entertainment industry. This is what perpetuates the capacity of the film industry to make an enormous impact on the discursive fields of Indian society.

In previous chapters, we have argued that the logic of the multiplex industry reflects a concerted shift away from mass audiences towards the targeting of niche audiences. We have also established that the multiplex crowd understands itself by comparison to a rump cinema audience from which its members wish to distance themselves for a variety of reasons. One of these reasons – if not the major motivation – arises from the long-standing perception that the old one-size-fits-all mode of filmmaking encouraged the perpetuation of vulgar, low-brow films that did not serve the tastes of middle-class viewers and their families (Sharma 2003). As such, the multiplex is implicated in the dispersal of the all-India *masala* movie into a more diverse range of themes and styles. This chapter, therefore, interrogates the dynamics of content at the multiplex in light of the ongoing separation of the film-going public facilitated by the multiplex. To begin with, we examine the programming regimen of the leading multiplex operators during 2007 and detail the relative popularity of particular types of films with multiplex audiences. Subsequently, we situate those films within the wider aesthetics of the contemporary Indian film, and in so doing we establish what is mainstream at the multiplex and what is marginal. Ultimately, we seek to illustrate how the multiplex enshrines a particular kind of taste culture within the wider world of Indian cinema.

Programming the multiplex

The global history of the multiplex is indisputably a symptom of the complex inter-weaving of profligate consumerism, the proliferation of media formats and the corporatisation of entertainment. Both architecturally and operationally, the mul-tiplex enshrines the privilege of choice, which has itself become the defining mantra of the consuming economy. In the process, the social practices surrounding the cin-ema have shifted away from the collective experience of a self-contained film text towards a menu-driven model of entertainment where the selection of visual enter-tainment is made in relation to wider patterns of consumption. The films them-selves, responding to this new reality, are now designed to operate across a range of media formats. Their presence further extends beyond the textual experience to incorporate a whole series of promotional tie-ins that lend the cultural capital of the movie to the wider field of consumption. Outside of India, the story of the multiplex has been one of vertical integration, where production and distribution interests took control of the exhibition sector and ensured the profitability and dominance of their flagship products. Paradoxically, the prerogative of choice that is intrinsic to multiplex exhibition has also opened up opportunities for a wider generic field of films addressing niche audiences in smaller auditoriums. As Kerrigan and Ozbilgin (2001) note, the multiplex format has been central to the survival of the independ-ent film sector in the UK over the past two decades. The multiplex has also been a primary factor for the emergence of a profitable audience for Indian cinema in the UK, taking the major Hindi releases out of the heavily-pirated home video market and into the exhibition mainstream (ibid.: 199–200). Aparna Sharma, writing in 2003, was optimistic that this side effect of improving the efficiency of blockbuster films was also being repeated in India since the multiplex:

> makes for a space that mirrors a complex cinematic multiplicity. The increas-ingly curious mix of parallel, regional and art cinema along with the main-stream, both domestic and foreign, is what distinguishes most multiplexes in India, such that the Indian multiplex has come to position itself, not so much by identifying with particular kinds of films, as by being a theatre for accessing the 'latest' from a wide spread of cinematic fare – mainstream or fringe – in comfortable, colourful and inviting surroundings.
>
> (Sharma 2003).

Sharma's praise is undertaken with an acute awareness of the social exclusivity of the multiplex. However, Sharma remains highly sympathetic to the demands from film buffs for a more aesthetically diverse, quality cinema in India. Since the days of Satyajit Ray and the Film Society movement of the 1950s, there has been a vocal minority calling for a new kind of Indian cinema that reflects the blend of social realism and literary *auteriste* filmmaking that has been the cause célèbre of non-Hollywood cinema worldwide (Ray 1976). The socialist Indian governments of the 1960s and 1970s were responsive to this agenda. Thus, the Film Finance Corporation (FFC) was established in 1960 to provide finance for the production of quality films. The Film Institute of India (FII) was set up in Pune in 1961 to develop the necessary production talent. The National Film Development Council (NFDC) initially operated as a canal agency for film exports and imports before taking on an overseeing role at the end of 1970s for supporting art films. Together these institutions were intended to provide the means for a 'New Indian Cinema' (Bannerjee 1982). According to Vasudevan, this alternative cinema, sometimes dubbed the 'parallel' cinema, was born out of a 'realist critique of the melodramatic and distractive form of Indian popular cinema, of its excessively pitched histrionic narratives punctuated by "untidily" placed musical and comedy sequences' and 'was very much part of a cultural-political project to develop a realist and rationalist disposition in the citizen-spectator' (Vasudevan 2000a: 123).

At the end of the 1960s, the modest success of low-budget FFC-financed art films directed by Mrinal Sen (*Bhuvan Shome*, 1969) and Mani Kaul (*Uski Roti*, 1969) seemed to offer some promise for the art film movement. However, the lack of an alternative exhibition infrastructure for the distribution of state-financed films and the continued preference for popular films amongst mass audiences meant that the vast majority of these art films received little exposure beyond film festivals. Thus, while the *masala* film effectively kept out foreign imports, it also stymied Indira's parallel cinema and perpetuated what Derne (1999) describes as a male-dominated cinema of exploitation. By the mid-1980s, the state-led parallel cinema project was moribund, with international film festivals and the state television broadcaster, Doordarshan, representing the only outlets for such films. Many of those trained for the parallel cinema relocated to work within the confines of the commercial industry, leading to the so-called 'middle cinema' of the early 1990s (associated with directors like J. P. Dutta and Mani Rathnam) that combined photographic realism and serious themes with the commercial narrative format (Chakravarty 2000, Athique 2008b).

The de-regulation of television in India during the 1990s saw a rapid growth of private entertainment-based television stations that drew heavily on the back catalogue of the commercial film industry. With state television being forced to adopt a more popular approach in response, the diffusion of quality films via this medium was further diminished, both in absolute terms and as a proportion of overall programming. Given these developments, and in light of the long-standing frustration of Indian cineastes over many years, the arrival of the multiplex appeared to provide a life raft, a high-quality alternative distribution circuit that provided the capacity for a more diverse cinema to reach the public. The fact that the Indian multiplex, as opposed to its international counterparts, intentionally separated out the middle-class audience from the mass of spectators seemed to make it even more suitable for reviving India's art house cinema, which had traditionally been associated with this group. The reduction of risks for which the multiplex format had been designed and its smaller auditoriums meant that a significant degree of experimentation with new kinds of films was now possible without inviting financial ruin.

After a decade of operation, however, the multiplex is no longer a blank slate. It has become clear that the multiplex chains have, for the most part, settled on a fairly uniform mix of programming that is subsequently adjusted for regional variations in demand. Deepak Srivastava, General Manager at INOX Goa, sums up the characteristics of this programming:

> Bollywood movies rule in all our multiplexes. More than 80 per cent of our revenues come out of Bollywood. Hollywood movies, we are very happy with the response that we have got . . . the numbers that we have generated. The distributors they were encouraged, so they started giving us a lot of latest release movies, Hollywood movies. *Casino Royale*, the latest Bond movie, *Beauty and the Beast, Happy Feet*. We have done a lot of movies in the past two years. So Hollywood is another thing. It goes to 15 per cent of Hollywood. 15 to 18 per cent of revenues. And then there is a small little balance of regional movies.
>
> (interview 28/12/2006)

The presence of Hollywood films in programming schedules for multiplexes across the country is a prominent feature of the multiplex menu. The capacity of the multiplexes to open up screen slots for American imports at a national level has led to several distribution deals being signed by the multiplex chains with American distributors. While a ten to 15 per cent share is very small when compared to US domination of global film markets, it is a considerably larger slice than Hollywood has been able to achieve in India since the 1930s. The Hollywood share of the multiplex market is also many times larger than their share of the overall audience, where Hollywood products have typically represented about two per cent of the overall box office. Despite a niche market for big special effects films since the success of dubbed prints of *Jurassic Park* in 1993, Hollywood films (which are referred to in linguistic terms as 'English' films in India) are usually relegated to the B circuit, where they are marketed as action or exploitation films. The multiplexes, by contrast, have experimented with a much wider range of Hollywood imports on the basis that their upmarket audience is English-speaking and more familiar with international cinema as a result of the cable and satellite television boom of the past decade (Mishra 1999, Butcher 2003, Kohli-Khandekar 2006: 61–105, Mehta 2008).

After screening Hollywood films nationwide over the past few years, the multiplex chains have been able to establish that the Indian multiplex crowd demonstrates a preference for the biggest Hollywood blockbusters along with animations and other features designed for children – an audience that has long been neglected by mainstream Indian cinema. This creates a useful synergy with the goal of the industry to promote the multiplex as a family-oriented domain, and their programming of imported films clearly favours US films that cater to a juvenile audience. In the major metros, American art house and indie films also get shown in spare programming slots, although their audience is tiny by any measure. Despite the fact that, in comparison to the last four decades, these are boom times for Hollywood in

India, imported films remain very much second-in-line to the big Hindi block-busters that dominate the cinema in north India, not only in terms of the overall market, but also within the box office returns of the multiplex sector.

The sheer size of Indian cinema is often invoked in reference to a production level that oscillates between 600 and 800 films per year, which is the largest output in the world in numerical terms. This can be a misleading figure, however, since Indian cinema is produced in a number of production centres by what are effec-tively half a dozen identifiable film industries. Thus, within this overall production figure, regional movies far outstrip the production of the Mumbai-based Hindi films with which Indian cinema is most commonly associated. Nonetheless, it is the top end of the Hindi cinema that enjoys the largest domestic and international audi-ences. Again, it is important to recognise that this top end is itself a numerically small component of overall Hindi-language production, representing around 60 films per year. It is in this narrow slice of overall Indian film production where the budgets are highest and the profits greatest. For the multiplex operators, it is these films specifically that draw the biggest audiences. Since there is one of these films coming onto the market each week, the multiplex in India emulates the global shift towards big opening weeks and shorter runs for each film (Acland 2003: 3–22). For this reason, multiplexes will usually devote a number of their screens to the big new release, with any other content running in a smaller auditorium or in daytime slots that are less popular.

The rapid turnover of high-budget blockbusters represents a major break with the old order of things. Traditionally, the limited number of prints made available to distributors in the Indian market meant that major films would take a long time to pass through the entire distribution circuit, and the biggest hits would run for many months at theatres with gradually decreasing prices until they had reached their full audience. Films would generate publicity on the basis of their capacity to go on drawing audiences for 25 or 50 weeks, with these landmarks being occasions for festivities at each site. In the context of the multiplex, however, the much smaller audience and the greater screen capacity mean that the demand for a film amongst the multiplex crowd can generally be fulfilled within a few weeks, although the film may subsequently run on in the traditional theatres for some time after that. The rapid turnover of films at the multiplex reflects an era in which films are now released on many more prints, and where the multiplex sector is first in line for prints due to its disproportionate clout at the box office. This can mean a hectic schedule for site managers, as Srivastava explains:

> In a multiplex situation, you get four or five days only to work a promotion around a movie. We come to know only on Monday or Tuesday which movies are going to release on Friday. So we have three days only.
>
> (interview 28/12/2006)

INOX organises its programming schedules at its offices in Mumbai, but this is not the case with all the multiplex operators. Their pan-India ambitions make all the multiplex companies keenly aware of the regional specificity of their market. On this basis, Tashur Dhingra, COO at Adlabs, devolves programming decisions to specific sites:

> Programming is again on a local level. You cannot programme the nation . . . So there are towns which start playing nine o'clock in the morning. There are towns that start from 12:30 onwards, okay, or there are five number of shows or six shows in a day in certain cinemas. Maybe only four in certain cinemas. And the language mix: How much of Tamil, how much of Telugu, how much of Hindi, how much of English? It's defined by the catchment. So it is not national programming.
>
> (Tashur Dhingra, interview 08/01/2007)

Dhingra is also keen to point out the opportunities provided by the multiplex for lower-budget films that cater to a niche audience. Like Sharma, he sees the multiplex format as allowing both international and local art house films to enter the market alongside the major Bollywood productions:

> Most of the big blockbusters have been commercial films. You see that is one part of it. The second part of it is that smaller films, experimental films, now get a release. And if the film is good enough they make a profit as well because we present an avenue to showcase a certain kind of cinema. See, there has been a satellite boom in India. So, and Indians are well-travelled, at least in metros. So there is that niche audience which is very open to watch movies in any language. The content has to be good. So, keeping that in view, any kind of cinema whether it is, it has not only helped the European or Hollywood cinema to come in but local industries, like the Bengali industry or the Punjabi industry. That is actually revived.
>
> (Ibid.)

Given the historical configuration of the Indian film market, the inclusion of regional-language films was the most obvious factor to be considered in assessing regional variation at the level of content. In terms of the programming at the sites visited across the Delhi-NCR, the dominance of Hindi films was readily apparent. PVR sites at Saket, Metropolitan Mall (Gurgaon) and Spice World (NOIDA) were all screening a range of English films alongside the major Hindi releases. However, other PVR sites in West Delhi, East Delhi and Faridabad were either showing Hindi films exclusively or offering dubbed Hollywood blockbusters like *Ghostrider* (2006) and *300* (2006) in one or two programming slots. This pattern was mirrored in the schedules at Adlabs, FUN Cinemas and Wave Cinemas. It is notable, therefore, that while single-screen cinemas typically draw audiences on the basis of the film on show, there was no discernible difference between the multiplex operators in terms of the programming on offer, making the multiplex menu constant across different operators and locations.

Only a handful of the premium PVR sites broke the mould by offering the wider range of content that Sharma identifies with the multiplex. Here the programming mix was widened in terms of offering a number of art house titles in both Hindi and English. We found that the presence of regional-language films in the NCR multi-plexes was negligible. Only a couple of regional films appeared in one-off screenings at multiplexes in the city each month. During our study period, these films were all Tamil-language films and their screening at sites like Wave Cinemas in Ghaziabad was being organised in partnership with the local community of migrants from that region of South India. In recognition of the obvious differences between the hand-ful of premium sites and the bulk of the multiplexes, Sharma relates the vagaries of multiplex programming to the relative wealth of different suburban districts:

> Within the different income regions of say a metropolis itself, one finds multi-plexes located in posh localities exhibiting foreign films along with substantial numbers of non-mainstream films. However, when located in the lower income group areas, multiplexes get smaller, being composed of fewer screens and English films (mostly well advertised ones) constitute a smaller portion of the assortment. As one moves away from the Hindi heartland, the film menu tilts correspondingly in favour of native languages and no longer reads bilin-gually (i.e. comprising only Hindi and English films).
>
> (Sharma 2003)

In terms of the regional dimension, we monitored the programming in Kolkata in Eastern India and at Panjim and Bangalore in South India. In Kolkata, we found that although local-language films were included in multiplex programming, the dominance of Hindi and English at the box office was much the same as it was in the Hindi belt. Bengali films in the popular mould which screen in local cinemas did not generate sufficient appeal from the multiplex crowd to earn them a significance presence at the multiplexes. The status of Kolkata as the undisputed capital of art cinema since the days of Satyajit Ray did appear to result in a larger presence for art house films in all languages at Kolkata's multiplexes. At the same time, this legacy has also made the city one of the few centres in India where there are long-estab-lished venues for such films already in operation. The state government-run Nandan and single-screen theatres like Priya in metropolitan Kolkata enjoy a loyal clientele (amongst the older generation in particular). This undoubtedly dilutes the performance of Indian art films at the multiplex. Perhaps as a result of these factors, along with a more youthful audience demographic, we found that the takings of the multiplexes for Bollywood, Hollywood or art house films closely matched the national pattern in terms of box office sales at the outset of 2007.

Cosmopolitan Bangalore, however, was an exception to the general rule of 85 per cent Bollywood, 13 per cent Hollywood and two per cent regional and art house. Located in markedly non-Hindi South India, films in the Southern Indian languages (Kannada, Tamil, Telugu and Malayalam) were showing on five of the ten screens at PVR Forum Mall. English films were also proving popular at this site. In terms of box office, the Hindi films brought the highest returns on a per film basis, but given the 80 per cent occupancy rate across all screens, their overall contribu-tion was much less than found elsewhere. For our survey group, South Indian films accounted for ten per cent of film choices during respondents' last visits to a multi-plex. Hollywood films achieved an impressive 33 per cent and Hindi films made up the remainder (56.4 per cent). This was by far the lowest proportion for Hindi films that we observed in all our sample sites, reflecting the linguistic realities of South India. Nonetheless, it is significant that Hindi films still made up the majority of selections by our survey group. On the this basis it seems highly probable that Hindi films are more popular with the multiplex crowd in Bangalore than they are with the local film-going public in general since the majority of single-screen cinemas in the city show Kannada, Tamil or Telugu films more or less exclusively.

The relatively slow expansion of the multiplexes in South India may well reflect the scenario that we found in Bangalore, which was a more limited market for Bollywood staples with the prospects for English films appearing to be somewhat better amongst the multiplex crowd in the South. The size of the city is clearly another factor in the market for imported films. In the smaller city of Baroda in the western state of Gujarat, English movies did not do nearly as well in overall returns as they did in big metros like Bangalore and Mumbai. Two of the three multiplexes in the city did not show them at all, with INOX being the exception. As with the more downmarket districts in Delhi, Hollywood films required dubbing for the local audience in Baroda, and they still remained limited in their appeal. Conversely, in terms of regional content, none of the multiplexes were screening Gujarati films since these were seen as being more suitable for lower-class and rural audiences (although INOX has experimented with occasional shows of South Indian films). In the absence of art house or regional content, 85 per cent of the group we surveyed in Baroda had last seen a Hindi film at the multiplex and 15 per cent had last seen an English movie at the multiplex, again reflecting almost exactly the general trend in the multiplex box office.

On the basis of this brief survey period, the regional dynamics emphasised by the multiplex operators were reflected to a certain extent in the varying success of different kinds of films in different regions. Overall, however, we found that these variations were far less marked than one would expect on the basis of the wider film market. With the important exception of Bangalore, it was big-budget Hindi blockbusters that monopolised the main auditoria in all of the 30 multiplexes we visited across the country. In the larger sites and the more upmarket locations – which were often one and the same – one screen was generally given over to Hollywood and one used for a mixture of smaller Hindi and regional films. In the bulk of sites however, Hollywood and alternative films were inserted into just a handful of programming slots, and these were often afternoon and weekday shows. Thus, in the schedules that we collected over the first three months of 2007, we observed a clear trend in the selection of films in terms of genre. A-list Bollywood films dominated schedules, with Hollywood blockbusters and children's films plus a range of lower-budget comedies and art house films appearing in off-peak shows or on smaller screens in more affluent areas.

If we compare this programming mix to the traditional exhibition sector, English films were a clear beneficiary, as were the alternative films that, despite their modest presence at the multiplex, were gaining a far greater degree of exposure than they have traditionally enjoyed. The biggest losers, by contrast, were regional-language cinemas and the so-called 'B films' that are seen as catering to the lower classes. Thus, multiplex programming is as notable for its exclusions as it is for the inclusions emphasised by Sharma. In this context, the demonstrable coherence of multiplex programming matches a defined audience segment with an appropriate range of aesthetic choices – a range that is, at the same time, appropriately restricted. The box office evidence to date suggests that this is not the audience of cineastes with whom film scholars are so frequently sympathetic. Instead, the multiplex proscribes a broader taste culture that addresses the urban middle classes. If we take the Hollywood imports out of this picture, we are left with Bollywood block-busters and niche multiplex films that have the mobilisation of a middle-class sensibility very much in common. Accordingly, the cinematic menu on offer becomes crucial for situating the multiplex within the shifting mythic terrain of Indian cinema. In order to make this apparent in qualitative terms, the following section describes a selection of the films that we saw at the multiplex, situating them within the broad context of contemporary Indian filmmaking.

The multiplex menu

The Bollywood blockbuster

Ashish Rajadhyaksha (2003) describes recent export trends and the international re-branding of Indian commercial cinema as a process of 'Bollywoodisation'. While the majority of popular discourse now presents Indian cinema and Bollywood as effectively synonymous, Rajadhyaksha is at pains to make a distinction between the two: 'the cinema has been in existence as a national industry of sorts for the past fifty years . . . *Bollywood* has been around for only about a decade now' (2003: 28). Rajadhyaksha differentiates between Indian cinema and Bollywood for two major reasons: 1) the cultural industry surrounding the Bollywood brand extends far beyond the production and consumption of feature films 2) the high-budget gloss and transnational themes of the major Bollywood films are far from representative of the majority of Indian film production.

> Bollywood is *not* the Indian film industry, or at least not the film industry alone. Bollywood admittedly occupies a space analogous to the film industry, but might best be seen as a more diffuse cultural conglomeration involving a range of distribution and consumption activities from websites to music cassettes, from cable to radio. If so, the film industry itself – determined here solely in terms of its box office turnover and sales of print and music rights, all that actually comes back to the producer – can by definition constitute only a part, and perhaps an *alarmingly small* part of the overall culture industry that is currently being created and marketed . . . While Bollywood exists for, and prominently caters to, a diasporic audience of Indians . . . the Indian cinema – much as it would wish to tap this 'non-resident' audience – is only occasionally successful in doing so, and is in almost every instance able to do so only when it, so to say,

Bollywoodises itself, a transition that very few films in Hindi, and hardly any in other languages, are actually able to do.

(2003: 27/29)

The Bollywood brand excludes the low-budget comedies and action films that predominate in the B circuit and the exploitation films made for the C circuit and matinee shows. It does not encompass India's small parallel cinema or the regional-language films which constitute the bulk of film production and consumption in the subcontinent. Instead, Bollywood is overwhelmingly defined in aesthetic terms by the high-budget saccharine upper middle-class melodrama, which from the 1990s onwards has (re)presented a tongue-in-cheek repackaging of the *masala* movie within an affluent, nostalgic and highly exclusive view of Indian culture and society. There is a significant number of players in the Mumbai film world who have been associated with the Bollywood project. The two major figures, however, are reigning megastar Shah Rukh Khan and the veteran director Yash Chopra.

Shah Rukh Khan's acting career began in television and his early appearances in film were characterised by villainous roles. These beginnings are not generally considered auspicious for the making of a major film hero. Khan's versatility as an actor, however, won him praise in the early 1990s. His re-invention as a sensitive and humorous romantic figure in Adiya Chopra's *Dilwale Dulhania Le Jayenge* catapulted him to the top of the Hindi A-list. Due to its sympathetic treatment of the NRI male lead (played by Khan), this film captured a large overseas following of expatriate Indian audiences (see Dwyer 2000). This market was to prove lucrative for a series of NRI films starring Khan during the late 1990s, including *Pardes* (1997), *Dil To Pagal Hai* (1997) and *Kuch Kuch Hota Hai* (1998). The NRI characterisation, exemplified by the roles played by Shah Rukh Khan, was transformed from a cipher for the corrupting influence of the West into a new ideal type where cultural conservatism was skilfully combined with Indian aspirations to occupy the cosmopolitan spaces of the West (see Mishra 2002: 235–269, Kaur 2005, Athique 2006). These films were also highly successful in India, capturing the imagination of the liberalisation generation with their international settings and contemporary consumer fashions. Even for films which did not do so well in India, such as *Dil Se* (1998) and *Mohabbatein* (2000), Khan provided a guarantee of success in overseas territories. In this decade, Shah Rukh Khan has remained Hindi cinema's most bankable star, whilst moving away from romantic roles to make more action-based films, such as *Main Hoon Na* (2004) and *Don* (2006).

An important part of Shah Rukh Khan's rise to the top of the film industry has been his alliance with a handful of key directors who have provided the impetus for the Bollywood industry, including Karan Johar and Subhash Ghai. It was Khan's association with Yash Raj Films, headed by director Yash Chopra and his sons Aditya Chopra (a director) and Uday Chopra (an actor), that put him at the heart of the Bollywood phenomenon. The Aditya Chopra-directed *Dilwale Dulhania Le Jayenge* inaugurated Khan as an international megastar, but it also heralded the emergence of Yash Raj Films as the premier production house. Yash Chopra, the founder of Yash Raj Films, was quick to recognise the importance of overseas territories in the new era. Chopra opened distribution offices in London, New York and Dubai during the 1990s (Dwyer 2000). Access to hard currency returns from these export markets provided Yash Raj Film with the capacity to produce bigger-budget films and to extend their interests from production into distribution (which also diminished the leakage of box office returns considerably).

The success of Yash Raj Films, however, has been as much a matter of style as it has been of business acumen. Yash Chopra had hits with romantic films like *Kabhi Kabhie* (1976) even at the height of the 'angry young man' era, and had long been associated with romantic themes (Dwyer 2002). Chopra was quick to spot the return to favour of such films after the success of Sooraj Barjatya's *Hum Aapke Hain Koon* in 1994. Working with his sons, and with major stars like Shah Rukh Khan, Kajol and industry stalwart Amitabh Bachchan, Yash Raj Films produced a series of big-budget films that located romantic themes within a melodramatic affirmation of the extended family. Combining these narratives with affluent overseas settings, Yash Raj Films was successful in appealing to both expatriate audiences and to domestic middle-class audiences who had been alienated by the vigilante-and-violence films of the 1980s. Yash Raj Films has subsequently become the heavyweight of the Mumbai industry and a champion of the corporate model, even if it remains far from a 'studio' in the Hollywood sense. In recent years, Yash Raj Films has augmented the work directed by Yash and Aditya Chopra by acting as producers and distributors for films by other directors, such as *Saathiya* (2002) and *Kabul Express* (2006). Like Shah Rukh Khan, Yash Raj recently made a move into action films with *Dhoom* (2004), a film with motorbikes and stunts starring Abhishek Bachchan (the son of the 1970s superstar) as a humourless policeman working alongside Yash Chopra's own son Uday, who played the comedic buddy role.

In this respect, it is worth noting that the rise of Bollywood can also be understood as an indication of generational change in the film industry, as the major stars and directors of the 1970s and 1980s hand over the reins to their children. Many of the current stars (such as Abhishek Bachchan, Karisma and Kareena Kapoor, Hrithik Roshan, Saif and Soha Ali Khan) come from established film families, as do many of the new directors (such as Aditya Chopra and Farhan Akhtar) working in the Bollywood vein. The explosion of transnational television, international brands and global aspirations during the 1990s has produced a very different outlook on the cinema amongst these younger players. This is very much a post-MTV generation that is acutely aware of international trends in the cinema. Thus, Bollywood films are more outward-looking in their film style than the films made by the previous generation, whose attention was much more focused on long-term trends in a closed domestic market. At the same time, the latest crop of filmmakers clearly remains conscious of the legacy that they are inheriting, and the prevalence of retro references to the formula films of the past is a notable feature of Bollywood films. Much of this attention to the old Indian cinema is expressed in terms of ironic affection, a trope that sometimes mobilises a surprisingly effective nostalgia for classic Indian cinema, but at other times has the effect of making contemporary Bollywood appear to be something of a slick parody of itself. Another notable feature of the Bollywood genre has been the revival of the 'multi-starrer' from the 1970s, where a number of big name stars share the billing within a narrative that combines a number of romantic narratives (examples include *Mohabbatein* (2000), *Kabhi Kushi Kabhie Gham* (2001), *Dil Chahta Hai* (2001)). Typically, this takes the form of a trio of heterosexual romances – of which one will be heroic, one tragic and one comedic – within a group of peers.

Bollywood gloss has not been restricted to sentiment alone. We have also witnessed the rise of the impossibly beautiful body as the central focus of contemporary films. This trend was led by the entry of a former Miss World, Aishwarya Rai, into the film industry with Subhash Ghai's *Taal* (1998). This trend has subsequently been augmented by the fetishistic representation of the male body in the forms of Hrithik Roshan and John Abraham. Impossibly beautiful bodies set in impossibly beautiful lives have been further augmented by the saturation of the Bollywood frame with impossibly beautiful products. As product placements have proliferated within the films themselves, for Coca Cola (in *Taal*) or for Mercedes (in *Dil Chahta Hai*), we begin to see Bollywood articulating the collapse of distinctions between advertising and narrative entertainment common to the media-saturated cultures of late capitalism found in Europe and North America. It seems that the bigger stars, like Shah Rukh Khan and Amitabh Bachchan, have advertised everything from axle oil to light aircraft over the last ten years. Aishwarya Rai also delivers considerable cultural capital for companies targeting affluent Indian consumers, as well as representing the preferred face of the new India for international advertisers. Thus, Bollywood operates as a symbolic performance of India in the liberalisation era and has increasingly been seen as iconic of India's global ambitions and as a major resource of soft power in the repertoire of global culture (see Bose 2006). There is no doubt, therefore, that the Bollywood blockbuster inhabits a universe that is light years away from the Manmohan Desai potboiler and the more visceral Indian cinema of the immediate past.

In the period preceding our study of the multiplexes, it was Shah Rukh Khan's re-make of the 1970s superhit gangster film, *Don*, that was dominating the box office at the multiplexes. In the period immediately following, Shah Rukh Khan's self-reflexive opus, *Om Shanti Om* (2008), was leading programming schedules and box office returns. During our study period, however, it was the Yash Raj action sequel, *Dhoom 2* (2006), that represented the Bollywood blockbuster. In *Dhoom 2*, the heroic but understated Mumbai policeman Jai Dixit (Abhishek Bachchan) and his humorous and hyperactive sidekick, Ali (Uday Chopra) attempt to foil the dramatic heists of an international art thief, Mr A (Hrithik Roshan). Outwitted in Mumbai in the first part of the film, they follow Mr A to Rio in the second part of the film, where the seduction of Mr A by cat burglar–turned-informer, Sunehri (Aishwarya Rai), is part of a plan to catch him in the act. The second love interest is played by the voluptuous Bipasha Basu, who plays an equally serious police colleague and admirer of Dixit in the first half and her dipsy NRI twin-sister, who falls in love with sidekick Ali in Rio, in the second half. Ultimately, Senehri finds herself unable to betray Mr A and they attempt to escape together, pursued by Dixit and Ali in a lengthy motorcycle chase reminiscent of the first *Dhoom* film. They are caught, however, and Sunehri shoots Mr A in order to save him from arrest. His death, however, proves to be another stunt. At the end of the film, Dixit tracks them down to Fiji where they have 'gone straight' to run a beach bar.

This rather unlikely plot scenario unfolds in what are relatively short dramatic interludes interspersed between the big stunt sequences and a series of lengthy musical numbers focusing on each of the stars in turn. For an action film, there is surprisingly little in the way of violence in *Dhoom 2*, which places its major focus on the famous bodies of its stars. The camera lingers particularly on Aishwarya and Bipasha, with Hrithik also receiving a fair amount of visual attention. The overt eroticism of the film, along with the glamorous locations and the super-bikes, makes *Dhoom 2* much more of a glamour film than a standard action feature. The film, along with its predecessor, also marks a move by Abhishek Bachchan away from the sensitive and romantic roles he has played to date towards the more powerful, taciturn figure which was defined by his father in the superhits of the 1970s. Aishwarya Rai is also uncharacteristically cast as the bad girl, Sunehri, although it must be said that neither is particularly convincing in making these transitions for this film. Equally, the musical sequences in *Dhoom 2* are much weaker than is normally the case in Bollywood features. As a conscious attempt to branch out from the romantic and familial narratives that have underpinned the success of Bollywood, the cast seems a bit adrift in the action scenario and the film produces very little in the way of dramatic tension. It certainly does not compete with Shah Rukh Khan's tongue-in-cheek action features of the past few years. Nonetheless, the roster of stars and the Yash Raj brand were enough to guarantee takings of almost a billion rupees, making this far and away the highest-grossing film in the market during our study.

Salaam E Ishq, which followed *Dhoom 2* on its release in January 2007 was, by contrast, a more traditional Bollywood film that remained firmly within the romance genre. Again, this was a multi-starrer with Salman Khan, Priyanka Chopra, Anil Kapoor, Juhi Chawla, Akshaye Khanna, John Abraham, Govinda and a host of minor stars. Taking the multi-starrer formula to its limits, *Salaam e Ishq* follows the romantic fortunes of six couples over three hours and 45 minutes. *Salaam E Ishq* was directed by Nikhil Advani, who had a debut hit with *Kal Ho Naa Ho* in 2003 and previously assisted on major Bollywood productions like *Khabhi Kushi Khabhie Gham*, *Mohabbatein* and *Kuch Kuch Hota Hai*. Intertextual references to all these films appear in *Salaam E Ishq*, although the major reference point is very clearly Richard Curtis' *Love Actually* (2003). The difficulty of keeping six stories moving and giving characters equal substance is evident, even though the technical quality of the film is high. The music is compelling, which is certainly more than could be said for *Dhoom 2*. By further comparison, *Salaam E Ishq* draws on the second tier of Bollywood stars, but Akshaye Khanna and Anil Kapoor put in strong performances. Govinda, who would not commonly be associated with the Bollywood set, also adds a lot to the film. Some of the performances by the other stars are less convincing, and not all the narrative components maintain interest, but *Salaam E Ishq* is a decent, if predictable, Bollywood production. The film was not a major success on release, however, making just one-quarter of the takings for *Dhoom 2*.

Taking note of Rajadhyaksha's observation that Bollywood is not the Indian cinema per se, it might best be described instead as the 'export lager' of the Indian cinema, since it is Bollywood productions which dominate India's film exports. The Bollywood film generates the vast majority of overseas returns and has, in the process, become centrally positioned as the trademark Indian film in the international imagination. Export earnings have, in turn, bolstered the production budgets and ambitions of the producers and stars associated with the Bollywood phenomenon, giving them a competitive edge over their contemporaries in India and yielding an impressive number of hit films over the past two decades. As such, the Bollywood brand has simultaneously reconfigured the sensibility of India's middle-class film audience. The highly effective combination of diasporic and higher-value metropolitan audiences has allowed the Bollywood blockbuster to put clear water between itself and the rump of the Indian film industry, in terms of its production resources, certainly, but also in terms of its cinematic *mise-en-scène* and the purchasing power of its primary audience. It is hardly surprising, then, that these are the films that absolutely dominate the Indian multiplex.

The multiplex film

While the multiplex menu has been closely aligned to Bollywood releases and reflective of deals with Hollywood distributors, it is the array of alternative films that occupies a very small proportion of metropolitan programming that has been most frequently associated with the multiplex by commentators such as Aparna Sharma. They represent something of a novelty to film fans since these are niche films which previously would not have been exhibited at any of the distribution tiers. The multiplex industry as a whole also frequently emphasises the importance of these films, with INOX COO Alok Tandon in close agreement with Adlabs' Tashur Dhingra on the opportunities offered by the multiplexes for non-blockbuster films:

> Because the multiplex is coming in, we have a new genre of movie and that genre is called the 'multiplex genre'. Where the producer knows that the multiplex will have seats ranging from 150 to 400 seats . . . and he is not dependent on those old cinema halls with 11 or 12 hundred seats all in one go . . . if he is making a movie for a niche audience, he knows only a certain number of people will come over there to watch this movie. Then he can target a multiplex for one screen with only two hundred seats, which will give him good occupancies and good revenues. Because he knows that for that kind of movie, 11 hundred people will never come at one time. Maximum could be two hundred, two hundred and fifty. And for that, multiplex is the best location to show it in. So there are also movies that are coming that are only for a niche audience. I would say that those kind of movies have really become popular after the advent of the multiplexes in India, and even directors and producers, want to make that movie.
>
> (Alok Tandon, interview 04/01/2007)

As a set of films that occupies a certain operational possibility within the economics of cinema, what the multiplex films have in common is the pursuit of a small, high-value audience that is supportive of films that situate themselves beyond the sphere of both the Bollywood blockbuster and the traditional *masala* film. In surveying the range of films that occupied this narrow programming slot at the multiplexes, three broad trends were apparent. First, there was a specifically middle-class comedy format that both celebrates and satirises the new realites of urban middle-class existence. Typical examples are films like *Joggers Park* (2003), *Jhankaar Beats* (2003), *Pyaar Ke Side Effects* (2006) and *Khosla Ka Ghosla* (2006). Second, there is the continuation of an art house style that stems from the legacy of the parallel cinema movement in India, with a stylistic imprint of 1950s neo-realism, an absence of songs and a penchant for themes of gender inequality and social justice. Perhaps the leading proponent of this kind of cinema amongst the younger generation would be Bengali director Rituparno Ghosh with his series of literary woman-centred films like *Dahan* (1997), *Utsab* (2000) and *Chokher Bali* (2003). In Third, there is an emergent film noir-style that is heavily influenced by contemporary US indie cinema. In these films, the dark underside of contemporary urban life is the subject matter for a faster-paced visual style. Dev Benegal's *English August* (1994) and *Split Wide Open* (1999), both narrated with an irreverent irony, would fit into this category, as would Anarag Kashyup's darker docu-drama, *Black Friday* (2004).

As with the Bollywood blockbuster, the multiplex films can also be seen to represent a generational shift. Although veterans of the parallel cinema movement of the 1970s, such as Naseeruddin Shah and Shabana Azmi, may appear within the same category of exhibition, the vast majority of the multiplex films are made by younger directors with a different stylistic and thematic agenda. The work of Madhur Bhandarkar is a good example of the milieu of this new alternative cinema. After working with Ram Gopal Varma, Bhandharkar began directing his own films in the late 1990s. Bhandharkar won critical acclaim with his film *Chandni Bar* (2001), which focused on the exploitation of women in the dancing bars of Mumbai. With its cast of petty villains, pimps and corrupt policeman, *Chandni Bar* made a powerful statement about the multi-layered exploitation of Mumbai's underclass. The film won a series of awards for Bhandharkar and lead actress Tabu. Bhandharkar subsequently embarked on a trilogy of films that took life in contemporary Mumbai as their subject. The first film, *Page 3* (2005), starring Konkana Sen Sharma, was a commercial success that brought more national awards for Bhandharkar. *Page 3* presents a critique of the glamour lifestyle surrounding Mumbai's media industries, with the female protagonists of the films suffering a series of sexual exploitations that destroy their shared ambition of entering the world of celebrity.

Page 3 was followed by *Corporate* (2006) which traces the self-interest and corruption of two Indian business houses chasing foreign investment opportunities and, in the process, colluding with local politicians to sell poisoned soft drinks to the Indian public. An ambitious young executive Nishi (Bipasha Basu) gets caught up in the intrigue and eventually ends up taking the fall for the crimes of her employers. The final film of the trilogy, *Traffic Signal* (2007), which was on release during our study, follows the lives of a group of street hawkers working at a Mumbai junction. In the course of the film, the collusion between underworld dons, local politicians and property developers sees the hawkers embroiled in a plan to murder an incorruptible urban engineer in order to ensure that a planned flyover gets re-routed to serve a luxury apartment development. The advent of this flyover will take away the middle-class commuters from the traffic signal and thus destroy the livelihoods of the street workers. Having been tricked into assisting the murder plot, Silsila (Khunal Khemu), the leader of the local street workers, agrees to give evidence against those behind the murder at the conclusion of the film.

Although less successful than *Page 3* in commercial terms, both *Corporate* and *Traffic Signal* received a degree of critical acclaim. Stylistically, Bhandharkar's films combine contemporary commercial style with hard-hitting themes of exploitation and injustice. By portraying the economic and social dynamics of the urban under-belly, the multiplex films bring those social classes excluded from the narratives of development economics into the elite spaces of the malls. They have this thematic agenda in common with the Indian art films of the 1970s, and like those films they have much shorter running times than the lengthy commercial films. However, unlike the self-consciously serious parallel films, Bhandharkar's works include light-hearted and musical sequences within their narratives. This makes for a more populist delivery of their unquestionably critical content. It is also significant that these films differ from old parallel films of the past by remaining firmly within an urban setting, reflecting a general trend in post-liberalisation Indian cinema of an absence of rural settings and narratives. What the new multiplex films do share with the old parallel films, however, is their niche market. Both generations of India's alternative cinema have employed the miseries of India's underclass as a cinematic subject for consumption by middle-class spectators.

The other side of the coin is the advent of more light-hearted multiplex films that are characterised by decidedly middle-class humour, settings and characters (and by the extensive use of both English and Hinglish). In both cases, multiplex films represent what is very much a middle-class film culture, as Mumbai-based director Kabir Khan explains:

> You no longer have to have films that cater to all segments of society. As you know, more so in India than in any other country, I would say, sensibilities will vary with, would vary with the classes and their economic background, you know, and where they are coming from. Earlier, you had to make a film and you had to sort of cater to everybody, but you ultimately ended up catering to the lowest common denominator. That sort of made sense, because then you would get back your money. But with multiplexes coming up, and multiplexes are now in an excess of a hundred across India, it is very possible to make a small film which is more urban in its sensibility. Might have a smattering of English. Might talk about subjects which are probably alien to some of our rural populations, and yet they do well, and they are accepted.
>
> (interview 09/01/2007)

Khan's recent contribution to this new kind of cinema was his film *Kabul Express* (2007). The film was a dramatisation loosely based on his own experiences as a documentary filmmaker in Afghanistan following the American-led invasion of 2002. It was the first international feature to be made in Afghanistan since the fall of the Taliban government. *Kabul Express* follows the attempts of two Indian journalists (John Abraham and Arshad Warsi) to gain an interview with a Taliban fighter. Along the way they befriend an American journalist (Jessica Beckham) and are subsequently held at gunpoint by a Taliban fugitive (Salman Shahid) who compels them to help him reach the border of his native Pakistan. Shot in the dramatic landscapes of Afghanistan, with dialogue outweighing action by a large margin and without and songs, the film bears the hallmark of an art house production (despite the presence of up-and-coming Bollywood star John Abraham). The film was backed by Yash Raj Films, who described it as a foray into the international film scene (Yash Raj Films 2007). Khan, however, is adamant that he made the film for an Indian audience, with the exposition of India–Pakistan relations being the central dialogue of the film. More specifically, Khan identifies that he saw the Indian multiplex crowd as the key audience for the film:

> The only reason for the scene in the last five years, of new cinema coming out of India, cinema without the song and dance, cinema without the traditional entertainment values, is because of the multiplexes. Suddenly film makers realise that, yes, we can make a small film. We can release fifty prints of that film, and hope to get the money back from the multiplexes because the multiplex prices are much higher . . . Multiplex audience is almost all of it for *Kabul Express*. Almost eighty percent. Initially it was thought that we would release only in the multiplex. We decided to go slightly wider and also release in what we call 'select' single screens. That is single screens that have been upgraded or the location is much better. But easily seventy-five percent was the multiplexes.
>
> (interview 09/01/2007)

Vipul Shah, another Mumbai-based director who made the comedy hit *Namastey London* (2007) is also keen to point out the importance of the multiplex crowd for encouraging the production of more low-budget, innovative films:

> Recently we saw two films doing pretty well. One was *Khosla Ka Ghosla*, the other one was *Joggers Park*. They would not have released in the era when multiplexes were not there. Nobody would have thought about making a film in that way. Now people are actually planning films like those for multiplex audience. For a very, very young audience, for an audience that is willing to accept a film purely on the basis of the script. Even if there are no stars connected to it.
>
> (Vipul Shah, interview 08/01/2007)

In the mainstream Indian cinema, the highest cost of filmmaking has for a long time been the recruitment of top-tier stars who have been the only consistent impetus for success at the box office. At the present time, the only films guaranteed opening day success are those featuring Shah Rukh Khan, Salman Khan, Aamir Khan, Akshay Kumar or Hrithik Roshan. Amitabh Bachchan, whose dominance over the film industry led to him being dubbed 'the one man industry' during the 1980s, also remains a strong performer at the box office, although not all of his films are hits nowadays. A small selection of female stars – most notably Aishwarya Rai, but also Preity Zinta and Rani Mukherjee – has the ability to attract audiences consistently, if not on the same scale. These stars are all beyond the budget of the smaller multiplex films, which as a consequence are less dependent upon the star formula for their success. However, the multiplex films have spawned some stars of their own, including Rahul Bose, who has been particularly associated with the genre. In addition, rising stars in the Mumbai film scene have begun turning their hands to these smaller films in recent years as a means of asserting their acting credentials. As such, minor stars such as Bipasha Basu and John Abraham, who are now appearing in Bollywood features, have appeared in films like *Corporate* and *Kabul Express*.

Vipul Shah's *Namastey London* had the benefit of star attraction from Akshay Kumar, who has worked with Shah on a number of films. The casting of Kumar enabled Shah's film to achieve a solid box office performance. There have also been a number of lower-budget comedies appearing within the multiplex film bracket. During our study, it was *Honeymoon Travels Pvt Ltd* (2007) that represented the lighter side of the multiplex film ethos. In this film, Shabana Azmi, a veteran of the parallel cinema, is teamed with Parsi comic Boman Irani and a clutch of minor stars in a narrative that follows the fortunes of six couples on a honeymoon excursion to Goa. A light-hearted take on making the adjustment to married life, *Honeymoon Travels* is a modest but well-made film that was popular with younger middle-class couples. Both *Honeymoon Travels* and Vipul Shah's bigger-budget film indicate the increasing popularity of comedies in recent years. While stars like Govinda have been producing comedies that have been popular in the B circuit for some time, the recent success of more middle-class comedies can be related to the focus of multiplexes on the family audience.

For the fuller range of multiplex films, it is the reduction of risks facilitated by screen-shifting and the availability of smaller auditoriums that allows the smaller productions to piggyback on the infrastructure paid for by the blockbuster releases. In return, for the multiplex operators, the uncertain longevity of each blockbuster can be balanced by increasing or decreasing the screenings of the smaller movies which produce lower returns, but which cost much less to acquire and can, in the best cases, generate a sufficient audience to guarantee a tidy profit. As Vipul Shah explains,

> Right now, there is still too small a number of screens to release two big films on the same Friday, because every multiplex books a big film on three or four screens. They don't have space for another big film to come in. So there is room for everybody today, because there will be one big film per week and a small film can come with it simultaneously. Both can survive happily. So in that sense it is a pretty good system.

(interview 08/01/2007)

There exists a productive tension between the way in which the multiplex reinforces and legitimates the overall dominance of the blockbuster film, whilst at the same time offering, through its excess capacity, a toehold to filmmakers producing small offbeat films. These films are too diverse to classify under the notion of a multiplex 'genre' in the classic sense of the term. It is the operating context of these films, rather than any set of cinematic features, that distinguishes them from other kinds of filmmaking. However, their targeting of a particular segment of the urban audience does engender a common mode of address, and the emergence of a commercially-viable Indian indie sector represents a major shift away from the aesthetic confines of the festival circuit for India's aspiring filmmakers. In this sense, the multiplex has opened up a wider space for films that tackle, however obliquely, many of the critical issues facing India today. At the same time, the logic of the multiplex paradoxically ensures that those films remain economically and numerically marginal to the cinematic industry as a whole.

Other middle-class films

Despite the dominance of the blockbuster/niche film combination and the growing divergence between multiplexes and single-screen cinemas at the level of content, there will still be occasional films that escape this paradigm. A cross-over film remains a possibility because there continues to be a significant lower middle-class and rural middle-class audience that lacks the access and/or the purchasing power to join the multiplex crowd. Sooraj R. Barjatya's film, *Vivah* (2006) is instructive in this regard. *Vivah* was made on a modest budget and received only a limited initial release without corresponding to the model of a niche film. The narrative of *Vivah* is centred on tried-and-tested themes of familial duty and romantic desire in the context of an arranged marriage between a wealthy industrialist family and a middle-class family from a rural town. Lacking the presence of any big stars or a big rollout in the multiplexes, *Vivah* eventually became a hit after a long run that relied predominantly on single-screen theatres to generate momentum. Although *Vivah* subsequently performed well in multiplexes, this is a film that bucked the general trend by collecting a substantial part of its revenue in the districts as well as in urban B centres.

In *Vivah*, the romance of Prem (Shahid Kapur) and Poonam (Amrita Rao) and the union of the two families receive a very traditional (and culturally conservative) treatment, particularly when compared to the modern relationships shown in multiplex films like *Page 3* and *Honeymoon Travels*. The comfortable affirmation of traditional gender roles and the institution of the extended family in *Vivah* may have some bearing upon its popularity in the districts. It is also significant that the union of the two families in the film endorses an alliance between the urban and rural middle classes. At one level, *Vivah* does this by reiterating the perennial promise of the redistribution of wealth and status from benevolent urban elites to deserving middle-class families in *mofussil* towns. In return, the upscale family undergoes a cultural renewal by accessing the Hindu traditions for which rural settings are seen to be a repository. This exchange is epitomised by Prem struggling to speak in chaste Hindi and by the symbolic coming together of the families in the rustic surrounds of the holiday house at San Sarovar. This narrative resolution of both urban/rural and class divides further underpins the broad appeal of the film to lower middle-class and district audiences. At the same time, *Vivah* also proved to be compatible with multiplex crowd due its solid espousal of middle-class aspiration and family values. This makes sense when we recall that Barjatya's early successes in the 1990s, such as *Hum Aapke Hain Koun* (1994), were seen as milestones in re-establishing middle-class values in the popular cinema, even though his family film business, Rajshri Productions, did not subsequently undertake the Bollywood metamorphosis.

The other major exception to the overall programming trend recorded during our study was Mani Rathnam's film *Guru* (2007). Mani Rathnam is an *auteur* who stands out in the Indian cinema precisely because of his capacity to deviate from the general pattern of filmmaking. He is one of the few directors originating in regional cinema to achieve a national profile. Working within the Tamil film industry in Chennai, Rathnam made films in all of the major South Indian languages for a decade before gaining national recognition for his film *Roja* (1992), which focuses on the insurgency in Kashmir. *Roja* was the first of three Rathnam's films that have been referred to as the 'terrorism trilogy' (Chakravarty 2000). The other two films were *Bombay* (1995) and *Dil Se* (1998). Rathnam's work in the past decade has been divided between Tamil- and Hindi-language films, employing stars from both industries. Besides crossing the linguistic divides of the Indian cinema, Rathnam is also known for his popular treatment of serious themes and for his blend of cinematic realism with the style of commercial films. Again, against the tide of recent fashion, Rathnam has shot almost all of his films exclusively within India, and his films continue to combine rural and urban settings. His films are much bigger in their scale and audience than the so-called 'multiplex films' and they do not correspond to the formula of the contemporary blockbuster.

Made in Hindi, *Guru* was released on the January 12 2007 and was still running alongside *Salaam E Ishq* in February. Like *Dhoom 2*, *Guru* features the pairing of Abhishek Bachchan with Aishwarya Rai, and thus benefited from the publicity generated by the announcement of their engagement two days after the film's release. *Guru* tells the story of a headmaster's son from a village, Gurukant Desai (Abhishek Bachchan), and his struggle to become a major business leader. Desai raises his start-up capital by working overseas in Turkey and by receiving a marriage dowry. He then goes to Mumbai to enter the world of business. There he is frequently frustrated by the discriminatory practices of trade union leaders, the established business houses and the public officials who seek to keep him out of the textile trade. Gurukant, who becomes known as Gurubhai, turns to India's middle classes by raising capital through a public share offering. His textile empire grows rapidly and receives ever greater levels of public investment. The dismayed establishment does everything it can to check his rise. Initially, Gurubhai gains support from the press, but the newspapers turn against him as they become convinced that his success is based upon the widespread use of bribes, the flouting of legal regulations and dishonest business practises. At the climax of the film, Gurubhai, much weakened by his constant struggle against the old elites, suffers a stroke. He is then forced to leave his sickbed to answer an enquiry accusing him of manipulating the stock exchange through the illegal conversion of shares.

Although *Guru* is presented as a fictional tale, it was widely perceived in India as a dramatisation of the life of Anil Dhirubhai Ambani. The striking correspondence between the fictional life of Gurubhai and the larger-than-life figure of Dhirubhai speak for themselves. After working in Yemen, Anil Dhirubhai Ambani entered the textile trade and raised large sums of capital from innovative public investment schemes to fund his Reliance Industries, which subsequently became the biggest company in India. Along the way, Reliance faced fierce opposition from the elite families who ran the older business houses. Dhirubhai himself publicly fell out with press magnate Ramnath Goenka, who waged a press campaign against him. Reliance was embroiled in the 1980s in a major controversy over its share dealings, leading to a public enquiry which Dhirubhai attended after suffering a debilitating stroke (McDonald 1999). Dhirubhai, who died in 2002, was a controversial figure who exemplified business acumen whilst also being associated with the widespread corruption that plagued the Indian economy during the 'license raj' era of the command economy. The elevation of a very similar figure to heroic status in the film *Guru* is itself telling of the current mood in India. This is not to say that Rathnam's film omits or skirts around the controversies associated with its main character, but it is certainly the case that *Guru* presents a very sympathetic account of the pursuit of wealth and of the various means necessary for an outsider to succeed in India's business world.

At the conclusion of the film, Gurubhai faces the panel of the public enquiry and delivers an impassioned speech in which he denounces the role played by the old elites in holding down the aspirations of the Indian people and in perpetuating India's subordination to the developed world in order to protect the interests of the establishment. Gurubhai accuses the government of presiding over a system where bribery and corruption are requisites of business dealings. Earlier in the film, he tells his shareholders at a public meeting that 'The rich hate that the middle class is now writing its own destiny'. Here at the film's conclusion, Gurubhai again equates the rise of his company with the 'common man's courage' in the face of state-sponsored nepotism. Comparing the battle against government regulations with Gandhi's struggle against colonial rule, he asserts that India has the right to be a First World country, and that if business is allowed to flourish unhindered, India could be a First World country. 'Our foot is in the door' says Gurubhai, and 'the whole country is moving ahead with me'. This central message of the film could not help but impart a particular resonance if you were watching it in one of the many Adlabs multiplexes that are majority-owned by Reliance Industries. Thus, of all of the films discussed in this chapter, *Guru* provides perhaps the most demonstrative example of the complex interweaving of social space, economic ideology and cultural narrative in the contemporary Indian cinema.

Table 8.1 Box office returns of key films January–March 2007

Title	Release date	Distributor	Director	Actors	Genre(s)	Collections (Rs)
Dhoom 2	24 Nov. 2006	Yash Raj Films	Sanjay Gadhvi	Abhishek Bachchan, Aishwarya Rai, Hrithik Roshan, Bipasha Basu, Uday Chopra	Action Drama	94,93,93,216
Guru	12 Jan. 2007	Madras Talkies	Mani Rathnam	Abhishek Bachchan, Aishwarya Rai, Mithun Chakraborty	Drama	53,83,74,272
Vivah	10 Nov. 2006	Rajshri Productions	Sooraj R. Barjatya	Shahid Kapur, Amrita Rao	Romantic Family Drama	45,60,33,376
Namastey London	23 Mar. 2007	Blockbuster Movie Entertainers	Vipul Shah	Akshay Kumar, Katrina Kaif	Comedy	31,68,71,488
Salaam-E-Ishq	25 Jan. 2007	Orion Pictures MAD Entertainment Ltd	Nikhil Advani	Salman Khan, Priyanka Chopra, Anil Kapoor, Juhi Chawla, Akshaye Khanna, John Abraham, Govinda et al	Romantic Drama	23,94,39,840
Kabul Express	15 Dec. 2006	Yash Raj Films	Kabir Khan	John Abraham, Arshad Warsi, Salman Shahid	Drama	15,00,19,408
Honeymoon Travels Pvt Ltd.	23 Feb. 2007	Excel Entertainment	Reema Kagti	Shabana Azmi, Boman Irani, Kay Kay Menon, Raima Sen, Amisha Patel, Karan Khanna, Vikram Chatwal et al	Comedy	14,06,10,176
Traffic Signal	2 Feb. 2007	Madhur Bhandarkar Motion Pictures	Madhur Bhandarkar	Kunal Khemu, Neetu Chandra, Konkona Sen Sharma, Naseer Abdullah, et al.	Drama	9,46,06,304

Source: Adapted from: http://www.ibosnetwork.com

The constitution of a taste culture

Our analysis of multiplex programming over the study period strongly supported the hypothesis that the defined socio-economic segment to which the multiplex caters, and the carefully targeted placement of the multiplexes themselves must necessarily be reflected by the emergence of a distinctive cinematic menu serving this particular context. We found that the taste culture enshrined by the multiplexes is highly distinctive due to its remarkable internal consistency in spatial, ritual and narrative organisation. The sensory environment of the architecture, the acceptable conventions of social behaviour that go with it and the selection of film content for (and by) this particular niche public all contribute to the cultural environment of the Indian multiplex. The film culture on offer can be easily distinguished in all these respects from the experience of cinema that is mobilised in the majority of the single-screen cinemas that cater to more modest income brackets. However, this is certainly not a distinction between art house and populist cinema. The critical arguments and economic realities that separate quality cinema and popular cinema remain in place at the multiplex. Rather, the more significant point of distinction is between the aspirations of the urban middle classes and the rest of the population.

As many of the interviewees in this chapter emphasise, in overruling the narrow common ground found that can be achieved in the larger market, the multiplex plays a vital role in facilitating new film styles. It could also be argued that the concentration by some producers on the multiplex sector is freeing up the availability of single-screen cinemas for other producers. Thus, while the multiplex naturally sidelines themes and genres that are seen as more suitable for the 'other' crowd, there are plenty of filmmakers who remain willing to cater to this audience. In this light, the particular taste culture associated with the multiplex can be positively seen as an indication of a more sophisticated media environment that has now matured to the point of being able to target different sectors of the market more effectively and to offer a wider range of choice to its defined customer base.

On a less optimistic note, it seems likely that the higher value of multiplex crowd will exert a disproportionate influence on filmmakers, and that the subculture of the multiplex will have more impact on the form and content of Indian films in the future than will the tastes and interests of the larger general audience. This has powerful implications for how we conceptualise the status of the Bollywood blockbuster as the inheritor of the all-India film of old. The divergence between the multiplex menu and the films made for the theatrical circuit clearly illustrates the segmentation of the cinema at different pricing points. Another divergence, between pan-Indian multiplex programming and the domains of the regional film industries, is also highly significant in this regard. Finally, the concentration of multiplexes in the larger cities and wealthier suburbs reflects a growing disjuncture between metropolitan and district audiences. As such, there are a number of fault lines now evident between different segments of the market, which fewer films appear to be capable of crossing. Consequently, the shift towards making films for a series of niche audiences is likely to continue, representing a change in the way that Indian film producers and directors conceive their work.

Conclusion

The multiplex and the leisure economy

In the course of this work, we have attempted to illuminate the phenomenon of the multiplex in terms of its demonstrable relationships to the cultural, economic and material aspects of social life. In doing so, we have sought to illustrate the wide range of trends within which the multiplex is situated: agendas for urban renewal, the ethos of corporatisation in the media sector, the cultural politics of aspiration, the pursuit of a consumer market and a services economy and the inevitable tensions arising from spatial and demographic disparities in an unevenly developing economy. Taken together, it is these intersecting concerns that constitute the conceptual environment that currently shapes the popular understanding of India today. As such, during the decade of its existence, the multiplex has been very much a sign of the times – both a symptom and a symbol of new social values. As the evidence presented here suggests, the Indian multiplex has been particularly indicative of a consistent, if not always coherent, push to create a globalised consuming middle class and a new urban environment. For this reason, multiplex theatres, like their single-screen predecessors, have become key sites in the long-running struggle over cultural legitimacy and the right to public space in Indian cities. The symbolic dominance of the consuming class in the social imagination is therefore played out in both textual and material realms in the changing themes of Indian films and in the redistributions of urban space that facilitate the new leisure infrastructure.

In this context, the Indian multiplex is not simply an imported format suturing global and local space (although it bears those apparent markings). We must be attentive to the fact that the cinema hall was itself a symbol of occidental modernity and decadence when it appeared in India's urban landscape in the early part of the twentieth century. Over the course of several decades the cinema hall nonetheless became embedded in India's social fabric in unique ways. There is no reason to suspect that the story of the multiplex will be different. Without neglecting in any way the symbolic power of the international provenance of the multiplex and the manifest desire of the Indian middle classes to inhabit Westernised cultural environments, we have sought to demonstrate here that the antecedents of the Indian multiplex, and its exclusivist nature in particular, also emerge from the specific history of the Indian cinema. From this perspective, the multiplex is just the latest part of an urban history which, in totality, provides a useful weather vane pointing to the prevailing currents in India's public culture over the last century, in turn accommodating (and thus spatialising) colonial and caste elites, a proto-nationalist public, urban mass migrants, disenfranchised agitators and, in the form of the multiplex, a consuming class that is wilfully segregated. It is in this context that the shifting ideological terrain within the parallel historiography presented by the films inspired, made and consumed in India makes most sense.

While the interwoven histories of urbanism, cinema and modern politics are crucial for situating the multiplex within social space, it remains equally crucial to understand the industrial nature of the cinematic medium and the economic logic that directs its operations. In exploring the contemporary dynamics of the media sector in India, we have seen how the rise of the multiplex is inextricably linked to the re-organisation of working practices and of capital investment within the leisure economy. The fact that the multiplex has become a reality at the very same moment that concerted efforts are being made to relocate the film industry away from the margins of India's informal economy and into the ambit of the big business houses is far from coincidental. The aggregation of interests within what has traditionally been a highly fragmented industry with largely informal organisation is a direct result of both the entry of outside concerns into the media business and the deregulation policies pursued by successive governments in this arena. The agenda of corporatisation has required a substantial degree of operational change within the film industry as it redefines its primary markets in terms of higher-value customers, both overseas and at the multiplex.

Corporatisation is a business model very much influenced by the post-Reagan Hollywood milieu but, given the highly fragmented nature of the Indian film industries as a starting point, this is an agenda which remains very much a work in progress. Nonetheless, as with other areas of the Indian economy, the transformation of the film industry is much more advanced now than it was even just a few years ago. Bollywood producers accessing international revenues and undertaking their own marketing and distribution are now able to access large volumes of legitimate finance. The multiplex companies raise significant share capital and attract corporate investors from India's big league. Overseas distributors such as Eros, Indian Films and UTV have raised significant sums on international exchanges and used some of this money to invest in production. These activities have transformed the relationships between exhibitors, distributors and producers, and unsurprisingly all of this has upset the balance of power in the film world.

In the US, the story of the multiplex in the 1980s was one where distributors tied to major studios took control of the exhibition sector. In the Indian case, there were (and still are) no juggernaut studios with the requisite capital or the organisational capacity for such an undertaking. As such, the rapid growth of the big multiplex companies and the major component of box office takings that they now represent has put them in a position to leverage domestic distributors, who are further pressured by the ability of producers to find new sources of production finance. Thus, while the bigger international distributors have prospered, the complex multi-layered domestic distribution structure is seeing a process of consolidation. Arijit Dutta, Chairman of the Eastern India Motion Pictures Association (whose company Priya Entertainment handles distribution for Sony, Paramount, UTV and others), explains the situation:

> Say 8–10 years ago we have 30–40 distributors in Bengal. And then there was Orissa, and then there was a separate set of distributors. You have Bihar, a separate set of distributors there. Now the corporatisation factor comes in and you get 4–5 distributors in Bengal. And indirectly 4–5 distributors in the East. Because when the corporates come in they are giving it to one person. Now we are expected to handle Assam, we are expected to handle Bihar, we are expected to handle Orissa.
>
> (interview 08/12/2007)

The distribution sector faces further pressures from the premier production houses, like Yash Raj, who now market and distribute their own films, as well as from the forays that the multiplex companies are themselves making into the distribution sector. The switch made by Shringar Films in 2004 from being one of the biggest distributors in India and the majority owner of Shringar Cinemas to becoming a subsidiary of its multiplex operations may well have been a shrewd recognition of this new situation. At present, it certainly appears that the multiplexes have the advantageous position in determining the new relationship between distribution and exhibition. Similarly, even Yash Raj Films has had to enter into protracted negotiations with the multiplex companies over revenue-sharing arrangements over the past two years, and no other film producers have anything like the same bargaining power. For this reason, it seems entirely possible that the integration process in India could work up the value chain rather than down it. Nonetheless, the growth in revenues from the multiplexes have clearly benefited producers, who remain generally optimistic about the corporate experiment which is equated with global expansion and increasing professionalism. As Kabir Khan puts it:

> Corporatisation is a very, very welcome change for people like me who are outsiders and haven't grown up in the film industry or have godfathers in the industry. I think there now is films being made by outsiders because there is a more corporate structure coming in. There is not so much funding going on from the underworld or black money being pushed into the film industry. This will make a huge difference to the way that films are being made. I am very, very happy with the corporatisation of the film industry. It permits progress to be made by the film industry.
>
> (interview 08/01/2007)

The trend towards integration of the various aspects of the film industry which is being driven by corporatisation has numerous other benefits. It has the potential to alleviate some of the conflicts of interest that have characterised the industry in the past and to reduce the problems of box office underreporting and endemic piracy that have plagued the industry for two decades. It is in this context that the diversification of multiplex companies like Adlabs and FUN into digital distribution technologies makes sense, given that digital delivery systems for the B and C circuits reduce the number of intermediaries, keep content under the control of the distributor and reduce the window for piracy by allowing simultaneous national release. Integrated media companies have both the interest and the wherewithal to invest in these kinds of systems in a way that the old disorganised industry did not.

The multiplex companies in particular are the most visible evidence of the impact of corporatisation in the film world, and their ambitions for growth in the exhibition sector is increasingly characterised by diversification into both production and distribution. PVR operates as a distributor in north India and was slated to invest a billion rupees in film production during 2008, although with the backing of its giant majority shareholder reliance, Reliance, competitor Adlabs is weighing in with five billion rupees in production finance, outstripping the investments of the leading film producers (PriceWaterhouseCoopers 2008). For the corporates, integration is the name of the game, as Shriram Krishnan at Shringar explains: 'any player in the entertainment industry needs to be in at least two or three related spheres' (interview 20/01/2007). INOX, by contrast, is less keen to rush into things, as Alok Tandon notes: 'We have dabbled a little with production. Distribution, yes, we have distributed quite a few films. But I would say our core competency is exhibition, and we are concentrating on that' (interview 04/01/2007). Tashur Dhingra at Adlabs, however, is adamant about the benefits of vertical integration:

> As you know, cinema exhibition is a very low margin business. So our company is currently forming the largest integrated company of India. As far as integration is concerned, we are holding a sixty percent share in processing of films, we have a large international distribution setup. We are into distribution set-up for India. We are into television programming. We are into exhibition, as you know. We are getting into studios. We are getting into rental services. And production obviously, production of films. So, Adlabs is very well hedged across the whole value chain.
>
> (interview 08/01/2007)

What has also become apparent in recent years is not only the integration of the previously distinct tiers of activity within the film industry, but also the increasing difficulty with which an object called 'the cinema' can be analysed in isolation from the interests of the wider economy. The early expositions of liberalisation in Indian during the 1990s tended to focus on projections for the consumption of consumer durables at the domestic level. In recent years there has been a decisive shift towards detailing the growing importance of India as a service provider to the global economy, particularly in the fields of computer software, back-office processing, advertising and others tropes of the so-called 'knowledge economy'. In both cases, the involvement of foreign companies has provided a major point of reference for understanding the New Economy. This emphasis on tangible consumption and the production of intangibles has served to neglect, until very recently, the growing importance of intangible consumption within India, particularly in the form of visual media, communications and financial services. The leisure economy has enjoyed substantive growth of around 20 per cent per annum since 2002, a rate that compares very favourably to growth in the consumption of manufactured goods (Price Waterhouse Coopers 2006, 2007, 2008). This provides quantitative support for the evidence that we found indicating that many Indians regard shopping malls primarily as facilities for entertainment and socialising.

Perhaps one reason for the delay in recognising leisure spending as a major focus of the New Economy overall is that, again until very recently, the impressive growth in these areas has been very much a story of Indian capital. This neglect of the leisure economy is now being revised as the focus on the potentials of the Indian economy begins to shift. The newfound interest of international investors in the global presence of the Indian media is stoking the ambitions of the film industry. For outside investors, the obvious saturation of markets for leisure and services in so many developed countries is driving a search for new markets. The massive growth in Indian television from the mid-1990s onwards has provided much of the impetus for re-evaluating the potentials of media and communications. We could also take the recent purchase of the Hutchison stake in Hutchison Essar by Vodafone as a further symptom of international recognition of the importance of leisure activities amongst the Indian middle classes, and we can certainly place foreign investments in Indian film and television production in this context. In light of these developments, capital interests in India have shown their willingness to make unprecedented investments in the leisure economy. Support from organisations such as IDBI and EXIM Bank are emblematic of a shift from the pre-liberalisation era, when banks displayed a marked aversion to the disorganised Indian film industry.

One result of this influx of capital is the collapsing distinction between the various media industries as the film industries find new profits in television schedules, as TV companies begin to invest in film production and multiplexes and as advertisers use film culture to market fashion and telecoms. Prior to the liberalisation era, there was a clear distinction between commercial cinema and state-owned television in India, and for the latter, the opportunities for non-box office revenues were limited. It was thus entirely defensible to describe the Indian media as distinct entities. This is clearly no longer the case as the commercial media industries expand and their fortunes become increasingly interlinked. The rise of media conglomerates under the auspices of business houses like the Essel Group and Reliance, who are expanding their interests rapidly in all the media sectors, is a logical response to an increasingly transmedia commercial sector. The ambitions of the bigger multiplex companies to combine their media interests with other sites of leisure, such as food courts, gaming and theme parks, indicates a growing interface between traditional media and a wider leisure economy.

There is, however, an even wider convergence surrounding the rise of the multiplex in terms of the integration of the media sector with other areas of economic activity. As we have shown, the fortunes of the multiplex have been dictated to a large extent by the dynamics of India's metropolitan property market, the ambitions of the retail sector and the diversification projects of companies originating in traditional industries such as textiles, chemicals, sugar and plastics. Thus, we not only need to recognise the expansion of the leisure economy and its growing importance within the wider economy, but we also need to remain aware of the ways in which the leisure economy is now being integrated into India's formal economy at the macrological scale.

At the same time that we consider the impact of private investment, it is worth paying attention to the degree to which the multiplex phenomenon has been facilitated by government policy at the federal and state levels. The term 'deregulation', which has been so commonly been associated with the transformation of India's media sphere, may be misleading at a certain level since it is not simply the repeal of legislative obstacles that has benefited the new leisure economy, but also the introduction of new legislation that has consciously favoured the development of a new leisure infrastructure. This intervention by government has functioned at a number of levels, from entertainment tax exemptions to the re-zoning of lands for development. The advent of these new facilities serves the interests of government in various ways, from the transferability of electronic accounting within the industry that allows for efficient tax collections to the increasing land values and duties in the upmarket districts (to which the multiplex significantly contributes). The encouragement given overall to the new leisure economy in recent years is also symptomatic of a larger shift towards a consumption-based regime of revenue collection intended to mitigate the failures of income-based taxation in India over many years.

As a flagship for the leisure economy, the multiplex is necessarily located at the intersection of new relationships being forged between the public and private sectors and between India's state and the federal governments. As such, the development clusters where the multiplexes have been constructed are a physical manifestation of a marked shift in development policy towards investment in the major urban centres. Equally, the dispersal of multiplex developments at the national level is reflective of the regional disparities that have been exacerbated by federal policies of resource allocation on the basis of prior success in attracting investment. In this sense, success builds success. By consciously targeting the pockets of disposable wealth arising in key metropolitan districts, the construction of a multiplex operates as an indicator of wealth and positive proof of private investment. This, in turn, attracts public-sector funding for new infrastructure. Perhaps most importantly, the popularity of multiplexes and malls with the middle-class public brings a political dividend, and their conspicuous visibility in urban space makes an important symbolic contribution to the zeitgeist of economic prosperity that legitimates the era of liberalisation along with the socio-spatial segregation of the city.

The semiological significance of the multiplex in India, and the role it plays in generating demand for these facilities, cannot be overstated. The Indian multiplex has become a potent symbol of middle-class profligacy in a country where austerity has ruled the day for generations. This gives the multiplex far greater symbolic importance than it has had in the First World countries. The Indian multiplex is neither a means of simply minimising risk and maximising returns in a shrinking mass market for cinema, nor an extension of consumer convenience and social engineering within retail environments. It is all of these, naturally, but the capacity of the multiplex operators to offer leisure environments that are luxurious by any standard makes a direct appeal to the keen sense of quality that infuses the imagination of India's middle classes. The construction of these facilities in the face of, and amidst, the long-standing pressures that impact upon the urban environment in Indian cities also makes a powerful rejoinder to those who have been sceptical about India's capacity to produce world class infrastructure. Similarly, after many years of lamenting the deficiency of anything made in India, the new leisure infrastructure is prompting the middle classes to acquire a newfound confidence in the capabilities of the domestic economy. In that sense, the multiplexes stand alongside the larger road, rail and residential developments that are transforming the living environment of their beneficiaries. Thus, despite the fact that the multiplexes are directly and conspicuously inspired by their international forebears, they nonetheless contribute to a growing confidence that the Indian economy can match its international competitors in terms of quality.

The differences between the Indian multiplex and the utilitarian and proletarian environments of many of the multiplexes found in American shopping malls are striking. There is, however, a number of important questions that arise in relation to the marked emphasis on delivering the highest quality facilities by the Indian multiplex operators. One of the most pressing questions lies in how they are able to pursue their expansion plans in light of the obvious importance of exclusivity, and its attendant cultural capital, to their present clientele. To date, the multiplex boom has been supported by the attraction of novelty and the attraction of status-spending amongst the younger metropolitan middle class. As we have indicated, the all-India ambitions of the major chains will necessarily take them into areas where the middle classes are either less affluent or less numerous and where their attitudes to conspicuous consumption are likely to be quite different.

Projections for middle-class growth that have been widely circulated in the liberalisation era have a decidedly blue-sky aspect to them, and it is immediately obvious that there are still clouds hanging over many parts of the country. It is worth reiterating, therefore, that this future prosperity is by no means assured, given that India's contemporary engagement with the global economy is partially built on the inflows of speculative capital. This is particularly the case in the real estate, retail and entertainment sectors that concern us here, bearing in mind the overheating of the commercial and real estate market in East Asia prior to the economic crisis of 1997–1998. A further question is the stability of 'hot money' activity. By the time that we prepared our final manuscript for press at the end of 2008, the potential for this speculative investment to dry up as quickly as it was promised was vividly illustrated by a global financial crisis that witnessed the collapse of many of the global funds discussed here. How systematic market failure in the West will effect the dynamics of India's economic growth is yet to become fully apparent.

Of course, the quality, rather than just the quantity, of India's growth in coming years remains critically important. Even as we have tried to assess the rise of the New Economy on its own merits, the social consequences of following the philosophy of 'betting on the strong' that the various liberalisation-era projects have typically entailed cannot be easily ignored. At a time when there is greater attention than ever before on energy usage and carbon footprints, it is also legitimate to question the sustainability of energy-hungry malls, as well as the rapidly increasing incidence of privately-owned cars and their accompanying infrastructure (e.g. carparks, fly-overs, and expressways) in India's cities. These wider questions are appropriate here since the flourishing of these kinds of projects is integral to the success or failure of the multiplexes.

Furthermore, the future of the multiplex industry in India must inevitably negotiate the obvious tension between the logic of cinema as a mass medium and the existing model of the multiplex as an exclusive and luxurious habitat. There is inevitably a pricing point at which luxury ceases to be a selling point and becomes an unacceptably high overhead for the operator. As such, it has already become clear that at a certain point trade-offs will have to be made on the scale and fitting of new multiplexes in smaller cities where middle-class incomes are more modest. In light of this problem, PVR has conceived a trimmed-down multiplex experience for their new customers in the smaller cities. It is a project that is currently headed by Ashish Shukla:

> PVR has got metropolitan cinemas, and it is primarily a metropolitan city type of company. Now we have gone into the B and C tier towns as well. So the mainstream as we call it, is PVR in the metros, and in the B and C towns we call it PVR Talkies . . . The way that PVR has gone about it is that we have actually positioned it as a separate product altogether. The idea being that the consumer cannot be confused that today X-brand is available at lets say a three dollar price and then you put the same brand at one dollar, and you still say that it is the same brand. Because, where are the brand values? Where are the brand associations? So, in order to get the consumer and the positioning of the product right, what we did was we did value-engineering and we did product-reengineering and we are the only company that has executed products which you see here at almost half the price of what our regular cinemas are. So we have been able to bring down the capital expenditure to about half, from 2.5 crores per screen to 1.1 crores per screen. And from a ticket price of about 130, 140 Rupees ATP, we have got it down to forty to sixty Rupees.
>
> (interview 14/03/2007)

There is a limit, however, to downscaling that goes beyond conventional economics. Given the attitudes that we found amongst multiplex patrons, there is clearly going to be a loss of appeal to some existing customers if multiplexes are priced down to accommodate patrons from lower income brackets. Perhaps for this reason, INOX intends to maintain its focus on the very top end of the exhibition spectrum. The new INOX sites will continue to focus on the wealthiest neighbourhoods and will seek to maintain their status as a luxury brand by ensuring a more expensive outfitting of their theatres, and a higher ticket price, in comparison to their competitors in each location. Clearly, INOX believes that there is still adequate room for growth, and fewer complications, within the more limited upscale audience demographic.

Where all the multiplex operators are in agreement is that they are not in any form of competition with the owners of traditional single-screen theatres for their audience. Again, this is a particularity of the multiplex phenomenon in India. In the UK, for example, the arrival of multiplexes in most cases quickly put older, single-screen theatres in the vicinity out of business. In the Indian case, the multiplexes are only interested in the decent crowd, an audience which they assert was lost to the single-screen cinemas a long time ago. The owners of traditional theatres that we interviewed in all of our study sites were in broad agreement with this claim, associating the multiplexes with the decent crowd and describing their own audiences as 'the poor', 'villagers', 'rickshaw wallahs' and the 'little classy people'. Only a handful of prestigious cinemas in long-established wealthy neighbourhoods saw the multiplexes as direct competition. At the same time, the single-screen owners all agreed that it was unlikely that anyone would seek to construct new single-screen theatres in the future or invest in existing ones, given the continuing problems of stagnant ticket prices and the high entertainment taxes to which they are subject. The multiplex boom is thus accompanied by a deepening gloom in the traditional theatrical industry, which, irrespective of the multiplex, continues to struggle in the face of endemic piracy and the growth of television.

The pressing question of whether the multiplex will eventually displace the traditional cinema hall in India remains debateable, however, since it would be dependent upon the capacity (and the desire) of organised leisure to cater to the bulk of Indian society. At present, there is little sign that multiplex operators would wish to do so. It is this selectivity in their customer base that explains why the multiplexes currently operating in India remain notably smaller in capacity than their international counterparts. The differences in ownership, operating procedures and (increasingly) programming between the multiplexes and the bulk of single-screen cinemas are glaringly apparent. The overall consensus amongst owners and operators on the distinctly different target audiences for the multiplexes and the single-screen cinemas seems to suggest space for the continuance of both organised and disorganised entertainment infrastructures.

On a cautionary note, however, our own findings from the limited audience research conducted in this study indicated that there appears to be a far greater overlap between the multiplex crowd and the general audience than was generally recognised by either the multiplex chains or the operators of single-screen cinemas. In part, the reason for this was the disjuncture between the spending capacity of many multiplex patrons and the popular ideal of the SEC A+ affluent spender. There were also indications, however, that an exclusive multiplex audience does now exist, with younger and female moviegoers from the upper middle classes most likely to belong to this group. The capacity of these new facilities to provide a safe environment where young women feel comfortable enough to publicly mix with their male and female peers clearly improves their quality of life and represents a significant social benefit. At the same time, the leisure space gained here inevitably represents a redistribution of resources from the overall majority, with both men and women from the lower classes consciously excluded from the crowd that the multiplex enshrines.

At the outset of this work, we noted Partha Chatterjee's theorisation of a long-running conflict between the middle classes and proletarian groups being played out in (and over) urban space. Chatterjee describes the mobilisation of politics amongst these two broad groupings as a contest between bourgeois civil society and lumpen political society. There is an obvious correlation to be found here in the discourses surrounding the multiplex, where the social expectations of the decent crowd are articulated in opposition to the bawdy behaviour of the cheap crowd that defines the general cinema audience. The historical perspectives drawn from the work of S. V. Srinivas and others tell us that this tension is not a product of the multiplex, but is in fact a long-standing feature of cinematic exhibition in India. Where the multiplex does make an intervention in this history is in its capacity to separate these parties and to filter out the undesirable elements of the cinema crowd. In the process, the carefully considered architecture of the multiplex transforms a social body that has long been associated with mob behaviour into a marketable commodity for retailers and advertisers. This reinvention of the public of the cinema necessarily entails a spatial separation between the decent crowd and the masses, from which the distinctive taste cultures of the multiplex and the cinema hall subsequently arise.

As we have demonstrated, the distinction between these two tiers of exhibition infrastructure, and the differential in their market value, has many implications for the creative professionals who work in the film industry. Much more importantly, it raises serious questions about the demise of a common cinematic culture operating across the different strata of Indian society or about the validity of the much-vaunted claims about Indian cinema as a force for social integration in the first place. Looking forward, it seems entirely possible that the middle and lower classes will become increasingly separated in terms of what they watch at the cinema and where they watch it. Further fault lines in the national audience can also be seen appearing between metropolitan and district audiences and between the older and younger generations. Again, the social significance of these divergences in the context of urban leisure is clearly indicative of much wider questions now facing a liberalising Indian economy.

For the multiplex operators, who cannot reasonably be appointed the task of engineering social cohesion, the business logic of a specifically middle-class cinema continues to make sense since this is where the wealth generated by the New Economy is to be found. Even if the imagined community of the consuming class fails to meet current growth projections, the considerable numbers of the Indian upper middle classes in absolute terms, their aversion to rubbing shoulders with the urban poor and the long-term underscreening of the Indian market in general provide support for the expansion plans of the multiplex companies. In the first ten years of the multiplex boom, the growth in screens that these new facilities represent has yet to offset the loss of screens from the closures of single-screen theatres across a wide range of locations. However, the sheer scale of the expansion programmes that are now underway may well contribute to a net growth in screens per capita over the next three years, even though the seating capacity per screen will always be lower than in the cinemas of the past. As Alok Tandon at INOX explains:

There is a lot of room for growth in India. See, if you look at India, we are about thirteen thousand nine hundred screens. I would say that for Indian people, movie watching is a religion. We produce one of the largest amount of movies in the world. And, still, we are the most under-screened nation in the world. If you look at places like America, there are about 127 screens per million. Europe has got about 35 to 40 screens per million. India has only 13 screens per million of population. So there is a lot of room for expansion.

(interview 04/01/2007)

With the number of multiplexes increasing so dramatically over the duration of our study, this book has attempted to capture the impetus behind these seismic shifts in the context of urban leisure. In doing so, we have provided the first comprehensive account of the multiplex phenomenon as it is being played out within the complex spatial and cultural politics of metropolitan India. It is important to recognise, however, that the work presented here was very much conceived as a pilot study that is intended to lay the ground for more sustained future research. Nonetheless, despite the fact that the Indian multiplex is only just emerging from its nascent stages of development, it is abundantly clear from the evidence that we have collated here that the deployment of the multiplex in India has already taken on a particular nature that requires further detailed consideration. This is a point reinforced by Adlabs' COO, Tashur:

I think India has built one of the better circuits in the world, because we have learned from other people. What they have done. So we benefit, in terms of being a follower, you have seen them commit mistakes etc. And we have the innate Asian intuitiveness to do some things differently. So I think we are in an interesting and advantageous position in that sense . . . Look at the location that we are sitting in. It was completely undeveloped six years back. So one of the top grossing cinemas started off in a location where there was nothing. India is going through a very particular change. We are moving from 386 to Pentium 5, in leaps and bounds, so it depends on where you are and what you're doing. It's not a sequential progress, okay, and there are things that you are re-defining and doing anew.

(interview 08/01/2007)

It has also been the intention of this book to demonstrate the salience of an interdisciplinary approach to contemporary urban society. The relevance of the multiplex to a wide range of disciplinary concerns has been reflected here in our analysis of the economic, environmental and cultural aspects of the phenomenon. Further, we have sought to elucidate the significance of their interaction within the particular social and historical contexts that have shaped the conditions in which the Indian multiplex operates. In subtitling this work 'a cultural economy of urban leisure', we have sought to emphasise the importance of understanding the human experience of social change. The cultural is imperative here not simply because our object of analysis facilitates the consumption of immaterial cultural products and operates within the category of the media industries. It is equally, if not more, critical to recognise the ways in which the story of the multiplex demonstrates important changes in the everyday culture of doing business in India. Furthermore, without wishing to state the obvious, the phenomenon of the Indian multiplex provides a powerful illustration of the ways in which the particularity of the wider social terrain shapes even the most globalised economic practices in distinctive ways. For all these reasons, this book makes a small contribution to the larger project of a much-needed anthropological account of the liberalisation era in India.

Prior to future work that enjoys the benefit of a longitudinal approach, we look forward with fascination to the ongoing transformation of the leisure economy in India. It remains beyond the scope of this work to make predictions about the ultimate future of the multiplex industry and the full social significance of the changes that are now taking place. This can only become apparent over a period of many years. Clearly, there are many questions yet to be answered, and many obstacles to be overcome, if the ambitions of the multiplex companies are to be realised. As with all aspects of India's New Economy, the real extent of the market for entertainment remains unknown and the divergences and disparities in wealth and taste between different parts of the country (and between different social groups) remain unresolved. Success carries its own risks, and the expansion of any industry at this rate in such uncertain conditions brings with it the risk of market failure proportionate to the promise of profitable growth. The intense competition between several large players to achieve an all-India presence makes the issue of market saturation already seen in some metropolitan districts a pressing one – a fact of which the industry is only too aware. The conclusion being drawn at the present moment seems to be that if any consolidation occurs in the future, the economic logic of the day will favour the bigger players as surely as the punitive regulations of the previous epoch favoured the smaller operators.

The exuberance of the multiplex industry is symptomatic of the energies unleashed by liberalisation as a doctrine and, without a doubt, there is a lot at stake in the recasting of India's leisure economy. After 17i years of liberalisation, large-scale investments in telecoms, television and cinema have bestowed the media industries with an entirely new social and economic status. As such, it is entirely logical that the commercial media have vocally celebrated the new regulatory environment, becoming an exemplar and cheerleader for the liberalisation economy. In turn, the influence of the new visual environment promulgated by the commercial media has become a powerful factor shaping the mindset of India's upcoming post-liberalisation generation. Thus, while Jawaharlal Nehru, India's first post-independence Prime Minister, saw cinema halls as (literally) a waste of concrete, it has become abundantly clear that the leisure economy has to be understood as much more than an ephemeral activity. For good or bad, the status of the multiplex in India today is a powerful indication of how the infrastructure of consumption has replaced industrial output as the symbolic measure of progress.

References

Abaza, M. (2001) 'Shopping Malls, Consumer Culture and the Reshaping of Public Space in Egypt' *Theory Culture and Society*, Vol. 18, No. 5, pp. 97–122.

Abbas, A. (2005) 'Cities And The Urban Imaginary' in Abbas, A. and Nguyet Erni, J., *Internationalising Cultural Studies: An Anthology*, Malden, MA: Blackwell.

Acland, C. (2000) 'Cinemagoing and the Rise of the Megaplex', *Television and New Media*, Vol. 1, No. 3, pp. 355–382.

Acland, C. (2003) *Screen Traffic: Movies, Multiplexes and Global Culture*, Durham and London: Duke University Press.

Adiga, A. (2004) 'India's Mania for Malls', *Time*, September 20 2004.

Adlabs Films Ltd. (2006a) 'About Us', Online. Available HTTP: <http://www.adlabsfilms.com/aboutus.htm> (accessed September 12 2006).

Adlabs Films Ltd. (2006b) 'Investor Share Pattern', Online. Available HTTP: <http://www.adlabsfilms.com/invsharepattern.htm> (accessed September 12 2006).

Adlabs Films Ltd. (2006c) *Annual Report 2006*, Online. Available HTTP: <http://www.adlabsfilms.com/Adlabs20-%20Annual%20Report%20%202005-2006.pdf> (accessed September 19 2006).

Adlabs Films Ltd. (2006d) 'Advertise', Online. Available HTTP: <http://www.adlabsmultiplex.com/advertise.asp> (accessed September 19 2006).

Adlabs Films Ltd. (2006e) 'Launch of R Adlabs', press release, Online. Available HTTP: <http://www.adlabsfilms.com/pre04.htm> (accessed September 19 2006).

Agrawal, B. C. (1984) 'Indianness of the Indian Cinema', in Dissanayake, W. and Wang, G. (eds.) *Continuity and Change in Communication Systems: An Asian Perspective*, Norwood, New Jersey: Ablex Publishing Group.

Ahmad, A. (1994) *In Theory: Nations, Classes Literature*, London: Verso.

Alasuutari, P. (ed.) (1999) *Rethinking the Media Audience: The New Agenda*, London: Sage.

Amin, A. and Thrift, N. (2003) *The Cultural Economy Reader*, Oxford: Blackwell.

Amin, A. and Thrift, N. (2007) 'Cultural-economy and Cities', *Progress in Human Geography*, Vol. 31, No. 2, pp. 143–161.

Anderson, B. (1991) *Imagined Communities: Reflections on the Origins and Spread of Nationalism* (2nd edn.), London: Verso.

Anderson, B. (1998) *The Spectre of Comparisons: Nationalism, Southeast Asia and the World*, London and New York: Verso.

Ansari, J. H., Sharma, A. K., Shaheer, M., Mahavir and Prakash, P. (2000) *Revised Master Plan for Noida -2021*, New Delhi: School of Planning and Architecture.

Appadurai, A. (1996) *Modernity At Large: Cultural Dimensions Of Globalisation*, Minneapolis and London: University of Minnesota Press.

Appadurai, A. (2000) 'Spectral Housing and Urban Cleansing: Notes on Millenial Mumbai', *Public Culture*, Vol. 12, No. 3, pp. 627–651.

Appadurai, A. (ed.) (2001) *Globalisation*, Durham and London: Duke University Press.

Aranya, R. (2003) 'Globalisation and Urban Restructuring of Bangalore, India', paper presented at the 39th ISOCARP Congress.

Armes, R. (1987) *Third World Filmmaking and the West*, Berkeley and Los Angeles: University of California Press.

Asian Development Bank (2007) '2005 International Comparison Programme in Asia and the Pacific Purchasing Power Parity Preliminary Report', Manila: Asian Development Bank, Economics and Research Department.

ASSOCHAM (2006) 'FDI's Share in Real Estate Will Touch 26% by March 2007', press release, Associated Chambers of Commerce and Industry of India, Online. Available HTTP: <www.assocham.org/prels/shownews.php?id=792> (accessed November 19 2006).

Athique, A. (2006) 'The Diasporic Audience for Indian Films: Addressing and Consuming Non-Resident Subjects', paper presented at the workshop on 'The Indian Diaspora: Culture, Identity and Performance', CAPSTRANS, Wollongong, University of Wollongong, November.

Athique, A. (2008a) 'The Global Dynamics of Indian Media Piracy: Export Markets, Playback Formats and the Informal Economy', *Media Culture and Society*, Vol. 30, No. 5, pp. 699–717.

Athique, A. (2008b) 'A Line in the Sand – The Border Films of J. P. Dutta', *South Asia: Journal of South Asian Studies*, Vol. 31 No. 3, pp. 472–499.

Athique, A. (2009) 'Monopoly to Polyphony: India in the Era of Television' in Turner, G. and Tay, J. (eds.) *Television After TV: Understanding Television in the Post-Broadcast Era*, London: Routledge.

Athique, A. M. and Hill, D. (2007) 'Multiplex Cinemas and Urban Redevelopment in India', *Media International Australia*, No. 124, August 2007, pp. 108–118.

Bagchi, A. K. (1998) 'Economy of West Bengal Since Independence', *Economic and Political Weekly*, Vol. 33, No. 47 and 48.

Bajwa, S. B. (2003) 'ICT Policy In India In The Era Of Liberalisation: Its Impact And Consequences', *GBER*, Vol. 3, No. 2. pp. 49–61.

Banerjee, D. (1998) 'Indian Industrial Growth and Corporate Sector Behaviour in West Bengal 1947–97', *Economic and Political Weekly*, Vol. 33, No. 47 and 48.

Bannerjee, S. (ed.) (1982) *New Indian Cinema*, New Delhi: National Film Development Council.

Banerjee, T. (2005) 'Understanding Planning Cultures: The Kolkata Paradox' in B. Sanyal (ed.) *Comparative Planning Cultures*, New York and London: Routledge.

Banerjee-Guha, S. (2002) 'Critical Geographical Praxis: Globalisation and Socio-spatial Disorder', *Economic and Political Weekly*, pp. 4504–4509.

Barnouw, E. and Krishnaswamy, S. (1980) *Indian Film*, New York: Oxford University Press.

Basu, P. P. (2007) 'Brand Buddha in India's West Bengal' *Asian Survey*, Vol. 47, No. 2, pp. 288–306.

Baviskar, A. (2003) *Between violence and desire: space, power, and identity in the making of metropolitan Delhi*, Oxford and Maulden: UNESCO/Blackwell.

BBC Online (2006) 'Bollywood Cinemas On Tax Strike', *BBC Online*, Online. Available HTTP: <http://news.bbc.co.uk/2/hi/entertainment/3550199.stm> (accessed September 7 2006).

Beattie, M. (2004) 'Patrick Geddes And Barra Bazaar: Competing Visions, Ambivalence And Contradiction', *The Journal of Architecture*, Vol. 9, Iss. 2, pp. 131–150.

Benjamin, S. (2005) *The Lifestyle Advertisement and the Marxist Manifesto as Trojan Horses in a City of Stealth*, New Delhi: Institute of Social Studies Trust.

Bhabha, H. (1994) *The Location of Culture*, London: Routledge.

Bhupta, M. with Parihar, R., Sen, S., Mishra, S., Mahurkar, U. and Vinayak. R. (2005) 'Mall Mania', *India Today*, November 21 2005, p. 58.

Bidwai, P. (2006) 'The Great Land Grab', *Frontline*, Vol. 23, Iss.18.

Bose, D. (2006) *Brand Bollywood: A New Global Entertainment Order*, New Delhi: Sage.

Bottomley, A. and Moore, N. (2007) 'From Walls To Membranes: Fortress Polis And The Governance Of Urban Space In 21st Century Britain', *Law and Critique*, Vol. 18, No. 2, pp. 171–206.

Bourdieu, P. (1993) *The Field Of Cultural Production*, Cambridge: Polity Press.

Breckenridge, C. (ed.) (1995) *Consuming Modernity: Public Culture In A South Asian World*, Bombay and New York: Oxford University Press.

Brenner, N. and Theodore, N. (2002) 'Cities and the Geographies of "Actually Existing Neoliberalism"', *Antipode*, Vol. 33, No. 3, pp. 349–379.

Brooker, W. and Jermyn, D. (eds.) (2002) *The Audience Studies Reader*, London and New York: Routledge.

Business Standard (2007) 'DLF Plans Expansion of Multiplex Biz', *Business Standard*, July 1 2007, Online. Available HTTP: <http://www.business-standard.com/india/news/dlf-plans-expansionmultiplex-biz/00/17/24938/> (accessed July 16 2007).

Business World (2007) 'Ansal Properties Has A Land Bank Of Close To 6,000 Acres, Which Is The Third Largest Among Realty Companies', *Business World*, June 11 2007, p. 61.

Butcher, M. (2003) *Transnational Television, Cultural Identity and Change: When STAR Came to India*, New Delhi: Sage.

Caplan, L. (2001) *Children of Colonialism: Anglo-Indians in a Postcolonial World*, Oxford: Berg.

Castells, M. (1996) *The Rise of the Network Society*, Oxford: Blackwell.

Castree, N. (2004) 'Economy And Culture Are Dead! Long Live Economy and Culture', *Progress in Human Geography*, Vol. 28, No. 2. pp. 204–226.

Chakrabarty, D. (1991) 'Open Space/Public Place: Garbage, modernity and India', *South Asia: Journal of South Asian Studies*, Vol. 14, No. 1, pp. 15–31.

Chakrabarty, D. (2000) *Provincialising Europe: Postcolonial Thought and Historical Difference*, Princeton, NJ: Princeton University Press.

Chakrabarty, D. (2007) '"In the Name of Politics": Democracy and the Power of the Multitude in India', *Public Culture*, Vol. 19, No. 1, pp. 35–57.

Chakravarty, S. S. (1993) *National Identity in Indian Popular Cinema 1947–1987*, Austin, TX: Texas University Press.

Chakravarty, S. S. (2000) 'Fragmenting The Nation: Images Of Terrorism In Indian Popular Cinema' in Hjort, M. and Mackenzie, S. (eds.) *Cinema & Nation*, London and New York: Routledge.

Chakravartty, P. (2008) 'In or as Civil Society: Workers and Subaltern Publics in India's Information Society' in P. Chakravartty and Y. Zhao (eds.) *Global Communications: Towards a Transcultural Politcal Economy*, New York: Rowan & Littlefield, pp. 285–308.

Chakravorty, S. (2000) 'From Colonial City to Global City? The Far-From-Complete Spatial Transformation of Calcutta' in P. Marcuse and R. Van Kempen (eds.) *Globalising Cities: A New Spatial Order?*, Oxford: Blackwell. pp. 56–77.

Chakravorty, S. and Lall, S.V. (2007) *Made in India: The Economic Geography and Political Economy of Industrialisation*, Oxford: Oxford University Press.

Chandavarkar, P. (2007) 'The "Background" in Bangalore: Architecture and Critical Resistance in a New Modernity', *Architectural Design*, Vol. 77, No. 6, pp. 78–83.

Chaplin, S. E. (1999) 'Cities, Sewers And Poverty: India's Politics Of Sanitation', *Environment and Urbanisation*, Vol. 11, No. 1, pp. 145–158.

Chatterjee, P. (1993) *The Nation & Its Fragments: Colonial & Postcolonial Histories*, New Delhi: Oxford University Press.

Chatterjee, P. (1998) 'Beyond the Nation? Or Within?', *Social Text*, No. 56, Autumn, pp. 57–69.

Chatterjee, P. (2004) *The Politics Of The Governed: Reflections On Popular Politics In Most Of The World*, New Delhi: Permanent Black.

Chattopadhyay, S. (2005) *Representing Calcutta: Modernity, Nationalism, And The Colonial Uncanny*, London: Routledge.

CII and TeamPro (2007) *Vadodora: Knowledge City*, Vadodora: Confederation of Indian Industry.

Cinemax (2006) 'Enjoy, Relax @ Cinemax', Online. Available HTTP: <http://www.cinemax.co.in/AboutUs.aspx> (accessed November 20 2006).

CityCentre (2007) 'CityCentre Kolkata', Online. Available HTTP: <http://www.citycentrekolkata.com> (accessed May 5 2007).

Collins, A., Hand, C. and Ryder, A. (2005) 'The Lure of the Multiplex? The Interplay of Time, Distance and Cinema Attendance', *Environment and Planning A*, Vol. 37, No. 3, pp. 483–501.

Correa, C. (1989) 'The Public, The Private and the Sacred', *Daedalus*, Vol. 118, No. 4, pp. 92–113.

Crewe, L. (2003) 'Geographies Of Retailing And Consumption: Markets In Motion', *Progress in Human Geography*, Vol. 27, No. 3, pp. 352–362.

CRIT (2006 and 2007) 'Collective Research Initiatives Trust' Online. Available HTTP: <www.crit.org.in/> (accessed February 1 2007).

Curtin, M. (2003) 'Media Capital: Towards the Study of Spatial Flows', *International Journal of Cultural Studies*, Vol. 6, No. 2, pp. 202–228.

Das, G. (2002) *India Unbound: The Social and Economic Revolution from Independence to the Global Information Age*, New York: Anchor.

Das, S. (2006) 'Partition And Punjabiyat In Bombay Cinema: The Cinematic Perspectives Of Yash Chopra And Others', *Contemporary South Asia*, Vol. 15, No. 4, pp. 453–471.

Dasgupta, K. (2007) 'City Divided? Planning and Urban Sprwal in the Eastern Fringes of Calcutta' in A. Shaw (ed.) *Indian Cities in Transition*, Hyderabad: Orient Longman.

Datt, G. and Ravallion, M. (2002) 'Is India's Economic Growth Leaving the Poor Behind?', *Journal of Economic Perspectives*, Vol. 16, No. 3, pp. 89–108.

De, B. (2005) 'The History of Kolkata Port and the Hooghly River and Its Future', Lecture delivered on the occasion of the 135th anniversary of Kolkata Port, Online. Available HTTP: <http://www.kolkataporttrust.gov.in/kopt_lecture2005.pdf> (accessed January 10 2006).

Deaton, A. (2003a) 'Adjusted Indian Poverty Estimates For 1999–2000' *Economic and Political Weekly*, 25 January, pp. 322–326.

Deaton, A. (2003b) 'Prices And Poverty In India, 1987–2000' *Economic and Political Weekly*, 25 January, pp. 362–368.

Debord, G. (1994) *The Society of the Spectacle*, New York: Zone Books.

Delhi Metro Rail Corporation (2007) 'Project Update', Online. Available HTTP: <http://www.delhimetrorail.com/corporates/projectupdate/phase1_network.html> (accessed November 29 2007).

Derne, S. (1999) 'Making Sex Violent: Love As Force in Recent Hindi Films', *Violence Against Women*, Vol. 5, No. 5, pp. 548–575.

Deshpande, S. (2005) 'The Consumable Hero Of Globalised India' in R. Kaur and A. Sinha (eds.) *Bollyworld: Indian Cinema Through A Transnational Lens* (pp. 186–203). New Delhi and London: Sage.

D'Essence Consulting (2006) *Industry Overview*, Online. Available HTTP: <www. dessenceconsulting.com/pdf/multiplex20industry%20in%20India.pdf> (accessed September 18 2006).

D'Monte, D. (2005) *Ripping the Fabric: The Decline of Mumbai and Its Mills*, New Delhi: Oxford India.

Dodson, B. (2000) 'Are we having Fun Yet? Leisure and Consumption in the Post Apartheid City', *Tijdscrift voor Economische en Sociale Geographfie*, Vol. 91, No. 4, pp. 412–425.

Dhareshwar, V. and Srivatsan, R. (1996) 'Rowdy-Sheeters: An Essay on Subalternity and Politics' in S. Amin and D. Chakrabarty (eds.) *Subaltern Studies IX*, New Delhi: Oxford University Press, pp. 201–231.

Dickey, S. (1993) 'The Politics of Adulation: Cinema and the Production of Politicians in South India', *Journal of Asian Studies* Vol. 52, Iss. 2, pp. 340–372.

Dixit, S. (2006) 'Delhi to be a world-class city, reasserts Sheila' *The Tribune*, Chandigarh, 16 August.

Dossal, M. (1991) *Imperial Designs and Indian Realities: The Planning of Bombay City 1845–1875*, Bombay: Oxford University Press.

Du Gay, P. and Prycke, M. (eds.) (2002) *Cultural Economy: Cultural Analysis and Commercial Life*, London: Sage.

Dupont, V. (2007) 'Conflicting Stakes And Governance In The Peripheries Of Large Indian Metropolises – An Introduction', *Cities*, Vol. 24, No. 2, pp. 89–94.

Dwyer, R. (2000) '"Indian Values" and the Diaspora: Yash Chopra's Films of the 1990s', *West Coast Line*, Autumn, pp. 6–27.

Dwyer, R. (2002) *Yash Chopra*, London: British Film Institute.

Dwyer, R. and Patel, D. (2002) *Cinema India: The Visual Culture of the Hindi Film*, London: Reaktion Books.

E-City Ventures (2006) 'E-City Ventures', Online. Available HTTP: <http:// funcinemas.com/corp_info.aspx> (accessed September 20 2006).

Erkip, F. (2003) 'The Shopping Mall as an Emergent Public Space in Turkey', *Environment and Planning A*, Vol. 35, No. 6, pp. 1073–1093.

Essel Group (2006) 'The Essel Group', Online. Available HTTP: <http://www. esselgroup.com> (accessed September 20 2006).

Essel World (2007) 'Essel World', Online. Available HTTP: <http://esselworld.com> (accessed April 4 2007).

Fame Cinemas (2006) 'Upcoming Projects', Online. Available HTTP: <http://www. famecinemas.com/UpcomingProject/UpcomingProject.aspx> (accessed September 15 2006).

Fernandes, L. (2004) The Politics of Forgetting: Class Politics, State Power and the Restructuring of Urban Space in India, *Urban Studies*, Vol. 41, No. 12, 2415–2430.

Fernandes, L. (2006) *India's New Middle Class: Democratic Politics in an Era of Democratic Reform*, Minneapolis and London: University of Minnesota Press.

Financial Express (2004) '89 Cinemas in the City of Joy', *Financial Express*, June 27 2004.

Financial Express (2007) 'Haryana Flooded With SEZ Proposals', *Financial Express*, August 3 2007.

Forum Mall (2008) 'The Forum: Your Time, Your Place', Online. Available HTTP: <http://www.thefprumexperience.com/forumbangalore.htm> (accessed April 23 2008).

Friedberg, A. (2000) 'The End of Cinema: Multi-media and Technological Change' in Gledhill, C. and Williams, L. (eds.) *Reinventing Film Studies*, London: Arnold.

Fun Cinemas Pvt. (2006) 'Fun Cinemas', Online. Available HTTP: <http://funcinemas.com/fun_multiplex.aspx> accessed November 20 2006.

Gajwani, K., Kanbur, R.and Zhang X. (2006) 'Comparing the Evolution of Spatial Inequality in China and India: A Fifty Year Perspective' *DSGD discussion papers*,Vol. 44, Washington: International Food Policy Research Institute.

Gandelsonas, M. (2005) 'Scene X: The Development of the X-Urban City' in Abbas, A. and Nguyet Erni, J., *Internationalising Cultural Studies: An Anthology*, Malden, MA: Blackwell.

Gokulsing, K. M. and Dissanayake, W. (1998) *Indian Popular Cinema: A Narrative of Cultural Change*, Stoke on Trent: Trentham Books.

Goldsmith, B. and O'Regan, T. (2004) 'Locomotives and Stargates: Inner-city Studio Complexes in Sydney, Melbourne and Toronto', *International Journal of Cultural Policy*, Vol. 10, No. 1, pp. 29–45.

Goss, J. (2004) 'Geographies of Consumption 1', *Progress in Human Geography*, Vol. 28, No. 3, pp. 369–380.

Government of Uttar Pradesh (1976) 'The Uttar Pradesh Industrial Area Development Act 1976', Online. Available HTTP: <http://wwww.noidaauthorityonline.com/upact/html/1.html> (accessed April 27 2007).

Graham, S. and Marvin, S. (2001) *Splintering Urbanism: Networked Infrastructure, Technological Mobilities and Urban Condition*, London: Routledge.

Grossberg, L. (1995) 'Cultural Studies vs. Political Economy: Is Anybody Else Bored with This Debate?' *Critical Studies in Mass Communication*, Vol. 12, No. 1, pp. 72–81.

Guback, T. (1987) 'The Evolution of the Motion Picture Business in the 1980s', *Journal of Communication*, Spring, Vol. 37, No. 2, pp. 60–77.

Gugler, J. (ed.) (2004) *World Cities Beyond the West: Globalisation, Development and Inequality*, Cambridge and New York: Cambridge University Press.

Guha, R. and Spivak, G. (1989) *Selected Subaltern Studies*, London and New York: Oxford University Press.

Gunter, B. (1999) *Media Research Methods: Measuring Audiences, Reactions and Impact*, London: Sage.

Guruswamy, M. (2005) 'FDI In Retailing- Short-Changing The Kirana Store?', *Hindu Businessline*, Online. Available HTTP: <http://www.thehindubusinessline.com/bline/2005/01/06/stories/2005010600050800.htm> (accessed January 6 2005).

Hardgrove, A. (2002) *Community and Public Culture: the Marwaris in Calcutta, 1897–1997*, New York: Columbia University Press.

Harriss-White, B. (2003) *India Working: Essays on Society and Economy*, Cambridge: Cambridge University Press.

Heitzman, J. (1999) 'Corporate Strategy and Planning in the Science City: Bangalore as "Silicon Valley"', *Economic and Political Weekly*, Vol. 34, No. 5, pp. PE2–PE11.

Hill, D. (2001) 'Rural Developments: A Case Study from Bankura', *South Asia: Journal of South Asian Studies*, Vol. 24, No. 1, pp. 117–140.

Hill, D. (2007) 'Urban Development and the Multiplex', paper presented at the British Association of South Asian Studies (BASAS) annual conference, St Catharines College, Cambridge, March 28–30.

Hill, D.P. (2008) 'Developing India's Ports: Blancing Social and Economic Objectives?' in J. Reveley and M. Tull (eds.) *Port Privatisation: The Asia-Pacific Experience*, London: Edward Elgar.

Hindustan Times (2006) 'Delhi High Court Refuses To Stay Demolition On MG2', *Hindustan Times*, February 6 2006.

Hobart, M. (2000) *After culture: anthropology as radical metaphysical critique*, Yogyakarta: Duta Wacana University Press.

Hornsby, S. J. (1997) 'Discovering The Merchantile City In South Asia: The Example Of Early Nineteenth-Century Calcutta', *Journal of Historical Geography* Vol. 23, No. 2, pp. 135–150.

Hubbard, P. (2002) 'Screen-Shifting: Consumption, 'Riskless Risks' And The Changing Geographies Of Cinema', *Environment and Planning A*, Vol. 34, No. 7, pp. 1239–1258.

Hubbard, P. (2003) 'A Good Night Out? Multiplex Cinemas as Sites of Embodied Leisure', *Leisure Studies*, Vol. 22, No. 3, pp. 255–272.

Hudson, R. (2004) 'Conceptualising Economies And Their Geographies: Spaces, Flows And Circuits', *Progress in Human Geography*, Vol. 28, No. 4, pp. 447–471.

Huggett, N. and Bowles, K. (2004) 'Cowboys, Jaffas and Pies: Researching Cinemagoing in the Illawarra', in *Hollywood Abroad: Audiences and Cultural Exchange*, London: British Film Institute.

Hughes, S. (2000) ' Policing Silent Film Exhibition in Colonial South India' in Vasudevan, R. (ed.) *Making Meaning In Indian Cinema*, New Delhi: Oxford University Press.

Hughes, S. (2003) 'Pride of Place', *Seminar*, 525, Online. Available HTTP: <http://www.india-seminar.com/2003/525/525%20stephen%20p.%20hughes.htm> (accessed November 22 2006).

IBEF – PriceWaterhouseCoopers (2004) Information Technology Enabled Services, Gurgaon, India Brand Equity Foundation.

IBEF (2008) IT and ITES, Gurgaon, Indian Brand Equity Foundation.

IGD (2007) 'Grocery Retailing in India', Online. Available HTTP: <http://www.igd.com/index.asp?id=1&fid=1&sid=17&tid=0&folid=0&cid=191> (accessed June 19 2007).

Inden, R. (1999) 'Transnational Class, Erotic Arcadia and Commercial Utopia in Hindi Films' in C. Brosius and M. Butcher (eds.) *Image Journeys: Audio-Visual Media and Cultural Change in India*, New Delhi: Sage, pp. 41–68.

India Infoline (2006) *Multiplexes – Big Picture Ahead*, Online. Available HTTP: <http://202.87.40.145/content/rep/Investment_Ideas/2006/7/1572006/multiplex_030406.pdf> (accessed September 8 2006).

Indian Cinematograph Committee (1928) *Indian Cinematograph Committee Evidence*, Vols. I, II and III, Calcutta: Government of India.

Indian Cinematograph Committee (1928) *Report of the Indian Cinematograph Committee*, Calcutta: Government of India.

Indian Express (2007) 'We Have Enough Reserves For 10 Years: DLF', *Indian Express*, May 29 2007.

India Infoline (2006) 'Multiplexes – Big picture ahead', Online. Available HTTP: <http://202.87.40.145/content/rep/
Investment_Ideas/2006/7/1572006/multiplex_030406.pdf> (accessed September 8 2006).

INOX Leisure Ltd. (2006a) *Annual Report 2005/6: Poised For Exponential Growth*, Online. Available HTTP: <http://www.inoxmovies.com/investor/AGM%20Report.pdf> (accessed September 12 2006).

INOX Leisure Ltd. (2006b) 'Existing Properties', Online. Available HTTP: <http://www.inoxmovies.com/Aboutus/ExpInox_UpEx.aspx?type=2> (accessed September 12 2006).

INOX Leisure Ltd. (2006c) 'Shareholding Pattern June 2006', Online. Available HTTP: <http://www.inoxmovies.com/RHP/index_SHP_June.htm> (accessed September 10 2006).

INOX Leisure Ltd. (2006d) 'Upcoming Properties', Online. Available HTTP:

<http://www.inoxmovies.com/Aboutus/ExpInox_UpEx.aspx?type=1>   (accessed September 12 2006).

INOX Leisure Ltd. (2006e) 'Branding@INOX', Online. Available HTTP: <http://www.inoxmovies.com/branding/Contact.aspx> (accessed September 11 2006).

INOX Leisure Ltd. (2007) 'INOX Kolkata – Salt Lake', Online. Available HTTP: <http://www.inoxmovies.com/inox/wcms/en/home/our-cinema/inox-city-centerkolkata.html> (accessed January 12 2007).

INR News Asian News Network (2006) 'FDI's share in Indian Real Estate to touch 26% by March 2007', Online. Available HTTP: <http://www.inrnews.com/realestateproperty/fdis_share_in_indian_real_esta.html> (accessed November 27 2006).

Jaikumar, P. (2006) *Cinema at the End of Empire: A Politics of Transition in Britain and India*, Durham and London: Duke University Press.

Jain, M. (1990) 'The 80s Cinema: Triumph Trauma and Tears', *India Today*, January 15 1990, pp. 44–49.

Jeffrey, R. (2008) 'The Mahatma Didn't Like The Movies and Why It Matters: Indian Broadcasting Policy 1920s–1990s' in Mehta, N. (ed.) *Television in India: Satellites, Politics and Cultural Change*, London and New York: Routledge, pp. 13–31.

Jones Lang Lasalle Meghraj (JLLM) (2007) *India Retail – The Geography of Opportunity: The India Top 50*, Online. Available HTTP: <http://www.inrnews.com/indianrealestate/reports/india_retail_research_jllm.pdf> (accessed April 23 2007).

Kaarsholm, P. (2004) *City Flicks: Indian Cinema and the Urban Experience*, Calcutta: Seagull Books.

Kanakia Group (2006) 'Kanakia: Constructing Lifestyles', Online. Available HTTP: <http://kanakia.com/> (accessed November 7 2006).

Kasbekar, A. (1996) 'An Introduction to Indian Cinema', in Nelmes, J. (ed) *An Introduction to Film Studies*, London: Routledge.

Kaul, P. and Prashant, M. (2007) 'The Real Story Of India's Retail Boom', *Outlook Business*, Online. Available HTTP: <http://www.rediff.com/cms/print.jspdocpath=/money/2007/jan/19bspec.htm> (accessed January 19 2007).

Kaur, R. (2005) 'Cruising On The Vilayati Bandwagon: Diasporic Representations and Reception of Popular Indian Movies India' in Kaur, R. and Sinha, A. (eds.) *Bollyworld: Popular Indian Cinema Through A Transnational Lens*, New Delhi: Sage.

Kazmi, F. (1999a) 'How Angry is the Angry Young Man?: "Rebellion" in Conventional Hindi Films', in Nandy, A. (ed.) *The Secret Politics of Our Desires: Innocence, Culpability and Indian Popular Cinema*, New Delhi: Zed Books.

Kazmi, F. (1999b) *The Politics of India's Conventional Cinema: Imaging a Universe, Subverting a Multiverse*, New Delhi: Sage.

Kearns, G. and Philo, C. (eds.) (1993) *Selling Places: The City As Cultural Capital*, Oxford: Pergamon.

Kerigan, F and Ozbilgin, M. F. (2002) 'Art for the Masses or Art for the Few? Ethical Issues of Film Marketing in the UK', *International Journal of Nonprofit and Voluntary Sector Marketing*, Vol. 7, No. 2, pp. 195–203.

King, A. D. (1975/2006) 'The Colonial Bungalow-Compound Complex in India' in S. Patel and K. Deb (eds.) *Urban Studies*, New Delhi: Oxford University Press, pp. 43–58 (reprinted from *Ekistics*, No. 234, May 1975, pp. 306–313).

King, A. D. (2004) *Spaces of Global Culture: Architecture, Urbanism, Identity*, London and New York: Routledge.

Kohli-Khandekar, V. (2006) *The Indian Media Business*, 2nd edition, New Delhi: Response Books.

Kong, L. and Law, L. (2002) 'Introduction: Contested Landscapes, Asian Cities', *Urban Studies*, Vol. 39, No. 9, pp. 1503–1512.

Koolhaas, R. (2005) 'The Generic City' in Abbas, A. and Nguyet Erni, J., *Internationalising Cultural Studies: An Anthology*, Malden, MA: Blackwell.

Kosambi, M. and Brush, J. E. (1988) 'Three Colonial Port Cities In India', *Geographical Review*, Vol. 78, No. 1, pp. 32–47.

KPMG and CII (2005) *Indian Entertainment Industry Focus 2010: Dreams To Reality*, Mumbai and New Delhi: KPMG India & Confederation of Indian Industry, Online. Available HTTP: <http://www.kpmg.de/library/pdf/050331_Focus_Dreams_to_Reality_en.pdf> (accessed April 25 2006).

KPMG and FICCI (2005) *Indian Retail On The Fast Track: Time For Bridging Capability Gaps*, Mumbai and New Delhi: KPMG India and Federation of Indian Chambers of Commerce and Industry, Online. Available HTTP: <http://www.scribd.com/doc/6710017/KPMG-Indian-Retail-2005> (accessed April 25 2006).

Kumar, A. (2000) 'Some Problems in the Co-ordination of Planning: Managing Interdependencies in the Planning of Delhi, India', *Space & Polity*, Vol. 4, No. 2, pp. 167–185.

Kumar, K. G. (2007) 'The Retailing Revolution' *Hindu Businessline*, Online. Available HTTP: <http://www.thehindubusinessline.com/2007/07/16/stories/2007071650800500.htm> (accessed July 16 2007).

Kuppinger, P. (2005) 'Globalisation And Extraterritoriality In Metropolitan Cairo', *The Geographical Review*, Vol. 95, No. 3, pp. 348–372.

Lefebvre, H. (1991) *The Production Of Space*, Oxford: Blackwell.

Legg, S. (2006) 'Postcolonial Developmentalities: From the Delhi Improvement Trust to the Delhi Development Authority' in S. Corbridge, S. Kumar and S. Raju (eds.) *Colonial and Postcolonial Indian Geographies*, London: Sage, pp. 182–204.

Liang, L. (2005) 'Cinematic citizenship and the illegal city', *Inter-Asia Cultural Studies*, Vol. 6, No. 3, pp. 366–385.

Luhrmann, T. (1996) *The Good Parsi: The Fate of a Colonial Elite in a Postcolonial Society*, Cambridge, MA and London: Harvard University Press.

Maltby, R., Stokes, M. and Allen, R. (2008) *Going to the movies: Hollywood and the social experience of cinema*, Exeter: University of Exeter Press.

Mawdsley, E. (2004) 'India's Middle Classes and the Environment', *Development and Change*, Vol. 35, No. 1, pp. 79–103.

Mayers, J. (2001) 'Economic Reform and the Urban/Rural Divide: Political Realignment in West Bengal 1977–2000', *South Asia*, Vol.XXIV, No. 1.

Mazumdar, R. (2000) 'From Subjectification to Schizophrenia: The "Angry Man" and the "Psychotic" Hero of Bombay Cinema,' in R. S. Vasudevan (ed.) *Making Meaning in Indian Cinema*, New Delhi: Oxford University Press, 2000: 238–264.

Mazzarella, W. (2003) *Shoveling Smoke: Advertising and Globalisation in Contemporary India*, Durham and London: Duke University Press.

McDonald, H. (1999) *The Polyester Prince: The Rise of Dhirubhai Ambani*, Melbourne: Allen and Unwin.

McLean, D. (2001) 'Tension between State and Capital in West Bengal', *South Asia*, New Series, Vol. XXIV, No. 1, pp. 93–115.

Mehta, N. (ed.) (2008) *Television in India: Satellites, Politics and Cultural Change*, London and New York: Routledge.

Mesbur, D. (2001) 'Principles of Multiplex Design for the Asian Marketplace', *Theatre World*, Oct–Dec, pp. 10–11.

Miller, T. (2006) 'Methodologies for Studying Migrating Media', Unpublished Paper, Migrating Media Roundtable, University of Queensland, 6 December.

Mishra, S. (1999) 'Dish is Life: Cable operators and the Neighbourhood', in Brosius, C. and Butcher, M. (eds.) *Image Journeys: Audio-Visual Media and Cultural Change in India*, New Delhi: Sage.

Mishra, V. (2002) *Bollywood Cinema: Temples of Desire*, London: Routledge.

Mittal, A. (1995) *Cinema Industry In India: Pricing and Taxation*, New Delhi: Indus Publishing Co.

Mohan, S. (2005) *Urban Development and New Localism: Politics in Mumbai*, Jaipur: Rawat Publications.

Moullier, B. (2007) 'Whither Bollywood?: IP Rights, Innovation and Economic Growth in India's Film Industries', Washington DC: The George Washington University Law School.

Mukherjee, R. (2008) 'Kolkata: Flowing Against The Tide' *Business Today*, May 18 2008.

Mukhija, V. (2001) 'Enabling Slum Redevelopment in Mumbai: Policy Paradox in Practice' *Housing Studies*, Vol. 16, No. 6, pp. 791–806.

Nandy, A. (1989) *The Intimate Enemy: Loss and Recovery of Self Under Colonialism*, Delhi: Oxford University Press.

Nandy, A. (1997) 'Indian Popular Cinema: A Slum's Eye View of Politics' in Nandy, A. (ed) *The Secret Politics of Our Desires: Innocence, Culpability and Indian Popular Cinema*, New Delhi: Zed Books, pp. 1–18.

Nandy, A. (2002) 'Telling the story of communal conflicts in South Asia: Interim Report on a Personal Search for Defining Myths', *Ethnic and Racial Studies*, Vol. 25, No. 1, pp. 1–19.

Nandy, A. (2003a) 'Notes Towards an Agenda for the Next Generation of Film Theorists in India', *South Asian Popular Culture*, Vol.1, No.1, pp. 79–84.

Nandy, A. (2003b) *The Romance of the State: And the Fate of Dissent in the Tropics*, Delhi: Oxford University Press.

Nandy, A. and Trivedy, S., Mayaram, S. and Yagnik, A. (1998) *The Ramjanmabhumi Movement and the Fear of the Self*, Delhi: Oxford University Press.

Narula, M. (2002) 'Sarai: One Year in the Public Domain', *Television & New Media*, Vol. 3 No. 4, pp. 404–412.

NASSCOM and Kearney, A. T. (2008) 'Location Roadmap For IT- BPO Growth: Assessment Of 50 Leading Cities', Online. Available HTTP: <http://www.nasscom.in/> (accessed July 24 2008).

Newman, P. and Thornley, A. (2005) *Planning World Cities: Globalisation and Urban Politics*, New York: Palgrave Macmillan.

Nye, J. S. (2005) 'Soft Power Matters in Asia', *Japan Times*, November 18 2005.

Olds, K. (2002) *Globalisation and Urban Change: Capital, Culture, and Pacific Rim Mega-Projects*, New York: Oxford University Press.

Pal, A. (2005) 'Mall Mania', *Business Today*, Online. Available HTTP: <http://www.india-today.com/btoday/20050130/features1> (html accessed January 30 2005).

Pandian, M. (1992) *The Image Trap: M. G. Ramachadran in Film and Politics*, New Delhi: Sage.

Patel, S. and Thorner, A. (eds.) (1995a) *Bombay: Metaphor for Modern India*, Bombay and New York: Oxford University Press.

Patel, S. and Thorner, A. (eds.) (1995b) *Bombay: Mosaic of Modern Culture*, Bombay and New York: Oxford University Press.

Paul, A., Shetty, P. and Krishnan, S. (2005) 'The City As Extra-Curricular Space: Re-Instituting Urban Pedagogy in South Asia' *InterAsia Cultural Studies*, Vol. 6, No. 3, pp. 386–409.

Peck, J. (2006) 'Why We Shouldn't Be Bored With The Political Economy Versus Cultural Studies Debate', *Cultural Critique*, Fall, Vol. 64, pp. 92–126.

Pendakur, M. (2003) *Indian Popular Cinema: Industry, Ideology and Consciousness*, Cresskill: Hampton Press.

Phadke, S. (2007) 'Dangerous Liaisons Women and Men: Risk and Reputation in Mumbai', *Economic and Political Weekly*, 28 April, pp. 1510–1518.

Potter, R. B. and Sinha, R. (1990) 'NOIDA: A Planned Industrial Township South-East of Delhi', Geography, Vol. 75, Pt. 1, pp. 63–65.

Potter, R. B. and Kumar, A. (2004) 'A Profile of NOIDA: A New Town in the National Capital Region of India', Geographical Paper No. 174, Reading: University of Reading.

Prakash, G. (2002) 'The Urban Turn' in Vasudevan, R., Sundaram, R., Bagchi, J., Narula, M., Sengupta, S. and Lovink, G. (eds.) *Sarai Reader 02: The Cities Of Everyday Life*, Delhi: Sarai, pp. 2–7.

Prasad, M. (1998) *Ideology of the Hindi Film: A Historical Construction*, New Delhi: Oxford University Press.

Pratt, A. (2004) 'The Cultural Economy: A Call For Spatialised Production of Culture Perspectives', *International Journal of Cultural Studies*, Vol. 7, No. 1, pp. 117–128.

Press Trust of India (2007) 'UCP Completes Acquisition Of Gurgaon Project', press release, 16 January.

Price Waterhouse Coopers and FICCI (2006) *The Indian Entertainment and Media Industry:Unravelling The Potential*, Online. Available HTTP: <www.businessworld.in/APR1706/frames_pwc_2006.pdf> (accessed September 18 2006).

Price Waterhouse Coopers and FICCI (2007) *The Indian Entertainment and Media Industry: A Growth Story Unfolds*, Online. Available HTTP: <www.pwc.com/extweb/pwcpublications.nsf/docid/7CBA381E2D53D85CA2572F000290722/$file/FICCIPwCReport2007Executive Summary.pdf> (accessed September 23 2007).

Price Waterhouse Coopers and FICCI (2008) *The Indian Entertainment and Media Industry: Sustaining Growth*, Online. Available HTTP: <www.pwc.com/extweb/pwcpublications.nsf/docid/BF27519CD3178AAACA2574210026EFAC/$file/ExecutiveSummary1.pdf> (accessed September 20 2008).

PVR Cinemas Ltd. (2006a) 'The PVR Story', Online. Available HTTP: <http://www.pvrcinemas.com/pvr/aboutus/thepvrstory.asp> (accessed September 3 2006).

PVR Cinemas Ltd. (2006b) *Company Profile July 2006*, Online. Available HTTP: <http://www.pvrcinemas.com/pvr/investor/Company%20Profile-July%202006.pdf> (accessed September 8 2006).

PVR Cinemas Ltd. (2006c) *Shareholding Pattern As of 31.03.2006*, Online. Available HTTP: <http://www.pvrcinemas.com/pvr/investor/shareholding_pattern1.pdf> (accessed September 8 2006).

PVR Cinemas Ltd. (2006d) *Report on the Performance for the Financial Year Ended March 31 2006*, Online. Available HTTP: <http://www.pvrcinemas.com/pvr/investor/pvrlimited-annualresults2005-06.pdf> (accessed September 8 2006).

PVR Cinemas Ltd. (2006e) *Report on the Performance for the Quarter Ended June 30 2006*, Online. Available HTTP: <http://www.pvrcinemas.com/pvr/investor/PVR%20Limited%20-%20Qtrly%20Results%20June%202006.pdf> (accessed September 8 2006).

PVR Cinemas Ltd. (2006f) 'PVR Bangalore', Online. Available HTTP: <http://www.pvrcinemas.com/pvr/ourtheaters/bangalore3.asp> (accessed September 7 2006).

PVR Cinemas Ltd. (2006g) *Consumer Profile*, Online. Available HTTP: <http://www.pvrcinemas.com/pvr/alliance yourbrand.asp> (accessed September 12 2006).

PVR Cinemas Ltd. (2007) 'Government of Haryana Reduces Tax Duty', Online. Available

HTTP: <http://www.pvrcinemas.com/pvr/investor/news1.asp> (accessed January 15 2007).

Rajadhyaksha, A. (2000) 'Viewership and Democracy in the Cinema' in R. Vasudevan (ed.), *Making Meaning in Indian Cinema*, New Delhi: Oxford University Press, pp. 267–296.

Rajadhyaksha, A. (2003) 'The 'Bollywoodisation' of the Indian Cinema: Cultural Nationalism in a Global Arena', *Inter-Asia Cultural Studies*, Vol. 4, No. 1, pp. 25–39.

Ranade, S. (2007) 'The Way She Moves: Mapping the Everyday Production of Gender-Space', *Economic and Political Weekly*, April 28, pp. 1519–1526.

Rao, C. N. R. (2007) 'If IT Is Going To Take Away Our Values, Burn Bangalore, Burn IT', *Outlook*, 12 December, p. 108.

Ravenscroft, N., Chua, S. and Wee, L. K. N. (2001) 'Going to The Movies: Cinema Development in Singapore' *Leisure Studies*, Vol. 20, No. 3, 215–232.

Ray, S. (1976) *Our Films, Their Films*, Hyderabad: Disha Books.

Ren, X. (2008) 'Architecture and China's Urban revolution', *Cities*, Vol. 12, No. 2, pp. 217–225.

Roy, A. (2003) *City Requiem, Calcutta: Gender and the Politics of Poverty*, Calcutta: Social Sciences Press.

Rushdie, S. (1991) *Imaginary Homelands*, London: Granta.

Saez, L. (2002) *Federalism Without A Center: The Impact Of Political And Economic Reform On India's Federal System*, New Delhi: Sage.

Sarai (2002) *Sarai Reader 2002: The Cities of Everyday Life*, New Delhi: Sarai.

Sarai (2007) 'Welcome to Sarai', Online. Available HTTP: <http://www.Sarai.net/> (accessed February 1 2007).

Scott, A. J. (2000) *The Cultural Economy of Cities: Essays on the Geography of Image-producing Industries*, London: Sage.

Scrase, T. R. and Ganguly-Scrase, R. (2001) 'Who Wins? Who Loses? And Who Even Knows? – Responses to Economic Liberalisation and Cultural Globalisation' (co-authored with T. Scrase) Special Issue *Globalisation and Economic Liberalisation in South Asia, South Asia*, Vol. 24, No.1, pp. 141–158.

Siemiatycki, M. (2006) 'Message in a Metro: Building Urban Rail Infrastructure and Image in Delhi, India', *International Journal of Urban and Regional Research*, Vol. 30, Iss. 2, pp. 277–292.

Sen, J. (1975/2001) 'The Unintended City', *Seminar*, 500, Online. Available HTTP: <http://www.india-seminar.com/2001/500/500%20jai%20sen.htm> (accessed August 15 2007).

Sen, A. and Himanshu (2004a) 'Poverty and Inequality in India– I', *Economic and Political Weekly*, September 18.

Sen, A. and Himanshu (2004b) 'Poverty and Inequality in India–II: Widening Disparities during the 1990s' *Economic and Political Weekly*, September 25.

Sharan, A. (2002) 'Claims On Cleanliness: Environment and justice in contemporary Delhi: The City As Spectacle' in Vasudevan, R., Sundaram, R., Bagchi, J., Narula, M., Sengupta, S. and Lovink, G. (eds.) *Sarai Reader 02: The Cities Of Everyday Life*, Delhi: Sarai, pp. 31–37.

Sharma, A. (2003) 'India's Experience With the Multiplex', *Seminar*, Vol. 525, Online. Available HTTP: <www.india-seminar.com/2003/525/525%20aparna%20sharma.htm/> (accessed April 18 2006).

Shaw, A. (2004) *The Making of Navi Mumbai*, New Delhi: Orient Longman.

Shaw, A. and Satish, M. K. (2007) 'Metropolitan Restructuring in Post-Liberalised India: Seperating the Global and The Local', *Cities*, Vol. 24, No. 2, pp. 148–163.

Shringar Cinemas Ltd. (2006a) 'Exhibition', Online. Available HTTP: <http://www.shringar.co.in/iic/exhibition.htm> (accessed September 15 2006).

Shringar Cinemas Ltd. (2006b) 'Investor Relations', Online. Available HTTP: <http://www.shringar.co.in/iic/financialinfo.htm> (accessed September 15 2006).

Shringar Cinemas Ltd. (2006c) *Shareholding Pattern As Of 30/06/2006*, Online. Available HTTP: <http://www.shringar.co.in/financial/ShareholdingPattern/ShareHoldingPatter30062006.pdf> (accessed September 15 2006).

Shrinivas, L. (1991) 'Land and Politics in India. Working of the Urban Land Ceiling Act, 1976', *Economic and Political Weekly*, Vol. XXVI, No. 43, 26 October.

Shrinivas, L. (2002) 'The Active Audience: Spectatorship, Social Relations And The Experience Of Cinema In India', *Media, Culture & Society*, Vol. 24, pp. 155–173.

Singhal, P. (2006). *Multiplexes*, Mumbai: Edelweiss Securities.

Skeers, J. (2006) 'India's Pro-Investor Plans for Urban Renewal' *World Socialist Web*, 25 March.

Sklair, L. (2006) 'Iconic Architecture And Capitalist Globalisation', *City*, Vol. 10, No. 1, pp. 21–47.

Srinivas, S. V. (2000a) 'Is There a Public in the Cinema Hall?", *Framework*, Online. Available HTTP: <www.frameworkonline.com/> (accessed November 10 2000).

Srinivas, S. V. (2000b) 'Devotion and Defiance in Fan Activity', in Vasudevan, Ravi S. (ed.) *Making Meaning in Indian Cinema*, New Delhi: Oxford University Press.

Srinivasaraju, S. (2007) 'Raiders Lost the Arc', *Outlook* 12 December, pp. 104–112.

Stallmeyer, J. C. (2006) *Architecture and Urban Form in India's Silicon Valley: A case study of Bangalore*, unpublished PhD thesis: Berkely: University of California Berkeley.

Stremlau, J. (1996) 'Bangalore: India's silicon city', *Monthly Labour Review*, Vol. 119, pp. 50–51.

Subramaniam, R. (2002) 'Urban Physiognomies' In Vasudevan, R., Sundaram, R., Bagchi, J., Narula, M., Sengupta, S. and Lovink, G. (eds.) *Sarai Reader 02: The Cities Of Everyday Life*, Delhi: Sarai, pp. 8–13.

Suchitra, J. Y. and Nandakumar, C. K. (2008) 'Pensioners' Paradise to IT: The Fallacy that is Bangalore', *Economic and Political Weekly*, 19 January, pp. 16–17.

Tanaja, A. V. (2008) 'The Multiplex Makers: Meeting Morphogenesis', Online. Available HTTP: <http://www.Sarai.net/research/media-city/field-notes/film-city/> (accessed April 23 2008).

Thoraval, Y. (2000) *The Cinemas of India 1896–2000*, New Delhi: Macmillan India.

Times of India (1998) 'Noida Land Deal Is Dubious- Lok Ayukta', *Times of India*, May 28 1998.

Times of India (2005) 'FDI in Construction Industry', Online. Available HTTP: <http://timesofindia.indiatimes.com/articleshow/1049608.cms> (accessed March 12 2005).

Times of India (2007) 'Price Paradox in New Town', *Times of India*, December 24 2007.

Tomic, P., Trumper, R.and Dattwyler, R. H. (2006) 'Manufacturing Modernity: Cleanliness, Dirt and Neoliberalism in Chile', *Antipode*, Vol. 38, No. 3, pp. 508–529.

UNESCO Institute for Statistics (1999) 'Films and Cinemas: Number, Seating Capacity and Annual Attendance, 1995–1999', Online. Available HTTP: <http://www.uis.unesco.org/http://www.uis.unesco.org/TEMPLATE/html/HTMLTables/culture/film.htm> (accessed March 22 2003).

Urs, A. (2007) 'Mall space supply to be 60mn. sq. ft. by 2008', *Business Standard*, July 3 2007.

Varma, P. K. (1998) *The Great Indian Middle Class*, New Delhi: Penguin.

Varma, P. K. (2006) *Being Indian: Inside The Real India*, London: Arrow Books.

Vasudevan, R. (2000a) 'The Politics of Cultural Address in a 'Transitional' Cinema: A Case Study of Indian Popular Cinema' in Gledhill, C. and Williams, L. (eds.) *Reinventing Film Studies*, London: Arnold.

Vasudevan, R. (ed.) (2000b) *Making Meaning in Indian Cinema*, New Delhi: Oxford University Press.

Vasudevan, R. (2003), 'Cinema In Urban Space' *Seminar*, Vol. 525, Online. Available HTTP: <http://www.india-seminar.com/2003/525/525%20ravi%20vasudevan.htm/> (accessed April 18 2006).

Vitali, V. (2004) 'Nationalist Hindi Cinema: Questions of Film Analysis and Historiography', *Kinema*, Online. Available HTTP: <http://www.kinema.uwaterloo.ca/vita042.htm> (accessed November 17 2006).

Voyce, M. (2007) 'Shopping Malls in India: New Social 'Dividing Practices', *Economic and Political Weekly*, 2 June, pp. 2055–62.

Wallack, J. and Singh, N. K. (2005) 'Moving India: Policies and Priorities in Transport Sector Reform' Paper presented at Sixth Annual Conference on Indian Economic Policy Reform, Stanford Center for International Development (SCID), June 3–4 2005.

Wave Cinemas (2006a) 'Wave Cinemas', Online. Available HTTP: <http://wavecinemas.com/> (accessed October 20 2006).

Wave Cinemas (2006b) 'The Chadha Group', Online. Available HTTP: <http://www.wavecinemas.com/chadha-group.php> (accessed October 20 2006).

Willeman, P. and Rajadhyaksha, A. (eds.) (1999) *Encyclopaedia of Indian Cinema*, London: British Film Institute.

World Bank (2005) *India Country Brief*, Online. Available HTTP: <http://www.worldbank.org.in/> (accessed June 5 2007).

Yash Raj Films (2007) 'Kabul Express', Online. Available HTTP: <http://www.yashrajfilms.com/microsites/kabulexpress/microflash.htm> (accessed March 20 2007).

Zarabi, S. (2006) 'Unitech's Noida Land Deal Questioned', *Business Standard*, May 25 2006.

ZEE TV (2006) 'ZEE TV', Online. Available HTTP: <http://www.zee-tv.com> (accessed March 4 2006).

Index

For Product Safety Concerns and Information please contact our EU
representative GPSR@taylorandfrancis.com
Taylor & Francis Verlag GmbH, Kaufingerstraße 24, 80331 München, Germany

www.ingramcontent.com/pod-product-compliance
Lightning Source LLC
Chambersburg PA
CBHW070358270326
41926CB00014B/2605